CROCK·POT.

· THE ORIGINAL SLOW COOKER ·

RECIPE COLLECTION

Publications International, Ltd.

Recipes and text on pages 5-7, 10 recipe 1, 14 recipe 2, 16 recipe 1, 20 recipe 2, 25 recipe 2, 27 recipe 1, 32 recipe 2, 33, 35 recipe 2, 36 recipe 1, 38 recipe 1, 40 recipe 1, 43, 48, 50 recipe 2, 52 recipe 2, 59 recipe 2, 61 recipe 1, 71 recipe 1, 74 recipe 2, 78 recipe 1, 79 recipe 2, 80 recipe 2, 87 recipe 1, 96 recipe 1, 100 recipe 1, 106 recipe 2, 108 recipe 1, 111 recipe 1, 113 recipe 1, 114 recipe 1, 118 recipe 1, 124 recipe 2, 126, 134, 137 recipe 1, 142 recipe 1, 144-145, 152 recipe 1, 154 recipe 1, 158, 162 recipe 2, 164 recipe 1, 166 recipe 1, 168 recipe 1, 171, 176, 187 recipe 1, 192 recipe 1, 196 recipe 2, 202, 204, 208 recipe 1, 213, 216, 220, 224-226, 228, 230 recipe 1, 235, 237 recipe 2, 238 recipe 2, 242 recipe 3, 246 recipe 2, 248 recipe 2, 250 recipe 1, 252 recipe 1, 256, 262 recipe 1, 264, 272 recipe 2, 282-283, 285, 288 recipe 1, 290 recipe 1, 292 recipe 1, 295 recipe 1, 296, 297 recipe 1, 298 recipe 1, 300, 302, 303 recipe 1, 304 recipe 2, 306 recipe 1, 308 recipe 1 and 310 © 2013 Sunbeam Products, Inc. doing business as Jarden Consumer Solutions. All rights reserved. All other recipes © 2013 Publications International, Ltd. Photographs © 2013 Publications International, Ltd.

Louis Weber, CEO
Publications International, Ltd.
7373 North Cicero Avenue
Lincolnwood, IL 60712

Pictured on the front cover (left to right, top to bottom): Lemon Dilled Parsnips and Turnips *(page 250)*, Hearty Chicken Chili *(page 54)*, Creamy Crab Bisque *(page 235)*, Caponata *(page 156)*, Cream Cheese Chicken with Broccoli *(page 205)*, Campfired-Up Sloppy Joes *(page 100)*, Pork Chops with Jalapeño-Pecan Cornbread Stuffing *(page 128)* and Easy Chocolate Pudding Cake *(page 294)*.

Pictured on the back cover (left to right, top to bottom): Mu Shu Turkey *(page 198)*, Hot Fudge Cake *(page 297)*, Panama Pork Stew *(page 47)*, Beef Roast with Dark Rum Sauce *(page 283)*, Mini Carnitas Tacos *(page 64)*, Pesto Rice and Beans *(page 169)*, Classic Beef and Noodles *(page 102)* and Big Al's Hot and Sweet Sausage Sandwich *(page 124)*.

ISBN-13: 978-1-4508-7054-2
ISBN-10: 1-4508-7054-6

Library of Congress Control Number: 2013932209

Manufactured in China.

8 7 6 5 4 3 2 1

Table of Contents

54

156

282

Slow Cooking Hints and Tips

How to get the best results from your
CROCK-POT® slow cooker

Your **CROCK-POT®** slow cooker can be the best kitchen assistant you've ever had. Your family will enjoy delicious meals, and you'll save time and effort, thanks to the flavorful cooking process that works while you're away from home.

Your **CROCK-POT®** slow cooker can also help you entertain guests. It makes a great server for hot beverages, appetizers, or dips. Just keep it on the WARM setting to maintain the proper serving temperature.

To get the most from your **CROCK-POT®** slow cooker, keep the following hints and tips in mind.

Adding Ingredients at the End of the Cooking Time

Certain ingredients are best added toward the end of the cooking time. These include:
- **Milk, sour cream, and yogurt:** Add during the last 15 minutes.
- **Seafood and fish:** Add during the last 15 to 30 minutes.
- **Fresh herbs:** Fresh herbs such as basil will darken with long cooking, so if you want colorful fresh herbs, add them during the last 15 minutes of cooking or directly to the dish just before serving it.

Pasta and Rice

For slow-cooked rice dishes, converted rice holds up best through longer cooking times. Most recipes suggest adding pasta or rice halfway through the cooking time for the best texture. If the rice doesn't seem completely cooked after the suggested time, add an extra ½ cup to 1 cup of liquid per cup of rice, and extend the cooking time by 30 to 60 minutes.

Cooking Temperatures and Food Safety

According to the U.S. Department of Agriculture, bacteria in food is killed at a temperature of 165°F. As a result, it's important to follow the recommended cooking times and to keep the cover on your **CROCK-POT®** slow cooker during the cooking process to maintain food-safe temperatures. Slow-cooked meats and poultry are best when simmered gently for the period of time that allows the connective tissues to break down, yielding meat that is fall-off-the-bone tender and juicy.

If your food isn't done after 8 hours when the recipe calls for cooking 8 to 10 hours, this could be due to altitude, extreme humidity, or voltage variations, which are commonplace. Slight fluctuations in power do not have a noticeable effect on most appliances, however, they can slightly alter the cooking times. Always allow your food to continue cooking until it's done.

If you arrive home and find the electrical power service to your home is out, check the **CROCK-POT®** slow cooker immediately. Check the temperature of the contents in the **CROCK-POT®** slow cooker with an instant-read thermometer. If the temperature is above 140°F, you can transfer the contents to a large saucepan or Dutch oven and finish cooking it on a gas range or gas grill. However, if the temperature of the contents is between 40° and 140°F, you should throw the food away.

If the electricity is on when you arrive home, but you can tell by the clocks that your home has been without power, the best thing to do is throw away the food. You'll never know what the temperature of the food was when the power went off or how long it was off; the food may have spent several hours in the danger zone. And, although the food is hot when you get home and looks done, it's better to err on the side of safety and throw it away.

Allow plenty of time for cooking. Remember, it's practically impossible to overcook food in a **CROCK-POT®** slow cooker. You'll learn through experience whether to decrease or increase cooking times for your recipes.

Browning Meat

Meat will not brown as it would if it were cooked in a skillet or oven at a high temperature. It's not necessary to brown meat before slow cooking. However, if you prefer the look and flavor of browned meat, just brown it in a large skillet coated with oil, butter, or nonstick cooking spray, then place the browned ingredients into the stoneware and follow the recipe as written.

Herbs and Spices

When cooking with your **CROCK-POT®** slow cooker, use dried and ground herbs and spices, which work well during long cooking times. However, the flavor and aroma of crushed or ground herbs may differ depending on their shelf life, and their flavor can lessen during the extended cooking time in the **CROCK-POT®** slow cooker. Be sure to taste the finished dish and add more seasonings if needed. If you prefer colorful fresh herbs, add them during the last 15 minutes of cooking time or as a garnish. Fresh herbs add color and flavor to most dishes.

Cooking for Larger Quantity Yields

If you want to make a bigger batch in a larger unit, such as a 5-, 6-, or 7-quart **CROCK-POT®** slow cooker, guidelines for doubling or tripling ingredients include:

• When preparing dishes with beef or pork in a larger unit, browning the meat in a skillet before adding it to the **CROCK-POT®** slow cooker yields the best results; the meat will cook more evenly.

• Roasted meats, chicken, and turkey quantities may be doubled or tripled, and seasonings adjusted by half. Caution: Flavorful dried spices such as garlic or chili powder will intensify during long, slow cooking. Add just 25 to 50 percent more spices, as needed, to balance the flavors.

• When preparing a soup or a stew, you may double all ingredients except the liquids, seasonings, and dried herbs. Increase liquid volume by half, or adjust as needed. The **CROCK-POT**® slow cooker lid collects steam, which condenses to keep foods moist and to maintain liquid volume.

• To avoid over or undercooking, always fill the stoneware one half to three fourths full and conform to the recommended cook times (unless instructed otherwise by our **CROCK-POT**® slow cooker recipes).

• Do not double thickeners, such as cornstarch, at the beginning. You may always add more thickener later if it's necessary.

Cooking with Frozen Foods

You may cook frozen foods in your **CROCK-POT**® slow cooker. For best results, use the following guidelines:

• Add at least 1 cup of warm or hot liquid to the stoneware before placing frozen meat in the **CROCK-POT**® slow cooker.

• Do not preheat the **CROCK-POT**® slow cooker.

• Cook recipes containing frozen meats for an additional 4 to 6 hours on LOW or 2 hours on HIGH.

• Slow cooking frozen foods requires a longer cooking time than fresh foods because the food needs more time to come up to safe internal temperatures. Meats also will require additional time to allow them to become tender. If there is any question about the cooking time, use a thermometer to ensure meats are cooking appropriately.

High-Altitude Adjustments

If you live at an altitude above 3,500 feet, you'll need to make some adjustments when slow cooking. Everything will take longer to cook, so plan for that. Tough meats take longer to become tender at high altitudes—sometimes much longer. Try cooking on the HIGH heat setting instead of LOW. Root vegetables also take longer to cook; for quicker cooking, cut them into smaller pieces than the recipe suggests.

Removable Stoneware

The removable stoneware in your **CROCK-POT**® slow cooker makes cleaning easy. However, the stoneware insert can be damaged by sudden changes in temperature. Here are tips on the use and care of your stoneware:

• Many stoneware cooking inserts are safe for use in a conventional or microwave oven.

• Because all **CROCK-POT**® slow cookers have wrap-around heat, there's no direct heat at the bottom. Always fill the stoneware at least half full to conform to recommended times for best results. Smaller quantities can still be cooked, but cooking times will be affected.

• Don't preheat the **CROCK-POT**® slow cooker. Don't place a cold insert into a preheated base.

• Don't place a hot insert on a cold surface or in the refrigerator; don't fill it with cold water.

• Never place stoneware in the freezer.

• If you place ingredients in the stoneware and refrigerate the stoneware overnight, additional cooking time will be required to cook the food safely and appropriately. If there is any question about the cooking time, use a thermometer to ensure meats have cooked appropriately.

• Don't use the stoneware insert if it's cracked; replace it.

• For further safety tips, please refer to the instruction manual that came with your **CROCK-POT**® slow cooker.

**APPLE-CINNAMON
BREAKFAST RISOTTO**

Breakfast and Brunch

Apple-Cinnamon Breakfast Risotto

- ¼ cup (½ stick) butter
- 4 medium Granny Smith apples (about 1½ pounds), peeled, cored and diced into ½-inch cubes
- 1½ teaspoons ground cinnamon
- ¼ teaspoon ground allspice
- ¼ teaspoon salt
- 1½ cups Arborio rice
- ½ cup packed dark brown sugar
- 4 cups unfiltered apple juice, at room temperature*
- 1 teaspoon vanilla
- Optional toppings: dried cranberries, sliced almonds, milk

If unfiltered apple juice is unavailable, use any apple juice.

1. Coat **CROCK-POT**® slow cooker with nonstick cooking spray; set aside. Melt butter in large skillet over medium-high heat. Add apples, cinnamon, allspice and salt. Cook and stir 3 to 5 minutes or until apples begin to release juices. Transfer to **CROCK-POT**® slow cooker.

2. Add rice and stir to coat. Sprinkle brown sugar evenly over top. Add apple juice and vanilla. Cover; cook on HIGH 1½ to 2 hours or until all liquid is absorbed. Ladle risotto into bowls; top with cranberries, almonds and milk.

Makes 6 servings

Mulled Cranberry Tea

- 2 tea bags
- 1 cup boiling water
- 1 bottle (48 ounces) cranberry juice
- ½ cup dried cranberries (optional)
- ⅓ cup sugar
- 1 lemon, cut into ¼-inch slices
- 4 cinnamon sticks
- 6 whole cloves
- Additional cinnamon sticks or thin lemon slices (optional)

1. Place tea bags in **CROCK-POT**® slow cooker. Pour boiling water over tea bags; cover and let steep 5 minutes. Remove and discard tea bags.

2. Stir in cranberry juice, cranberries, if desired, sugar, 1 sliced lemon, 4 cinnamon sticks and cloves. Cover; cook on LOW 2 to 3 hours or on HIGH 1 to 2 hours.

3. Remove and discard cooked lemon slices, cinnamon sticks and cloves. Serve in warm mug with additional cinnamon stick or fresh lemon slice, if desired.

Makes 8 servings

Tip: The flavor and aroma of crushed or ground herbs and spices may lessen during a longer cooking time. So, for slow cooking in your **CROCK-POT**® slow cooker, you may use whole herbs and spices. Be sure to taste and adjust seasonings before serving.

Hawaiian Fruit Compote

    3 **cups coarsely chopped fresh pineapple**
    3 **grapefruits, peeled and sectioned**
    1 **can (21 ounces) cherry pie filling**
    2 **cups chopped fresh peaches**
    2 to 3 **limes, peeled and sectioned**
    1 **mango, peeled and chopped**
    2 **bananas, sliced**
    1 **tablespoon lemon juice**
       Slivered almonds (optional)

1. Place all ingredients except almonds in **CROCK-POT**® slow cooker and toss lightly. Cover; cook on LOW 4 to 5 hours or on HIGH 2 to 3 hours.

2. Serve with slivered almonds, if desired.

Makes 6 to 8 servings

Serving Suggestion: Try warm, fruity compote in place of maple syrup on your favorite waffles or pancakes for a great way to start your day. This sauce is also delicious served over roasted turkey, pork roast or baked ham.

French Toast Bread Pudding

    2 **tablespoons packed dark brown sugar**
  2½ **teaspoons ground cinnamon**
    1 **loaf (24 ounces) Texas toast-style bread***
    2 **cups whipping cream**
    2 **cups half-and-half**
    2 **teaspoons vanilla**
    ¼ **teaspoon salt**
  1¼ **cups granulated sugar**
    4 **egg yolks**
    ¼ **teaspoon ground nutmeg**
       Maple syrup (optional)
       Whipped cream (optional)

*If unavailable, cut day-old 24-ounce loaf of white sandwich bread into 1-inch-thick slices.

1. Coat inside of **CROCK-POT**® slow cooker with nonstick cooking spray. Combine brown sugar and cinnamon in small bowl. Reserve 1 tablespoon; set aside.

2. Cut bread slices in half diagonally. Arrange bread slices in single layer in bottom of **CROCK-POT**® slow cooker, keeping as flat as possible. Evenly sprinkle rounded tablespoon of cinnamon mixture over bread. Repeat layering with remaining bread and cinnamon mixture, keeping layers as flat as possible. Tuck bread into vertical spaces, if necessary.

3. Place cream, half-and-half, vanilla and salt in large saucepan over medium heat, stirring occasionally. Reduce heat to low.

4. Meanwhile, whisk granulated sugar and egg yolks in medium bowl. Continue to whisk quickly while adding ¼ cup of hot cream mixture.** Add warmed egg mixture to saucepan. Increase heat to medium-high; cook and stir 5 minutes or until mixture thickens slightly. Do not boil.

5. Remove cream mixture from heat; stir in nutmeg. Pour cream mixture over bread; press bread down lightly. Sprinkle reserved cinnamon mixture on top. Cover; cook on LOW 3 to 4 hours or on HIGH 1½ to 2 hours or until toothpick inserted into center comes out clean.

6. Turn off heat; uncover. Let pudding rest 10 minutes before spooning into bowls. Serve with maple syrup and whipped cream, if desired.
**Place bowl on damp towel to prevent slipping.

Makes 6 to 8 servings

Tip: Allow breads, cakes and puddings to cool at least 5 minutes before scooping or removing them from the **CROCK-POT**® slow cooker.

HAWAIIAN FRUIT COMPOTE

Glazed Cinnamon Coffee Cake

STREUSEL

¼ cup biscuit baking mix

¼ cup packed light brown sugar

½ teaspoon ground cinnamon

BATTER

1½ cups biscuit baking mix

¾ cup granulated sugar

½ cup vanilla or plain yogurt

1 egg, lightly beaten

1 teaspoon vanilla

GLAZE

1 to 2 tablespoons milk

1 cup powdered sugar

½ cup sliced almonds (optional)

1. Generously coat 4-quart **CROCK-POT**® slow cooker with nonstick cooking spray.

2. Prepare streusel: Blend ¼ cup baking mix, brown sugar and cinnamon in small bowl; set aside.

3. Prepare batter: Mix 1½ cups baking mix, granulated sugar, yogurt, egg and vanilla in medium bowl until well blended. Spoon ½ of batter into **CROCK-POT**® slow cooker. Sprinkle one half of streusel over top. Repeat with remaining batter and streusel.

4. Line lid with two paper towels. Cover tightly; cook on HIGH 1¾ to 2 hours or until toothpick inserted into center comes out clean and cake springs back when gently pressed. Allow cake to rest 10 minutes. Invert onto serving plate.

5. Prepare glaze: Whisk milk into powdered sugar, 1 tablespoon at a time, until desired consistency. Spoon glaze over top of cake. Garnish with sliced almonds. Cut into wedges. Serve warm or cold.

Makes 6 to 8 servings

Whole-Grain Banana Bread

¼ cup plus 2 tablespoons wheat germ, divided

1 cup sugar

⅔ cup butter, softened

2 eggs

1 cup mashed bananas (2 to 3 bananas)

1 teaspoon vanilla

1 cup all-purpose flour

1 cup whole wheat pastry flour

1 teaspoon baking soda

½ teaspoon salt

½ cup chopped walnuts or pecans (optional)

1. Coat inside of 1-quart soufflé dish that fits inside of **CROCK-POT**® slow cooker with nonstick cooking spray. Sprinkle dish with 2 tablespoons wheat germ.

2. Beat sugar and butter in large bowl with electric mixer until fluffy. Add eggs, one at a time; beat until blended. Add bananas and vanilla; beat until smooth.

3. Gradually stir in flours, remaining ¼ cup wheat germ, baking soda and salt. Stir in walnuts, if desired. Pour batter into prepared dish; place in 4½-quart **CROCK-POT**® slow cooker. Cover; cook on LOW 4 to 6 hours or on HIGH 2 to 3 hours or until edges begin to brown and toothpick inserted into center comes out clean.

4. Remove dish from **CROCK-POT**® slow cooker. Cool on wire rack 10 minutes. Remove bread from dish; cool completely on wire rack.

Makes 1 loaf

GLAZED CINNAMON COFFEE CAKE

Ham and Cheddar Brunch Strata

8 ounces French bread, torn into small pieces

2 cups (8 ounces) shredded reduced-fat sharp Cheddar cheese, divided

1½ cups diced lean ham

½ cup finely chopped green onions, divided

4 eggs

1 cup fat-free half-and-half

1 tablespoon Worcestershire sauce

⅛ teaspoon ground red pepper

1. Coat **CROCK-POT®** slow cooker with nonstick cooking spray.

2. Layer in following order: bread, 1½ cups cheese, ham and all but 2 tablespoons green onions.

3. Whisk eggs, half-and-half, Worcestershire sauce and ground red pepper in small bowl. Pour evenly over layered ingredients in **CROCK-POT®** slow cooker. Cover; cook on LOW 3½ hours or until knife inserted into center comes out clean. Turn off heat. Sprinkle evenly with remaining ½ cup cheese and reserved 2 tablespoons green onions. Let stand, covered, 10 minutes or until cheese is melted.

4. To serve, run a knife or rubber spatula around outer edges, lifting bottom slightly. Invert onto serving plate.

Makes 6 to 8 servings

Tip: When preparing ingredients for the **CROCK-POT®** slow cooker, cut into uniform pieces so everything cooks evenly.

Gingerbread

½ cup sugar

½ cup (1 stick) butter, softened

2½ cups all-purpose flour

1 cup light molasses

1 egg, lightly beaten

2 teaspoons ground ginger

1½ teaspoons baking soda

1 teaspoon ground cinnamon

½ teaspoon salt

½ teaspoon ground cloves

1 cup hot water

Whipped cream (optional)

1. Coat inside of 4½-quart **CROCK-POT®** slow cooker with nonstick cooking spray. Beat sugar and butter in large bowl with electric mixer at medium speed 3 to 5 minutes or until well blended. Add flour, molasses, egg, ginger, baking soda, cinnamon, salt and cloves; beat until well blended. Stir in water; mix well. Pour batter into **CROCK-POT®** slow cooker.

2. Cover; cook on HIGH 1½ to 1¾ hours or until toothpick inserted into center of cake comes out clean. Serve warm; top with whipped cream, if desired.

Makes 6 to 8 servings

HAM AND CHEDDAR BRUNCH STRATA

BREAKFAST BERRY BREAD PUDDING

Breakfast Berry Bread Pudding

6 cups bread, preferably dense peasant-style or sourdough, cut into ¾- to 1-inch cubes

1 cup raisins

½ cup slivered almonds, toasted*

6 eggs, beaten

1½ cups packed light brown sugar

1¾ cups milk (1% or greater)

1½ teaspoons cinnamon

1 teaspoon vanilla

3 cups sliced fresh strawberries

2 cups fresh blueberries

Fresh mint leaves (optional)

To toast almonds, spread in single layer in heavy skillet. Cook over medium heat 1 to 2 minutes or until nuts are lightly browned, stirring frequently.

1. Coat inside of **CROCK-POT**® slow cooker with nonstick cooking spray or butter. Add bread, raisins and almonds; toss to combine.

2. Whisk eggs, brown sugar, milk, cinnamon and vanilla in large bowl. Pour egg mixture over bread mixture; toss to blend. Cover; cook on LOW 4 to 4½ hours or on HIGH 3 hours.

3. Remove stoneware from **CROCK-POT**® base and allow bread pudding to cool and set before serving. Serve with berries and garnish with mint leaves.

Makes 10 to 12 servings

Spiced Citrus Tea

4 tea bags

Peel of 1 orange

4 cups boiling water

2 cans (6 ounces each) orange-pineapple juice

3 tablespoons honey

3 cinnamon sticks

3 star anise

Place tea bags, orange peel and boiling water in **CROCK-POT**® slow cooker; cover and let steep 10 minutes. Remove and discard tea bags and orange peel. Add juice, honey, cinnamon sticks and star anise. Cover; cook on LOW 3 hours. Remove cinnamon sticks and star anise before serving.

Makes 6 servings

APPLE AND GRANOLA
BREAKFAST COBBLER

Apple and Granola Breakfast Cobbler

4   Granny Smith apples, peeled, cored and sliced
½   cup packed light brown sugar
1   tablespoon lemon juice
1   teaspoon ground cinnamon
2   cups granola cereal, plus additional for garnish
2   tablespoons butter, cut into small pieces
    Cream, half-and-half or vanilla yogurt (optional)

1. Place apples in **CROCK-POT®** slow cooker. Sprinkle brown sugar, lemon juice and cinnamon over apples. Stir in 2 cups granola and butter.

2. Cover; cook on LOW 6 hours or on HIGH 2 to 3 hours. Serve hot with additional granola sprinkled on top. Serve with cream, if desired.

Makes 4 servings

Hot Mulled Cider

½   gallon apple cider
½   cup packed brown sugar
1½ teaspoons balsamic or cider vinegar (optional)
1   teaspoon vanilla
1   cinnamon stick
6   whole cloves
½   cup applejack or bourbon (optional)

Combine cider, brown sugar, vinegar, if desired, vanilla, cinnamon stick and cloves in **CROCK-POT®** slow cooker. Cover; cook on LOW 5 to 6 hours. Remove and discard cinnamon stick and cloves. Stir in applejack just before serving, if desired. Serve warm in mugs.

Makes 16 servings

MOCHA
SUPREME

Mocha Supreme

- **2 quarts strong brewed coffee**
- **½ cup instant hot chocolate beverage mix**
- **1 cinnamon stick, broken in half**
- **1 cup heavy cream**
- **1 tablespoon powdered sugar**

1. Place coffee, hot chocolate mix and cinnamon stick halves in **CROCK-POT®** slow cooker; stir. Cover; cook on HIGH 2 to 2½ hours or until heated through.

2. Remove and discard cinnamon stick halves.

3. Beat cream in medium bowl with electric mixer on high speed until soft peaks form. Add powdered sugar; beat until stiff peaks form. Ladle mocha mixture into mugs; top with whipped cream.

Makes 8 servings

Tip: To whip cream more quickly, chill the beaters and bowl in the freezer for 15 minutes.

Pear Crunch

- **1 can (8 ounces) crushed pineapple in juice, undrained**
- **¼ cup pineapple or apple juice**
- **3 tablespoons dried cranberries**
- **1½ teaspoons quick-cooking tapioca**
- **¼ teaspoon vanilla**
- **2 pears, cored and halved**
- **¼ cup granola with almonds**

1. Combine pineapple, juice, cranberries, tapioca and vanilla in **CROCK-POT®** slow cooker; mix well. Top with pears, cut sides down.

2. Cover; cook on LOW 3½ to 4½ hours. Arrange pear halves on serving plates. Spoon pineapple mixture over pear halves. Sprinkle with granola.

Makes 4 servings

WHOA
BREAKFAST

Whoa Breakfast

3 cups water
2 cups chopped peeled apples
1½ cups steel-cut or old-fashioned oats
¼ cup sliced almonds
½ teaspoon ground cinnamon

Combine water, apples, oats, almonds and cinnamon in **CROCK-POT®** slow cooker. Cover; cook on LOW 8 hours.

Makes 6 servings

Mucho Mocha Cocoa

4 cups whole milk
4 cups half-and-half
1 cup chocolate syrup
⅓ cup instant coffee granules
2 tablespoons sugar
2 whole cinnamon sticks

Combine all ingredients in **CROCK-POT®** slow cooker; stir until well blended. Cover; cook on LOW 3 hours. Remove and discard cinnamon sticks. Serve warm in mugs.

Makes 9 servings

Wake-Up Potato and Sausage Breakfast Casserole

1 pound kielbasa or smoked sausage, diced
1 cup chopped onion
1 cup chopped red bell pepper
1 package (20 ounces) refrigerated Southwestern-style hash browns*
10 eggs
1 cup milk
1 cup (4 ounces) shredded Monterey Jack or sharp Cheddar cheese

*You may substitute O'Brien potatoes and add ½ teaspoon chile pepper.

1. Coat inside of **CROCK-POT**® slow cooker with nonstick cooking spray. Heat large skillet over medium-high heat. Add sausage and onion; cook and stir until sausage is browned. Drain fat. Stir in bell pepper.

2. Place one third of potatoes in **CROCK-POT**® slow cooker. Top with half of sausage mixture. Repeat layers. Spread remaining one third of potatoes evenly on top.

3. Whisk eggs and milk in medium bowl. Pour evenly over potatoes. Cover; cook on LOW 6 to 7 hours.

4. Turn off heat. Sprinkle cheese over casserole; let stand 10 minutes or until cheese is melted.

Makes 8 servings

Tip: To remove casserole from **CROCK-POT**® slow cooker, omit step 4. Run a rubber spatula around the edge of casserole, lifting the bottom slightly. Invert onto a plate. Place a serving plate on top and invert again. Sprinkle with the cheese and let stand until cheese is melted. To serve, cut into wedges.

Poached Autumn Fruits with Vanilla-Citrus Broth

2 Granny Smith apples, peeled, cored and halved (reserve cores)
2 Bartlett pears, peeled, cored and halved (reserve cores)
1 orange, peeled and halved
⅓ cup sugar
5 tablespoons honey
1 vanilla bean, split and seeded (reserve seeds)
1 cinnamon stick

1. Place apple and pear cores in **CROCK-POT**® slow cooker. Squeeze juice from orange halves into **CROCK-POT**® slow cooker. Add orange halves, sugar, honey, vanilla bean and seeds and cinnamon stick. Add apples and pears. Pour in enough water to cover fruit. Stir gently to combine. Cover; cook on HIGH 2 hours or until fruit is tender.

2. Remove apple and pear halves; set aside. Strain cooking liquid into large saucepan. (Discard solids.) Simmer gently over low heat until liquid is reduced by half and thickened.

3. Dice apple and pear halves. Add to saucepan to rewarm fruit. To serve, spoon fruit with sauce into bowls. Top with vanilla ice cream, if desired.

Makes 4 to 6 servings

WAKE-UP POTATO
AND SAUSAGE
BREAKFAST
CASSEROLE

Chocolate-Stuffed Slow Cooker French Toast

Butter, softened

6 slices (¾-inch-thick) day-old challah*

½ cup semisweet chocolate chips

6 eggs

3 cups half-and-half

⅔ cup granulated sugar

1 teaspoon vanilla

¼ teaspoon salt

Powdered sugar or warm maple syrup

Fresh fruit (optional)

*Challah is usually braided. If you use brioche or another rich egg bread, slice bread to fit baking dish.

1. Coat 2½-quart baking dish that fits inside **CROCK-POT®** slow cooker with butter. Arrange 2 bread slices in bottom of dish. Sprinkle with ¼ cup chocolate chips. Add 2 more bread slices. Sprinkle with remaining ¼ cup chocolate chips. Top with remaining 2 bread slices.

2. Beat eggs in large bowl. Stir in half-and-half, granulated sugar, vanilla and salt. Pour egg mixture over bread layers. Press bread into liquid. Set aside 10 minutes or until liquid is absorbed. Cover dish with buttered foil, butter side down.

3. Pour 1 inch hot water into **CROCK-POT®** slow cooker. Add baking dish. Cover; cook on HIGH 3 hours or until toothpick inserted into center comes out clean. Remove dish and let stand 10 minutes. Serve with powdered sugar. Garnish with fresh fruit.

Makes 6 servings

Tip: Any oven-safe casserole or baking dish is safe to use in your **CROCK-POT®** slow cooker. Place directly inside the stoneware and follow the recipe directions.

Apple-Date Crisp

6 cups thinly sliced peeled apples (about 6 medium, preferably Golden Delicious)

2 teaspoons lemon juice

⅓ cup chopped dates

1⅓ cups uncooked quick oats

½ cup all-purpose flour

½ cup packed light brown sugar

½ teaspoon ground cinnamon

¼ teaspoon ground ginger

¼ teaspoon salt

Dash ground nutmeg

Dash ground cloves (optional)

4 tablespoons (½ stick) cold butter, cut into small pieces

1. Coat **CROCK-POT®** slow cooker with nonstick cooking spray. Place apples in medium bowl. Sprinkle with lemon juice; toss to coat. Add dates and mix well. Transfer mixture to **CROCK-POT®** slow cooker.

2. For topping, combine oats, flour, brown sugar, cinnamon, ginger, salt, nutmeg and cloves, if desired, in medium bowl. Cut in butter with pastry blender or two knives until mixture resembles coarse crumbs. Sprinkle oat mixture over apples; smooth top. Cover; cook on LOW 4 hours or on HIGH 2 hours or until apples are tender.

Makes 6 servings

CHOCOLATE-STUFFED SLOW COOKER FRENCH TOAST

English Bread Pudding

16 slices day-old, firm-textured white bread (1 small loaf)

1¾ cups milk

1 package (8 ounces) mixed dried fruit, cut into small pieces

1 medium apple, chopped

½ cup chopped nuts

⅓ cup packed brown sugar

¼ cup (½ stick) butter, melted

1 egg, lightly beaten

1 teaspoon ground cinnamon

¼ teaspoon ground nutmeg

¼ teaspoon ground cloves

Apple slices (optional)

1. Tear bread, with crusts, into 1- to 2-inch pieces; place in **CROCK-POT®** slow cooker. Pour milk over bread; let soak 30 minutes. Stir in dried fruit, apple and nuts.

2. Combine remaining ingredients except apple slices in small bowl; pour over bread mixture. Stir well to blend. Cover; cook on LOW 3½ to 4 hours or until toothpick inserted into center of pudding comes out clean. Garnish with apple slices.

Makes 6 to 8 servings

Note: To make chopping dried fruits easier, cut fruit with kitchen scissors or chef's knife sprayed with nonstick cooking spray to prevent sticking.

BACON AND CHEESE
BRUNCH POTATOES

Bacon and Cheese Brunch Potatoes

3 medium russet potatoes (about 2 pounds), cut into 1-inch cubes

1 cup chopped onion

½ teaspoon seasoned salt

4 slices bacon, crisp-cooked and crumbled

1 cup (4 ounces) shredded sharp Cheddar cheese

1 tablespoon chicken broth or water

1. Coat **CROCK-POT®** slow cooker with cooking spray. Place half of potatoes in **CROCK-POT®** slow cooker. Sprinkle half of onion and seasoned salt over potatoes; top with half of bacon and cheese. Repeat layers. Sprinkle broth over top.

2. Cover; cook on LOW 6 hours or on HIGH 3½ hours or until potatoes and onion are tender. Stir gently to mix; serve warm.

Makes 6 servings

Classic Baked Apples

¼ cup packed dark brown sugar

2 tablespoons golden raisins

1 teaspoon grated lemon peel

6 small to medium baking apples, cored

1 teaspoon ground cinnamon

2 tablespoons butter, cubed

¼ cup orange juice

¼ cup water

Whipped cream (optional)

1. Combine brown sugar, raisins and lemon peel in small bowl. Fill core of each apple with mixture. Place apples in **CROCK-POT®** slow cooker. Sprinkle with cinnamon and dot with butter. Pour orange juice and water over apples. Cover; cook on LOW 7 to 9 hours or on HIGH 2½ to 3½ hours.

2. To serve, place apples in individual bowls. Top with sauce. Garnish with whipped cream.

Makes 6 servings

CINNAMON LATTÉ

Cinnamon Latté

- 6 cups double-strength brewed coffee*
- 2 cups half-and-half
- 1 cup sugar
- 1 teaspoon vanilla
- 3 cinnamon sticks, plus additional for garnish
  Whipped cream (optional)

Double the amount of coffee grounds normally used to brew coffee. Or substitute 8 teaspoons instant coffee dissolved in 6 cups boiling water.

1. Blend coffee, half-and-half, sugar and vanilla in 3- to 4-quart **CROCK-POT**® slow cooker. Add 3 cinnamon sticks. Cover; cook on HIGH 3 hours.

2. Remove and discard cinnamon sticks. Serve latté in tall coffee mugs. Garnish with additional cinnamon sticks and whipped cream.

Makes 6 to 8 servings

Chai Tea

- 2 quarts (8 cups) water
- 8 bags black tea
- ¾ cup sugar*
- 8 slices fresh ginger
- 5 cinnamon sticks
- 16 whole cloves
- 16 whole cardamom seeds, pods removed (optional)
- 1 cup milk

Chai tea is typically sweet. For less sweet tea, reduce sugar to ½ cup.

1. Combine water, tea bags, sugar, ginger, cinnamon sticks, cloves and cardamon, if desired, in **CROCK-POT**® slow cooker. Cover; cook on HIGH 2 to 2½ hours.

2. Strain mixture; discard solids. (At this point, tea may be covered and refrigerated up to 3 days.)

3. Stir in milk just before serving.

Makes 8 to 10 servings

BREAKFAST BAKE

Breakfast Bake

3 to 4 cups diced crusty bread
  (¾- to 1-inch dice)

½ pound bacon, cut into ½-inch dice

2 cups sliced mushrooms

2 cups torn fresh spinach

8 eggs

½ cup milk

1 cup (4 ounces) shredded Cheddar or
  Monterey Jack cheese

¾ cup roasted red peppers, drained and
  chopped

  Salt and black pepper

1. Coat inside of **CROCK-POT**® slow cooker with nonstick cooking spray. Add bread.

2. Heat large skillet over medium heat. Add bacon; cook and stir until crisp. Remove to **CROCK-POT**® slow cooker using slotted spoon. Discard all but 1 tablespoon drippings. Add mushrooms and spinach to skillet; cook and stir 1 to 2 minutes or until spinach wilts. Transfer to **CROCK-POT**® slow cooker; toss to combine.

3. Beat eggs and milk in medium bowl. Stir in cheese and red peppers. Season with salt and black pepper. Pour into **CROCK-POT**® slow cooker. Cover; cook on LOW 3 to 3½ hours or on HIGH 2 to 2½ hours or until eggs are firm but still moist. Adjust seasonings.

Makes 6 to 8 servings

Spiced Apple Tea

3 bags cinnamon herbal tea

3 cups boiling water

2 cups unsweetened apple juice

6 whole cloves

1 cinnamon stick

1. Place tea bags in **CROCK-POT**® slow cooker. Pour boiling water over tea bags; cover and let stand 10 minutes. Remove and discard tea bags.

2. Add apple juice, cloves and cinnamon stick to **CROCK-POT**® slow cooker. Cover; cook on LOW 2 to 3 hours. Remove and discard cloves and cinnamon stick. Serve warm in mugs.

Makes 4 servings

Orange Cranberry Nut Bread

2 cups all-purpose flour

1 teaspoon baking powder

½ cup chopped pecans

½ teaspoon baking soda

¼ teaspoon salt

1 cup dried cranberries

2 teaspoons dried orange peel

⅔ cup boiling water

¾ cup sugar

2 tablespoons shortening

1 egg, lightly beaten

1 teaspoon vanilla

1. Coat inside of 3-quart **CROCK-POT®** slow cooker with nonstick cooking spray. Combine flour, pecans, baking powder, baking soda and salt in medium bowl.

2. Combine cranberries and orange peel in another medium bowl; stir in boiling water. Add sugar, shortening, egg and vanilla; stir just until blended. Add flour mixture; stir just until blended.

3. Pour batter into **CROCK-POT®** slow cooker. Cover; cook on HIGH 1¼ to 1½ hours or until edges begin to brown and toothpick inserted into center comes out clean.

4. Remove stoneware insert from **CROCK-POT®** slow cooker. Cool on wire rack 10 minutes. Remove bread from insert; cool completely on rack.

Makes 8 to 10 servings

Tip: This recipe works best in round **CROCK-POT®** slow cookers.

Note: Not all **CROCK-POT®** slow cookers have removable stoneware. For those that don't, use a prepared casserole, soufflé dish or other high-sided baking dish that fits in the **CROCK-POT®** slow cooker.

Honey Whole-Grain Bread

3 cups whole wheat bread flour, divided

2 cups warm (not hot) whole milk

¾ to 1 cup all-purpose flour, divided

¼ cup honey

2 tablespoons vegetable oil

3 packets (¼ ounce each) active dry yeast

¾ teaspoon salt

1. Make foil handles using three 18×3-inch strips of heavy-duty foil or use regular foil folded to double thickness. Crisscross foil to form spoke design across bottom and up sides; place in **CROCK-POT®** slow cooker. Coat inside of 1-quart soufflé dish that fits inside 4½-quart **CROCK-POT®** slow cooker with nonstick cooking spray.

2. Beat 1½ cups whole wheat flour, milk, ½ cup all-purpose flour, honey, oil, yeast and salt in large bowl with electric mixer at medium speed 2 minutes. Add remaining 1½ cups whole wheat flour and ¼ cup to ½ cup all-purpose flour until dough is no longer sticky. (If mixer has difficulty mixing dough, mix in remaining flours with wooden spoon.) Transfer to prepared dish.

3. Place dish in **CROCK-POT®** slow cooker. Cover; cook on HIGH 3 hours or until edges are browned.

4. Use foil handles to lift dish from **CROCK-POT®** slow cooker. Let stand 5 minutes. Invert onto wire rack to cool.

Makes 1 loaf

ORANGE CRANBERRY NUT BREAD

Oatmeal Crème Brûlée

4 cups boiling water

3 cups quick-cooking oatmeal

½ teaspoon salt

6 egg yolks

½ cup granulated sugar

2 cups whipping cream

1 teaspoon vanilla

¼ cup packed light brown sugar

   Fresh berries (optional)

1. Coat inside of **CROCK-POT®** slow cooker with nonstick cooking spray. Pour water into **CROCK-POT®** slow cooker. Stir in oatmeal and salt; cover.

2. Combine egg yolks and granulated sugar in medium bowl; mix well. Heat cream and vanilla in medium saucepan over medium heat until small bubbles begin to form at edge of pan. Do not boil. Remove from heat. Whisking constantly, pour ½ cup hot cream into egg yolk mixture in thin stream. Whisk egg mixture back into cream in saucepan, stirring rapidly to blend well. Spoon mixture over oatmeal. Do not stir.

3. Turn **CROCK-POT®** slow cooker to LOW. Line lid with two paper towels. Cover; cook on LOW 3 to 3½ hours or until custard is set.

4. Sprinkle brown sugar over surface of custard. Line lid with two dry paper towels. Cover tightly; cook on LOW 10 to 15 minutes or until brown sugar melts. Serve with fresh berries, if desired.

Makes 4 to 6 servings

Triple Delicious Hot Chocolate

3 cups milk, divided

⅓ cup sugar

¼ cup unsweetened cocoa powder

¼ teaspoon salt

¾ teaspoon vanilla

1 cup whipping cream

1 square (1 ounce) bittersweet chocolate, chopped

1 square (1 ounce) white chocolate, chopped

   Whipped cream

6 teaspoons mini semisweet chocolate chips or shaved bittersweet chocolate

1. Combine ½ cup milk, sugar, cocoa and salt in **CROCK-POT®** slow cooker; whisk until smooth. Stir in remaining 2½ cups milk and vanilla. Cover; cook on LOW 2 hours.

2. Stir in cream. Cover; cook on LOW 10 minutes. Stir in bittersweet and white chocolate until melted.

3. Pour hot chocolate into mugs. Top each serving with whipped cream and 1 teaspoon chocolate chips.

Makes 6 servings

OATMEAL CRÈME BRÛLÉE

VIENNESE
COFFEE

Viennese Coffee

- 3 cups strong freshly brewed hot coffee
- 3 tablespoons chocolate syrup
- 1 teaspoon sugar
- ⅓ cup whipping cream
- ¼ cup crème de cacao or Irish cream (optional)
  Whipped cream (optional)
  Chocolate shavings (optional)

1. Combine coffee, chocolate syrup and sugar in **CROCK-POT®** slow cooker. Cover; cook on LOW 2 to 2½ hours.

2. Stir whipping cream and crème de cacao, if desired, into **CROCK-POT®** slow cooker. Cover; cook on LOW 30 minutes or until heated through. Ladle coffee into coffee cups. Garnish with whipped cream and chocolate shavings.

Makes 4 servings

Cinn-Sational Swirl Cake

- 1 box (about 21 ounces) cinnamon swirl cake mix
- 1 cup sour cream
- 1 cup cinnamon-flavored baking chips
- 1 package (4-serving size) instant French vanilla pudding and pie filling mix
- 1 cup water
- ¾ cup vegetable oil

1. Coat inside of 4½-quart **CROCK-POT®** slow cooker with nonstick cooking spray. Set cinnamon swirl mix packet aside. Place remaining cake mix in **CROCK-POT®** slow cooker.

2. Add sour cream, cinnamon chips, pudding mix, water and oil; stir well to combine. Batter will be slightly lumpy. Add reserved cinnamon swirl mix, slowly swirling through batter with knife. Cover; cook on LOW 3 to 4 hours or on HIGH 1½ to 1¾ hours or until toothpick inserted into center of cake comes out clean.

3. Serve warm with cinnamon ice cream, if desired.

Makes 10 to 12 servings

Banana Nut Bread

⅓ cup butter or margarine

3 ripe bananas, well mashed

⅔ cup sugar

2 eggs, well beaten

2 tablespoons dark corn syrup

1¾ cups all-purpose flour

2 teaspoons baking powder

½ teaspoon salt

¼ teaspoon baking soda

½ cup chopped walnuts

1. Grease and flour inside of **CROCK-POT®** slow cooker. Beat butter in large bowl with electric mixer at medium speed until fluffy. Gradually beat in bananas, sugar, eggs and corn syrup until smooth.

2. Sift flour, baking powder, salt and baking soda in small bowl. Slowly beat flour mixture into banana mixture. Add walnuts; mix thoroughly. Pour batter into **CROCK-POT®** slow cooker. Cover; cook on HIGH 2 to 3 hours. Let cool before turning bread out onto serving platter.

Makes 1 loaf

Tip: Recipe can be doubled for a 5-, 6- or 7-quart **CROCK-POT®** slow cooker.

Note: Banana Nut Bread has always been a favorite way to use up those overripe bananas. Not only is it delicious, but it also freezes well for future use.

THREE-BEAN
TURKEY CHILI

Soups, Stews and Chilies

Three-Bean Turkey Chili

1 pound ground turkey
1 small onion, chopped
1 can (28 ounces) diced tomatoes
1 can (about 15 ounces) chickpeas, rinsed and drained
1 can (about 15 ounces) kidney beans, rinsed and drained
1 can (about 15 ounces) black beans, rinsed and drained
1 can (8 ounces) tomato sauce
1 can (4 ounces) diced mild green chiles
1 to 2 tablespoons chili powder

1. Place turkey and onion in medium skillet over medium-high heat; cook and stir until turkey is browned. Drain fat. Transfer to **CROCK-POT®** slow cooker.

2. Add tomatoes, chickpeas, beans, tomato sauce, chiles and chili powder to **CROCK-POT®** slow cooker; mix well. Cover; cook on HIGH 6 to 8 hours.

Makes 6 to 8 servings

Easy Beef Stew

2 pounds cubed beef stew meat
1 can (10¾ ounces) condensed cream of mushroom soup, undiluted
1 can (4 ounces) mushrooms
⅓ cup dry red or white wine
1 envelope (1 ounce) dry onion soup mix
   Hot cooked noodles

Combine all ingredients except noodles in **CROCK-POT®** slow cooker. Cover; cook on LOW 8 to 12 hours. Serve over noodles.

Makes 4 to 6 servings

Tip: Browning the beef before cooking it in the **CROCK-POT®** slow cooker isn't necessary, but it helps to enhance the flavor and appearance of the stew. If you have time, heat oil in large skillet and brown the meat before placing it in the **CROCK-POT®** slow cooker. Follow the recipe as directed.

Northwest Beef and Vegetable Soup

2 tablespoons olive oil

1 pound lean cubed stew beef

1 onion, chopped

1 clove garlic, minced

3½ cups canned crushed tomatoes, undrained

1 butternut squash, peeled and diced

1 can (about 15 ounces) white beans, rinsed and drained

1 turnip, peeled and diced

1 large potato, diced

8 cups water

2 stalks celery, sliced

2 tablespoons minced fresh basil

1½ teaspoons salt

1 teaspoon black pepper

1. Heat oil in large skillet over medium heat. Brown beef on all sides. Add onion and garlic during last few minutes of browning. Transfer to **CROCK-POT**® slow cooker.

2. Add remaining ingredients; stir until blended. Cover; cook on HIGH 2 hours. Turn **CROCK-POT**® slow cooker to LOW. Cook on LOW 4 to 6 hours, stirring occasionally and adjusting seasonings to taste.

Makes 6 to 8 servings

Three-Bean Mole Chili

1 can (about 15 ounces) chili beans in spicy sauce, undrained

1 can (about 15 ounces) pinto beans, rinsed and drained

1 can (about 15 ounces) black beans, rinsed and drained

1 can (about 14 ounces) Mexican or chili-style diced tomatoes

1 large green bell pepper, chopped

1 small onion, chopped

½ cup vegetable broth

¼ cup prepared mole paste*

2 teaspoons minced garlic

2 teaspoons ground cumin

2 teaspoons chili powder

2 teaspoons ground coriander (optional)

Optional toppings: crushed tortilla chips, chopped fresh cilantro, shredded cheese

***Mole paste is available in the Mexican section of large supermarkets and at specialty markets.**

Combine all ingredients except toppings in **CROCK-POT**® slow cooker; mix well. Cover; cook on LOW 5 to 6 hours or until vegetables are tender. Serve with desired toppings.

Makes 4 to 6 servings

Tip: Opening the lid and checking on food in the **CROCK-POT**® slow cooker can affect both cooking time and results. Due to the nature of slow cooking, there's no need to stir the food unless the recipe method says to do so.

NORTHWEST BEEF
AND VEGETABLE SOUP

Wild Mushroom Beef Stew

1½ to 2 pounds cubed beef stew meat
2 tablespoons all-purpose flour
½ teaspoon salt
½ teaspoon black pepper
1½ cups beef broth
1 teaspoon Worcestershire sauce
1 clove garlic, minced
1 whole bay leaf
1 teaspoon paprika
4 shiitake mushrooms, sliced
2 medium carrots, sliced
2 medium potatoes, diced
1 small white onion, chopped
1 stalk celery, sliced

1. Place beef in **CROCK-POT**® slow cooker. Mix flour, salt and pepper in small bowl; sprinkle over meat. Stir to coat meat with flour. Add remaining ingredients and stir to mix well.

2. Cover; cook on LOW 10 to 12 hours or on HIGH 4 to 6 hours. Remove and discard bay leaf.

Makes 5 servings

Tip: You may double the amount of meat, mushrooms, carrots, potatoes, onion and celery for a 5-, 6- or 7-quart **CROCK-POT**® slow cooker.

Note: This classic beef stew is given a twist with the addition of flavorful shiitake mushrooms. If shiitake mushrooms are unavailable in your local grocery store, you can substitute other mushrooms of your choice. For extra punch, add a few dried porcini mushrooms.

Chicken and Chile Pepper Stew

1 pound boneless, skinless chicken thighs, cut into ½-inch pieces
1 pound small potatoes, cut lengthwise into halves, then crosswise into slices
1 cup chopped onion
2 poblano peppers, seeded and cut into ½-inch pieces*
1 jalapeño pepper, seeded and finely chopped*
3 cloves garlic, minced
3 cups fat-free, reduced-sodium chicken broth
1 can (about 14 ounces) no-salt-added diced tomatoes
2 tablespoons chili powder
1 teaspoon dried oregano

Poblano and jalapeño peppers can sting and irritate the skin, so wear rubber gloves when handling peppers and do not touch your eyes.

1. Place chicken, potatoes, onion, poblano peppers, jalapeño pepper and garlic in **CROCK-POT**® slow cooker.

2. Combine broth, tomatoes, chili powder and oregano in large bowl; stir. Pour into **CROCK-POT**® slow cooker. Cover; cook on LOW 8 to 9 hours.

Makes 6 servings

WILD MUSHROOM BEEF STEW

Mama's Beer Chili

2 tablespoons olive oil

1 large onion (preferably Vidalia), diced

4 cloves garlic, crushed

1½ to 2 pounds ground turkey

1 can (28 ounces) crushed tomatoes

1 package (10 ounces) frozen corn

1 can (about 15 ounces) pink or kidney beans, rinsed and drained

1 cup beer (preferable dark)

⅓ cup honey

⅓ cup diced mild green chiles

3 tablespoons chili powder

3 tablespoons hot pepper sauce

3 beef bouillon cubes

1 to 2 tablespoons all-purpose flour

1 teaspoon curry powder

Sliced green onions

1. Heat oil in large skillet over medium-low heat. Add onion; cook and stir 5 minutes. Add garlic; cook and stir 2 minutes.

2. Add turkey to skillet; cook and stir until turkey is no longer pink. Drain fat.

3. Stir in remaining ingredients except green onions. Transfer to **CROCK-POT**® slow cooker. Cover; cook on LOW 8 to 10 hours or on HIGH 4 to 6 hours. Garnish with green onions.

Makes 4 to 6 servings

Serving Suggestion: Serve with corn bread and jam or a loaf of fresh bread, if desired.

Beef Stew with Bacon, Onion and Sweet Potatoes

1 pound cubed beef stew meat

1 can (about 14 ounces) beef broth

2 medium sweet potatoes, cut into 2-inch pieces

1 large onion, chopped

2 slices thick-cut bacon, diced

1 teaspoon dried thyme

1 teaspoon salt

¼ teaspoon black pepper

2 tablespoons water

2 tablespoons cornstarch

1. Coat inside of **CROCK-POT**® slow cooker with nonstick cooking spray. Combine all ingredients except water and cornstarch in **CROCK-POT**® slow cooker; mix well.

2. Cover; cook on LOW 7 to 8 hours or on HIGH 4 to 5 hours or until meat and vegetables are tender. Remove beef and vegetables to serving bowl using slotted spoon. Cover and keep warm.

3. Stir water into cornstarch in small bowl until smooth. Whisk into cooking liquid in **CROCK-POT**® slow cooker. Cover; cook on HIGH 15 minutes or until thickened. Serve sauce evenly over beef and vegetables.

Makes 4 servings

MAMA'S BEER CHILI

Black and White Chili

Nonstick cooking spray

1 pound chicken tenders, cut into ¾-inch pieces

1 cup coarsely chopped onion

1 can (about 15 ounces) Great Northern beans, rinsed and drained

1 can (about 15 ounces) black beans, rinsed and drained

1 can (about 14 ounces) Mexican-style stewed tomatoes, undrained

2 tablespoons Texas-style chili powder seasoning mix

1. Spray large skillet with cooking spray; heat over medium heat. Add chicken and onion; cook and stir 5 minutes or until chicken is browned.

2. Combine chicken mixture, beans, tomatoes and chili seasoning in **CROCK-POT®** slow cooker. Cover; cook on LOW 4 to 4½ hours.

Makes 6 servings

Serving Suggestion: For a change of pace, serve this delicious chili over cooked rice or pasta.

Weeknight Chili

1 pound ground beef or turkey

1 package (about 1 ounce) chili seasoning mix

1 can (about 15 ounces) red kidney beans, rinsed and drained

1 can (about 14 ounces) diced tomatoes with mild green chiles

1 can (8 ounces) tomato sauce

1 cup (4 ounces) shredded Cheddar cheese (optional)

1. Brown beef 6 to 8 minutes in large skillet over medium-high heat, stirring to break up meat. Drain fat. Stir in seasoning mix.

2. Place beef, beans, tomatoes and tomato sauce in **CROCK-POT®** slow cooker. Cover; cook on LOW 4 to 6 hours or on HIGH 2 to 3 hours. Garnish with cheese.

Makes 4 servings

Thai-Style Chicken Pumpkin Soup

1 tablespoon extra virgin olive oil

6 boneless, skinless chicken breasts, cut into 1-inch cubes

1 large white onion, thinly sliced

3 cloves garlic, minced

1 tablespoon minced fresh ginger

½ to ¾ teaspoon red pepper flakes

2 stalks celery, diced

2 carrots, diced

1 can (15 ounces) solid-pack pumpkin*

½ cup creamy peanut butter

4 cups low-sodium chicken broth

½ cup mango nectar

½ cup fresh lime juice

3 tablespoons rice vinegar

½ cup minced fresh cilantro, divided

½ cup heavy cream

1 tablespoon cornstarch

2 to 4 cups hot cooked rice (preferably jasmine or basmati)

3 green onions, minced

½ cup roasted unsalted peanuts, coarsely chopped

Lime wedges (optional)

Do not use pumpkin pie filling.

1. Heat oil in large skillet over medium heat. Add chicken and cook, stirring occasionally, about 3 minutes. Add onion, garlic, ginger and red pepper flakes; cook 1 or 2 minutes or until fragrant. Transfer chicken mixture to **CROCK-POT®** slow cooker.

2. Stir in celery, carrots, pumpkin, peanut butter, broth, mango nectar and lime juice. Cover; cook on LOW 8 hours or on HIGH 4 hours.

3. Stir in rice vinegar and ¼ cup cilantro. Stir together cream and cornstarch in small bowl. Stir into soup. Simmer, uncovered, on HIGH 10 minutes or until soup is thickened.

4. To serve, place rice in soup bowls. Ladle soup around rice. Sprinkle with remaining ¼ cup cilantro, green onions and peanuts. Squeeze fresh lime juice over soup, if desired.

Makes 4 to 6 servings

Greek Braised Beef Stew

¼ cup all-purpose flour

2 teaspoons Greek seasoning

¼ teaspoon salt

¼ teaspoon black pepper

2 pounds cubed beef stew meat or boneless beef chuck roast

2 tablespoons olive oil

2 cups fat-free, reduced-sodium beef broth

2 onions, each cut into 8 wedges

1 container (10 ounces) grape or cherry tomatoes

1 jar (8 ounces) pitted kalamata olives, drained

10 sprigs fresh oregano, divided

1 lemon, divided

1. Combine flour, Greek seasoning, salt and pepper in large resealable food storage bag. Add beef; shake to coat. Heat oil in large skillet over medium-high heat. Brown beef on all sides. Transfer to **CROCK-POT®** slow cooker.

2. Add broth, onions, tomatoes, olives, 4 sprigs oregano and juice of ½ lemon. Cover; cook on HIGH 6 to 7 hours or until beef is tender. Cut remaining ½ lemon into wedges and serve with stew. Garnish with remaining 6 sprigs oregano.

Makes 6 servings

Tip: Removing the lid from your **CROCK-POT®** slow cooker, even for just a few minutes to check on the progress of the dish inside, can allow significant amounts of heat to escape, requiring additional cooking time.

Chicken and Black Bean Chili

1 pound boneless, skinless chicken thighs, cut into 1-inch pieces

2 teaspoons chili powder

2 teaspoons ground cumin

¾ teaspoon salt

1 green bell pepper, diced

1 small onion, chopped

3 cloves garlic, minced

1 can (about 14 ounces) diced tomatoes

1 cup chunky salsa

1 can (about 15 ounces) black beans, rinsed and drained

Optional toppings: sour cream, diced ripe avocado, shredded Cheddar cheese, sliced green onions or chopped fresh cilantro, crushed tortilla chips or corn chips

1. Combine chicken, chili powder, cumin and salt in **CROCK-POT®** slow cooker; toss to coat.

2. Add bell pepper, onion and garlic; mix well. Stir in tomatoes and salsa. Cover; cook on LOW 5 to 6 hours or on HIGH 2½ to 3 hours or until chicken is tender.

3. Stir in beans. Cover; cook on HIGH 5 to 10 minutes or until heated through. Ladle into shallow bowls; serve with desired toppings.

Makes 4 servings

GREEK BRAISED BEEF STEW

Chicken Stew with Herb Dumplings

2 cups sliced carrots

1 cup chopped onion

1 green bell pepper, sliced

½ cup sliced celery

2 cans (about 14 ounces each) chicken broth, divided

⅔ cup all-purpose flour

1 pound boneless, skinless chicken breasts, cut into 1-inch pieces

1 large red potato, unpeeled and cut into 1-inch pieces

6 ounces mushrooms, halved

¾ cup frozen peas

1¼ teaspoons dried basil, divided

1 teaspoon dried rosemary, divided

½ teaspoon dried tarragon, divided

¼ cup heavy cream

¾ to 1 teaspoon salt

¼ teaspoon black pepper

1 cup biscuit baking mix

⅓ cup reduced-fat (2%) milk

1. Combine carrots, onion, bell pepper, celery and all but 1 cup broth in **CROCK-POT**® slow cooker. Cover; cook on LOW 2 hours.

2. Stir remaining 1 cup broth into flour in small bowl until smooth. Stir into vegetable mixture. Add chicken, potato, mushrooms, peas, 1 teaspoon basil, ¾ teaspoon rosemary and ¼ teaspoon tarragon. Cover; cook on LOW 4 hours or until vegetables and chicken are tender. Stir in cream, salt and black pepper.

3. Combine baking mix, remaining ¼ teaspoon basil, ¼ teaspoon rosemary and ¼ teaspoon tarragon in small bowl. Stir in milk until soft dough forms. Add dumpling mixture to top of stew in 4 large spoonfuls. Cook on LOW, uncovered, 30 minutes. Cover; cook on LOW 30 to 45 minutes or until dumplings are firm and toothpick inserted into center comes out clean. Serve in shallow bowls.

Makes 4 servings

PANAMA
PORK STEW

Panama Pork Stew

2 small sweet potatoes (about ¾ pound),
   cut into 2-inch pieces

1 package (10 ounces) frozen corn

1 package (9 ounces) frozen cut green
   beans

1 cup chopped onion

1¼ pounds cubed pork stew meat

1 can (about 14 ounces) diced tomatoes

¼ cup water

1 to 2 tablespoons chili powder

½ teaspoon salt

½ teaspoon ground coriander

1. Place potatoes, corn, green beans and onion
in **CROCK-POT®** slow cooker. Top with pork.

2. Combine tomatoes, water, chili powder, salt
and coriander in medium bowl. Pour over pork.
Cover; cook on LOW 7 to 9 hours.

Makes 6 servings

Pizza Soup

2 cans (about 14 ounces each) stewed
   tomatoes with Italian seasonings,
   undrained

2 cups beef broth

1 cup sliced mushrooms

1 small onion, chopped

1 tablespoon tomato paste

¼ teaspoon salt

¼ teaspoon black pepper

½ pound turkey Italian sausage, casings
   removed

   Shredded mozzarella cheese

1. Combine tomatoes, broth, mushrooms, onion,
tomato paste, salt and pepper in **CROCK-POT®**
slow cooker.

2. Shape sausage into marble-size balls. Gently
stir into soup mixture. Cover; cook on LOW 6 to
7 hours. Adjust salt and pepper to taste. Top with
cheese.

Makes 4 servings

CHIPOTLE
CHICKEN STEW

Chipotle Chicken Stew

- 1 **pound boneless, skinless chicken thighs, cut into cubes**
- 1 **can (about 15 ounces) navy beans, rinsed and drained**
- 1 **can (about 15 ounces) black beans, rinsed and drained**
- 1 **can (about 14 ounces) crushed tomatoes, undrained**
- 1½ **cups chicken broth**
- ½ **cup orange juice**
- 1 **medium onion, diced**
- 1 **canned chipotle pepper in adobo sauce, minced**
- 1 **teaspoon** *each* **salt and ground cumin**
- 1 **whole bay leaf**
  Sprigs fresh cilantro (optional)

1. Combine chicken, beans, tomatoes, broth, orange juice, onion, chipotle pepper, salt, cumin and bay leaf in **CROCK-POT**® slow cooker.

2. Cover; cook on LOW 7 to 8 hours or on HIGH 3½ to 4 hours. Remove and discard bay leaf. Garnish with cilantro.

Makes 6 servings

Lentil Soup with Ham and Bacon

- 8 **cups beef broth**
- 3 **cups dried lentils, rinsed and sorted**
- 2 **cups chopped ham**
- 8 **ounces chopped bacon, crisp-cooked and crumbled**
- 1 **cup chopped carrots**
- ¾ **cup chopped celery**
- ¾ **cup chopped tomatoes**
- ½ **cup chopped onion**
- 2 **teaspoons salt**
- 2 **teaspoons black pepper**
- ½ **teaspoon dried marjoram**

Add broth, lentils, ham, bacon, carrots, celery, tomatoes, onion, salt, pepper and marjoram to **CROCK-POT**® slow cooker. Cover; cook on LOW 8 to 10 hours or on HIGH 6 to 8 hours or until lentils are tender.

Makes 8 servings

Italian Hillside Garden Soup

- 1 tablespoon extra virgin olive oil
- 1 cup chopped green bell pepper
- 1 cup chopped onion
- ½ cup sliced celery
- 1 can (about 14 ounces) diced tomatoes with basil, garlic and oregano
- 1 can (about 15 ounces) navy beans, rinsed and drained
- 1 medium zucchini, chopped
- 1 cup frozen cut green beans, thawed
- 2 cans (about 14 ounces each) chicken broth
- ¼ teaspoon garlic powder
- 1 package (9 ounces) refrigerated sausage- or cheese-filled tortellini pasta
- 3 tablespoons chopped fresh basil

  Grated Asiago or Parmesan cheese (optional)

1. Heat oil in large skillet over medium-high heat. Add bell pepper, onion and celery. Cook and stir 4 minutes or until onions are translucent. Transfer to **CROCK-POT®** slow cooker.

2. Add tomatoes, navy beans, zucchini, green beans, broth and garlic powder. Cover; cook on LOW 7 hours or on HIGH 3½ hours.

3. Add tortellini. Cover; cook on HIGH 20 to 25 minutes or until pasta is tender. Stir in basil. Top with cheese.

Makes 6 servings

Tip: Cooking times are guidelines. **CROCK-POT®** slow cookers, just like ovens, cook differently depending on a variety of factors, including capacity. For example, cooking times will be longer at higher altitudes.

Jerk Pork and Sweet Potato Stew

2 tablespoons all-purpose flour

¼ teaspoon salt

¼ teaspoon black pepper

1¼ pounds pork shoulder, cut into bite-size pieces

2 tablespoons vegetable oil

1 large sweet potato, diced

1 cup frozen or canned corn

¼ cup minced green onions (green parts only), divided

1 clove garlic, minced

½ medium Scotch bonnet pepper or jalapeño pepper, seeded and minced (about 1 teaspoon)*

⅛ teaspoon ground allspice

1 cup chicken broth

1 tablespoon lime juice

2 cups cooked rice (optional)

*Scotch bonnet peppers can sting and irritate the skin, so wear rubber gloves when handling peppers and do not touch your eyes.

1. Combine flour, salt and black pepper in large resealable food storage bag; add pork. Seal bag; shake well to coat. Heat oil in large skillet over medium heat. Cook pork in batches in single layer 5 minutes or until browned. Transfer to **CROCK-POT**® slow cooker.

2. Stir sweet potato, corn, 2 tablespoons green onions, garlic, Scotch bonnet pepper and allspice. Stir in broth. Cover; cook on LOW 5 to 6 hours.

3. Stir in lime juice and remaining 2 tablespoons green onions. Adjust salt and black pepper to taste. Serve stew with rice, if desired.

Makes 4 servings

Tip: To reduce the amount of fat in **CROCK-POT**® slow cooker meals, trim excess fat from meats and degrease canned broth before using.

Cheesy Tavern Soup

4 tablespoons olive oil

½ cup chopped celery

½ cup chopped carrot

½ cup chopped onion

½ cup chopped green bell pepper

2 quarts chicken broth

2 cans (12 ounces each) beer, at room temperature

¼ cup (½ stick) butter

2 teaspoons salt

2 teaspoons black pepper

½ cup all-purpose flour

4 cups (16 ounces) shredded Cheddar cheese

1. Heat oil in medium skillet over medium heat. Add celery, carrot, onion and bell pepper. Cook and stir until tender. Transfer to **CROCK-POT**® slow cooker.

2. Add broth, beer, butter, salt and black pepper to **CROCK-POT**® slow cooker. Cover; cook on LOW 6 hours or on HIGH 2 to 4 hours.

3. Stir small amount of water into flour in small bowl until smooth. Whisk into **CROCK-POT**® slow cooker. Cover; cook on HIGH 10 to 15 minutes or until thickened.

4. Preheat broiler. Ladle soup into individual broiler-safe bowls. Top each with ½ cup cheese. Broil 10 to 15 minutes or until cheese is melted.

Makes 8 servings

**JERK PORK AND
SWEET POTATO STEW**

HEARTY LENTIL
AND ROOT
VEGETABLE STEW

Hearty Lentil and Root Vegetable Stew

2 cans (about 14 ounces each) chicken broth

1½ cups turnips, cut into 1-inch cubes

1 cup dried red lentils, rinsed and sorted

1 medium onion, cut into ½-inch wedges

2 medium carrots, cut into 1-inch pieces

1 medium red bell pepper, cut into 1-inch pieces

½ teaspoon dried oregano

⅛ teaspoon red pepper flakes

1 tablespoon olive oil

½ teaspoon salt

4 slices bacon, crisp-cooked and crumbled

½ cup finely chopped green onions

1. Combine broth, turnips, lentils, onion, carrots, bell pepper, oregano and red pepper flakes in **CROCK-POT**® slow cooker; mix well. Cover; cook on LOW 6 hours or on HIGH 3 hours or until lentils are tender.

2. Stir in oil and salt. Sprinkle each serving with bacon and green onions.

Makes 8 servings

Savory Chicken and Oregano Chili

3 cans (about 15 ounces each) Great Northern or cannellini beans, rinsed and drained

3½ cups chicken broth

2 cups chopped cooked chicken

2 red bell peppers, chopped

1 onion, chopped

1 can (4 ounces) diced mild green chiles, drained

3 cloves garlic, minced

2 teaspoons ground cumin

1 teaspoon salt

1 tablespoon minced fresh oregano

1. Place beans, broth, chicken, bell peppers, onion, chiles, garlic, cumin and salt in **CROCK-POT**® slow cooker; mix well. Cover; cook on LOW 8 to 10 hours or on HIGH 4 to 5 hours.

2. Stir in oregano just before serving.

Makes 8 servings

CHILI VERDE

Chili Verde

Nonstick cooking spray

¾ pound boneless lean pork, cut into 1-inch cubes

1 pound fresh tomatillos, husks removed, rinsed and coarsely chopped

1 can (about 15 ounces) Great Northern beans, rinsed and drained

1 can (about 14 ounces) chicken broth

1 large onion, halved and thinly sliced

1 can (4 ounces) diced mild green chiles

6 cloves garlic, sliced

1 teaspoon ground cumin

Salt and black pepper

½ cup lightly packed fresh cilantro, chopped

1. Spray large skillet with cooking spray. Heat over medium-high heat. Add pork; cook until browned on all sides.

2. Combine pork and remaining ingredients except cilantro in **CROCK-POT**® slow cooker. Cover; cook on HIGH 3 to 4 hours.

3. Season to taste with additional salt and pepper. Turn **CROCK-POT**® slow cooker to LOW. Stir in cilantro. Cover; cook on LOW 10 minutes.

Makes 4 servings

Kick'n Chili

2 pounds ground beef

2 cloves garlic, minced

1 tablespoon *each* salt, ground cumin, chili powder, paprika, dried oregano and black pepper

2 teaspoons red pepper flakes

¼ teaspoon ground red pepper

1 tablespoon vegetable oil

3 cans (about 14 ounces each) diced tomatoes with mild green chiles

1 jar (16 ounces) salsa

1 onion, chopped

1. Combine beef, garlic, salt, cumin, chili powder, paprika, oregano, black pepper, red pepper flakes and ground red pepper in large bowl.

2. Heat oil in large skillet over medium-high heat. Brown beef 6 to 8 minutes, stirring to break up meat. Drain fat. Add tomatoes, salsa and onion; mix well.

3. Transfer to **CROCK-POT**® slow cooker. Cover; cook on LOW 4 to 6 hours.

Makes 6 servings

Tip: This chunky chili is perfect for the spicy food lover in your family. Reduce red pepper flakes for a milder flavor.

Hearty Chicken Chili

- 1 medium onion, finely chopped
- 1 small jalapeño pepper, seeded and minced*
- 1 clove garlic, minced
- 1½ teaspoons chili powder
- ¾ teaspoon salt
- ½ teaspoon ground cumin
- ½ teaspoon dried oregano
- ½ teaspoon black pepper
- 2 cans (about 15 ounces each) hominy, rinsed and drained**
- 1 can (about 15 ounces) pinto beans, rinsed and drained
- 1½ pounds boneless, skinless chicken thighs, cut into 1-inch pieces
- 1 cup chicken broth
  Chopped fresh parsley or cilantro (optional)

*Jalapeño peppers can sting and irritate the skin, so wear rubber gloves when handling peppers and do not touch your eyes.

**Hominy is corn that has been treated to remove the germ and hull. It can be found with the canned vegetables or beans in most supermarkets.

1. Combine onion, jalapeño pepper, garlic, chili powder, salt, cumin, oregano and black pepper in **CROCK-POT**® slow cooker.

2. Stir in hominy, beans, chicken and broth. Cover; cook on LOW 7 hours. Garnish with parsley.

Makes 6 servings

Tip: For a hotter dish, add ¼ teaspoon red pepper flakes with the seasonings. For thicker chili, stir 3 tablespoons cooking liquid into 1 tablespoon flour in small bowl until smooth. Stir into cooking liquid; cook on HIGH 10 minutes or until thickened.

Italian Sausage Soup

SAUSAGE MEATBALLS

- 1 pound mild Italian sausage, casings removed
- ½ cup dry bread crumbs
- ¼ cup grated Parmesan cheese, plus additional for garnish
- ¼ cup milk
- 1 egg
- ½ teaspoon dried basil
- ½ teaspoon black pepper
- ¼ teaspoon garlic salt

SOUP

- 4 cups hot chicken broth
- 1 tablespoon tomato paste
- 1 clove garlic, minced
- ¼ teaspoon red pepper flakes
- ½ cup uncooked mini pasta shells*
- 1 bag (10 ounces) fresh baby spinach

*Or use other tiny pasta, such as ditalini (mini tubes) or farfallini (mini bowties).

1. For meatballs, combine sausage, bread crumbs, ¼ cup cheese, milk, egg, basil, black pepper and garlic salt in large bowl. Roll into ½-inch balls.

2. Combine broth, tomato paste, garlic and red pepper flakes in **CROCK-POT**® slow cooker. Add meatballs. Cover; cook on LOW 5 to 6 hours.

3. Add pasta; cook on LOW 30 minutes. Stir in spinach leaves when pasta is tender. Ladle into bowls; sprinkle with additional cheese.

Makes 4 to 6 servings

HEARTY
CHICKEN CHILI

Fresh Lime and Black Bean Soup

2 cans (about 15 ounces each) black beans, undrained
1 can (about 14 ounces) vegetable broth
1½ cups chopped onions
1½ teaspoons chili powder
¾ teaspoon ground cumin
¼ teaspoon garlic powder
⅛ to ¼ teaspoon red pepper flakes
½ cup sour cream
2 tablespoons extra virgin olive oil
2 tablespoons chopped fresh cilantro
1 medium lime, cut into wedges

1. Coat **CROCK-POT**® slow cooker with nonstick cooking spray. Add beans, broth, onions, chili powder, cumin, garlic powder and red pepper flakes. Cover; cook on LOW 7 hours or on HIGH 3½ hours or until onions are very soft.

2. Process 1 cup soup mixture in blender until smooth and return to **CROCK-POT**® slow cooker. Stir, check consistency and repeat with additional 1 cup soup as desired. Turn off heat. Let stand 15 to 20 minutes before serving.

3. Ladle soup into bowls. Divide sour cream, oil and cilantro evenly among servings. Squeeze juice from lime wedges over each.

Makes 4 servings

Tip: Brighten the flavor of dishes cooked in the **CROCK-POT**® slow cooker by adding fresh herbs or fresh lemon or lime juice before serving.

New Mexican Green Chile Pork Stew

1½ pounds boneless pork shoulder, cut into 1-inch cubes
2 medium baking potatoes or sweet potatoes, cut into large cubes
1 cup chopped onion
1 cup frozen corn
1 can (4 ounces) diced mild green chiles
1 jar (16 ounces) salsa verde (green salsa)
2 teaspoons sugar
2 teaspoons ground cumin or chili powder
1 teaspoon dried oregano
   Hot cooked rice
¼ cup chopped fresh cilantro (optional)

1. Place pork, potatoes, onion, corn and chiles in **CROCK-POT**® slow cooker. Stir salsa, sugar, cumin and oregano in medium bowl; pour over pork and vegetables. Stir gently to mix.

2. Cover; cook on LOW 6 to 8 hours or on HIGH 4 to 5 hours or until pork is tender. Serve stew over rice. Garnish with cilantro.

Makes 6 servings

Tip: Root vegetables such as potatoes can sometimes take longer to cook in a **CROCK-POT**® slow cooker than meat. Place uniformly cut vegetables on the bottom or along the sides of the **CROCK-POT**® slow cooker when possible.

FRESH LIME AND
BLACK BEAN SOUP

Classic Chili

1½ pounds ground beef

1½ cups chopped onion

 1 cup chopped green bell pepper

 2 cloves garlic, minced

 3 cans (about 15 ounces each) dark red kidney beans, rinsed and drained

 2 cans (about 15 ounces each) tomato sauce

 1 can (about 14 ounces) diced tomatoes

 2 to 3 teaspoons chili powder

 1 to 2 teaspoons ground mustard

 ¾ teaspoon dried basil

 ½ teaspoon black pepper

 1 to 2 dried red chiles (optional)

1. Brown beef, onion, bell pepper and garlic in large skillet over medium-high heat, stirring to break up meat. Drain fat. Transfer beef mixture to **CROCK-POT®** slow cooker.

2. Add beans, tomato sauce, tomatoes, chili powder, mustard, basil, black pepper and chiles, if desired, to **CROCK-POT®** slow cooker; mix well. Cover; cook on LOW 8 to 10 hours or on HIGH 4 to 5 hours. If used, remove chiles before serving.

Makes 6 servings

Simmering Hot and Sour Soup

 2 cans (about 14 ounces each) chicken broth

 1 cup chopped cooked chicken or pork

 4 ounces shiitake mushroom caps, thinly sliced

 ½ cup thinly sliced bamboo shoots

 3 tablespoons rice wine vinegar

 2 tablespoons soy sauce

1½ teaspoons chili paste *or* 1 teaspoon hot chili oil

 4 ounces firm tofu, drained and cut into ½-inch pieces

 2 teaspoons dark sesame oil

 2 tablespoons cold water

 2 tablespoons cornstarch

    Chopped fresh cilantro or sliced green onions

1. Combine broth, chicken, mushrooms, bamboo shoots, vinegar, soy sauce and chili paste in **CROCK-POT®** slow cooker. Cover; cook on LOW 3 to 4 hours or on HIGH 2 to 3 hours or until chicken is heated through.

2. Stir in tofu and sesame oil. Stir water into cornstarch in small bowl until smooth; stir into soup. Cover; cook on HIGH 10 minutes or until thickened. Sprinkle with cilantro.

Makes 4 servings

SWEET AND SOUR
BRISKET STEW

Sweet and Sour Brisket Stew

- 1 jar (12 ounces) chili sauce
- 1½ tablespoons packed dark brown sugar
- 1½ tablespoons lemon juice
- ¼ cup beef broth
- 1 tablespoon Dijon mustard
- ¼ teaspoon paprika
- ½ teaspoon salt
- ¼ teaspoon black pepper
- 1 beef brisket, trimmed and cut into 1-inch cubes*
- 2 carrots, cut into ½-inch slices
- 1 onion, chopped
- 1 clove garlic, minced
- 1 tablespoon all-purpose flour (optional)

Beef brisket has a thick layer of fat, which some supermarkets trim off. If the meat is well trimmed, buy 2½ pounds; if not, purchase 4 pounds, then trim and discard excess fat.

1. Combine chili sauce, brown sugar, lemon juice, broth, mustard, paprika, salt and pepper in **CROCK-POT®** slow cooker.

2. Add beef, carrots, onion and garlic; mix well. Cover; cook on LOW 8 hours.

3. For thicker gravy, turn **CROCK-POT®** slow cooker to HIGH. Stir 3 tablespoons cooking liquid into flour in small bowl until smooth. Stir into **CROCK-POT®** slow cooker. Cover; cook on HIGH 10 minutes or until thickened.

Makes 6 to 8 servings

Cream of Scallop Soup

- 1½ pounds red potatoes, cubed
- 3 cups water
- 1½ cups milk
- 2 onions, chopped
- 2 carrots, shredded
- ½ cup vegetable broth
- 2 tablespoons dry white wine
- ½ teaspoon garlic powder
- ½ teaspoon dried thyme
- 2 egg yolks, lightly beaten
- 1 pound sea scallops
- 1 cup (4 ounces) shredded Cheddar cheese

1. Combine potatoes, water, milk, onions, carrots, broth, wine, garlic powder and thyme in **CROCK-POT®** slow cooker. Cover; cook on LOW 6 to 8 hours or HIGH 3 to 5 hours.

2. Stir in egg yolks. Cover; cook on LOW 1 hour.

3. Add scallops and cook, uncovered, on LOW 10 minutes. Mix in cheese and cook, uncovered, on LOW 5 minutes or until cheese is melted and scallops are opaque.

Makes 4 to 6 servings

Tip: Scallops cook very quickly. Over cooking will make them tough, so check for doneness early.

WARM
BLUE CRAB
BRUSCHETTA

Party Starters

Warm Blue Crab Bruschetta

    4 cups peeled, seeded and diced plum
       tomatoes
    1 cup diced white onion
    ⅓ cup olive oil
    2 tablespoons sugar
    2 tablespoons balsamic vinegar
    2 teaspoons minced garlic
    ½ teaspoon dried oregano
    1 pound lump blue crabmeat, picked over
       for shells
 1½ teaspoons kosher salt
    ½ teaspoon cracked black pepper
    ⅓ cup minced fresh basil
    2 baguettes, sliced and toasted

1. Combine tomatoes, onion, oil, sugar, vinegar,
garlic and oregano in **CROCK-POT®** slow cooker.
Cover; cook on LOW 2 hours.

2. Stir crabmeat, salt and pepper into
CROCK-POT® slow cooker, taking care not to
break up crabmeat. Cover; cook on LOW 1 hour.
Fold in basil. Serve on toasted baguette slices.

Makes 16 servings

Serving Suggestion: Crab topping can
also be served on Melba toast or whole grain
crackers.

Creamy Cheesy Spinach Dip

    2 packages (10 ounces each) frozen
       chopped spinach, thawed and undrained
    2 cups chopped onions
    1 teaspoon salt
    ½ teaspoon garlic powder
    ¼ teaspoon black pepper
  12 ounces pasteurized process cheese
       spread with jalapeño peppers, cubed
       Cherry tomatoes with pulp removed
       (optional)
       Sliced cucumbers (optional)
       Assorted crackers (optional)

1. Drain spinach and squeeze dry, reserving
¾ cup liquid. Place spinach, reserved liquid,
onions, salt, garlic powder and black pepper in
1½-quart or other small-sized **CROCK-POT®**
slow cooker; stir to blend. Cover; cook on HIGH
1½ hours.

2. Stir in cheese spread. Cover; cook on HIGH
30 minutes or until melted. Fill cherry tomato
shells, spread on cucumber slices or serve with
crackers, if desired.

Makes about 4 cups

Tip: To thaw spinach quickly, remove paper
wrapper from spinach containers. Microwave on
HIGH 3 to 4 minutes or just until thawed.

Steamed Pork Buns

½ (18-ounce) container refrigerated cooked shredded pork in barbecue sauce*

1 tablespoon Asian garlic chili sauce

1 package (about 16 ounces) refrigerated big biscuit dough (8 biscuits)

Dipping Sauce (recipe follows)

Sliced green onions (optional)

Look for pork in plain, not smoky, barbecue sauce. Substitute chicken in barbecue sauce, if desired.

1. Combine pork and chili sauce in medium bowl. Split biscuits in half. Roll or stretch each biscuit into 4-inch circle. Spoon 1 tablespoon pork onto center of each biscuit. Gather edges around filling and press to seal.

2. Generously butter 2-quart baking dish that fits inside 5- to 6-quart **CROCK-POT®** slow cooker. Arrange filled biscuits in single layer, overlapping slightly if necessary. Cover dish with buttered foil, butter side down.

3. Place small rack in **CROCK-POT®** slow cooker. Add 1 inch hot water (water should not touch top of rack). Place baking dish on rack. Cover; cook on HIGH 2 hours.

4. Meanwhile, prepare Dipping Sauce. Garnish pork buns with green onions and serve with Dipping Sauce.

Makes 16 servings

Tip: Straight-sided round casserole or soufflé dishes that fit into the **CROCK-POT®** stoneware make excellent baking dishes.

Dipping Sauce

Stir together 2 tablespoons rice vinegar, 2 tablespoons soy sauce, 4 teaspoons sugar and 1 teaspoon toasted sesame oil in small bowl until sugar dissolves. Sprinkle with 1 tablespoon minced green onion just before serving.

Bean Dip for a Crowd

1½ cups dried black beans, rinsed and sorted

1½ cups dried pinto beans, rinsed and sorted

5 cups water, plus additional as needed

1 package (about 1¼ ounces) taco seasoning mix

2 tablespoons dried minced onion

3 vegetable bouillon cubes

1 tablespoon dried parsley flakes

2 whole bay leaves

1 jar (16 ounces) thick and chunky salsa

2 tablespoons lime juice

1. Place beans in large bowl; cover with water. Soak 6 to 8 hours or overnight. (To quick-soak beans, place in large saucepan; cover with water. Bring to a boil over high heat. Boil 2 minutes. Remove from heat; let soak, covered, 1 hour.)

2. Drain beans; discard water. Combine beans, 5 cups water, taco seasoning, onion, bouillon cubes, parsley flakes and bay leaves in **CROCK-POT®** slow cooker. Cover; cook on LOW 9 to 10 hours or until beans are tender. Add additional water, ½ cup at a time, as needed.

3. Remove and discard bay leaves. Carefully transfer half of bean mixture to food processor. Add salsa and lime juice. Cover; process until smooth. Stir into **CROCK-POT®** slow cooker.

Makes about 6 cups

Tip: Salt, sugar and acidic ingredients can toughen dried beans as they cook, so dried beans must be cooked and tender before you can add these ingredients. You may substitute canned beans for the dried beans in this recipe. Canned beans are ideal for **CROCK-POT®** slow cookers because they're already soft.

STEAMED PORK BUNS

Mini Carnitas Tacos

1½ pounds boneless pork loin, cut into 1-inch cubes

1 onion, finely chopped

½ cup chicken broth

1 tablespoon chili powder

2 teaspoons ground cumin

1 teaspoon dried oregano

½ teaspoon minced canned chipotle peppers in adobo sauce

½ cup pico de gallo

2 tablespoons chopped fresh cilantro

½ teaspoon salt

12 (6-inch) flour or corn tortillas

¾ cup (3 ounces) shredded sharp Cheddar cheese

3 tablespoons sour cream

1. Combine pork, onion, broth, chili powder, cumin, oregano and chipotle peppers in **CROCK-POT**® slow cooker. Cover; cook on LOW 6 hours or on HIGH 3 hours or until pork is very tender. Pour off excess cooking liquid.

2. Remove pork to cutting board; shred pork with two forks. Return to **CROCK-POT**® slow cooker. Stir in pico de gallo, cilantro and salt. Cover; keep warm on LOW or WARM setting.

3. Cut three circles from each tortilla with 2-inch biscuit cutter. Top each with pork, cheese and sour cream. Serve warm.

Makes 12 servings

Tip: Carnitas, or "little meats" in Spanish, are a festive way to spice up any gathering. Carnitas traditionally include a large amount of lard, but slow cooking makes the dish healthier by eliminating the need to add lard, oil or fat, while keeping the meat tender and delicious.

Slow Cooker Cheese Dip

1 pound ground beef

1 pound bulk Italian sausage

1 package (16 ounces) pasteurized process cheese product, cubed

1 can (11 ounces) sliced jalapeño peppers, drained

1 onion, diced

8 ounces Cheddar cheese, cubed

1 package (8 ounces) cream cheese, cubed

1 container (8 ounces) cottage cheese

1 container (8 ounces) sour cream

1 can (about 14 ounces) diced tomatoes

3 cloves garlic, minced

Salt and black pepper

Crackers or tortilla chips

1. Brown ground beef and sausage in medium skillet 6 to 8 minutes over medium-high heat, stirring to break up meat. Drain fat. Transfer to **CROCK-POT**® slow cooker.

2. Add process cheese, jalapeño peppers, onion, Cheddar cheese, cream cheese, cottage cheese, sour cream, tomatoes and garlic to **CROCK-POT**® slow cooker. Cover; cook on HIGH 1½ to 2 hours or until cheeses are melted. Season with salt and black pepper. Serve with crackers.

Makes 16 to 18 servings

MINI CARNITAS TACOS

Mini Swiss Steak Sandwiches

  2 **tablespoons all-purpose flour**
  ¼ **teaspoon salt**
  ¼ **teaspoon black pepper**
 1¾ **pounds boneless beef chuck steak, about 1 inch thick**
  2 **tablespoons vegetable oil**
  1 **medium onion, sliced**
  1 **green bell pepper, sliced**
  1 **clove garlic, sliced**
  1 **cup stewed tomatoes**
  ¾ **cup condensed beef consommé, undiluted**
  2 **teaspoons Worcestershire sauce**
  1 **whole bay leaf**
  2 **tablespoons cornstarch**
  2 **packages (12 ounces each) sweet Hawaiian-style dinner rolls**

1. Coat inside of **CROCK-POT**® slow cooker with nonstick cooking spray. Combine flour, salt and black pepper in large resealable food storage bag. Add steak. Seal bag; shake to coat.

2. Heat oil in large skillet over high heat. Brown steak on both sides. Transfer to **CROCK-POT**® slow cooker.

3. Add onion and bell pepper to skillet; cook and stir over medium-high heat 3 minutes or until softened. Add garlic; cook and stir 30 seconds. Pour mixture over steak.

4. Add tomatoes, consommé, Worcestershire sauce and bay leaf to **CROCK-POT**® slow cooker. Cover; cook on HIGH 3½ hours or until steak is tender. Transfer steak to cutting board. Remove and discard bay leaf.

5. Stir 2 tablespoons cooking liquid into cornstarch in small bowl until smooth. Stir into cooking liquid in **CROCK-POT**® slow cooker. Cover; cook on HIGH 10 minutes or until thickened.

6. Thinly slice steak against the grain to shred. Return steak to **CROCK-POT**® slow cooker; mix well. Serve steak mixture on rolls.

Makes 16 to 18 servings

Tip: Browning meat and poultry before cooking them in the **CROCK-POT**® slow cooker is not necessary but helps to enhance the flavor and appearance of the finished dish.

Easiest Three-Cheese Fondue

  2 **cups (8 ounces) shredded Cheddar cheese**
  ¾ **cup milk**
  ½ **cup crumbled blue cheese**
  1 **package (3 ounces) cream cheese, cut into cubes**
  ¼ **cup finely chopped onion**
  1 **tablespoon all-purpose flour**
  1 **tablespoon butter or margarine**
  2 **cloves garlic, minced**
  4 **to 6 drops hot pepper sauce**
  ⅛ **teaspoon ground red pepper**
     Breadsticks and assorted cut-up fresh vegetables

1. Combine Cheddar cheese, milk, blue cheese, cream cheese, onion, flour, butter, garlic, hot pepper sauce and ground red pepper in **CROCK-POT**® slow cooker. Cover; cook on LOW 2 to 2½ hours, stirring once or twice, until cheeses are melted and smooth.

2. Turn **CROCK-POT**® slow cooker to HIGH. Cover; cook on HIGH 1 to 1½ hours or until heated through. Serve with breadsticks and fresh vegetables.

Makes 8 servings

MINI SWISS STEAK
SANDWICHES

Shrimp Fondue Dip

1 pound medium raw shrimp, peeled and deveined

½ cup water

½ teaspoon salt, divided

2 tablespoons butter, softened

4 teaspoons Dijon mustard

6 slices thick-sliced white bread, crusts removed*

1 cup milk

2 eggs, beaten

¼ teaspoon black pepper

2 cups (8 ounces) shredded Gruyére or Swiss cheese

French bread slices

*Often labeled as Texas toast.

1. Coat inside of **CROCK-POT®** slow cooker with nonstick cooking spray. Place shrimp, water and ¼ teaspoon salt in large saucepan. Cover; cook over medium heat 3 minutes or until shrimp are pink and opaque. Drain shrimp, reserving ½ cup broth.

2. Combine butter and mustard in small bowl. Spread mixture onto bread slices. Cut bread into 1-inch cubes. Beat milk, eggs, reserved ½ cup broth, remaining ¼ teaspoon salt and pepper in medium bowl until well blended.

3. Spread one third of bread cubes in bottom of **CROCK-POT®** slow cooker. Top with one third of shrimp and sprinkle with one third of cheese. Repeat layers twice. Pour egg mixture over top. Press down on bread mixture to absorb liquid. Line lid with two paper towels. Cover; cook on LOW 2 hours or until mixture is heated through and thickened. Serve with French bread.

Makes 5 cups

Tip: For a party, use a **CROCK-POT®** slow cooker on the LOW or WARM setting to keep hot dips and fondues warm.

Honey-Mustard Chicken Wings

3 pounds chicken wings, tips removed and split at joints

1 teaspoon salt

1 teaspoon black pepper

½ cup honey

½ cup barbecue sauce

2 tablespoons spicy brown mustard

1 clove garlic, minced

3 to 4 thin lemon slices

1. Preheat broiler. Season wings with salt and pepper; place on broiler pan. Broil 4 to 5 inches from heat about 5 minutes per side. Transfer to **CROCK-POT®** slow cooker.

2. Combine honey, barbecue sauce, mustard and garlic in small bowl; mix well. Pour sauce over wings; top with lemon slices. Cover; cook on LOW 4 to 5 hours. Remove and discard lemon slices. Serve wings with sauce.

Makes 4 servings

Spicy Sweet & Sour Cocktail Franks

2 packages (8 ounces each) cocktail franks

½ cup ketchup or chili sauce

½ cup apricot preserves

1 teaspoon hot pepper sauce

Combine cocktail franks, ketchup, perserves and hot pepper sauce in 1½-quart **CROCK-POT®** slow cooker; mix well. Cover; cook on LOW 2 to 3 hours. Serve warm or at room temperature.

Makes 10 to 12 servings

SHRIMP FONDUE DIP

BACON-
WRAPPED
FINGERLING
POTATOES

Bacon-Wrapped Fingerling Potatoes

1 **pound fingerling potatoes**

2 **tablespoons olive oil**

1 **tablespoon minced fresh thyme**

½ **teaspoon black pepper**

¼ **teaspoon paprika**

½ **pound bacon slices, cut crosswise into halves**

¼ **cup chicken broth**

1. Toss potatoes with oil, thyme, pepper and paprika in large bowl. Wrap half slice of bacon tightly around each potato.

2. Heat large skillet over medium heat; add potatoes. Reduce heat to medium-low; cook until lightly browned and bacon has tightened around potatoes. Place potatoes in **CROCK-POT®** slow cooker. Add broth. Cover; cook on HIGH 3 hours.

Makes 4 to 6 servings

Asian Barbecue Skewers

2 **pounds boneless, skinless chicken thighs**

½ **cup soy sauce**

⅓ **cup packed brown sugar**

2 **tablespoons sesame oil**

3 **cloves garlic, minced**

½ **cup thinly sliced green onions (optional)**

1 **tablespoon toasted sesame seeds (optional)**

1. Cut each thigh into 4 pieces, about 1½ inches thick. Thread chicken onto 7-inch-long wooden skewers, folding thinner pieces, if necessary. Place skewers into **CROCK-POT®** slow cooker, layering as flat as possible.

2. Combine soy sauce, brown sugar, oil and garlic in small bowl. Reserve ⅓ cup sauce; set aside. Pour remaining sauce over skewers. Cover; cook on LOW 2 hours. Turn skewers over. Cover; cook on LOW 1 hour.

3. Transfer skewers to serving platter. Discard cooking liquid. Pour reserved sauce over skewers; sprinkle with sliced green onions and sesame seeds, if desired.

Makes 4 to 6 servings

TERIYAKI CHICKEN WINGS

Teriyaki Chicken Wings

- 3 to 4 pounds chicken wings
- ¼ cup soy sauce
- ¼ cup dry sherry
- ¼ cup honey
- 1 tablespoon hoisin sauce
- 1 tablespoon orange juice
- 2 cloves garlic, minced
- 1 fresh red chile pepper, finely chopped* (optional)

*Chile peppers can sting and irritate the skin, so wear rubber gloves when handling and do not touch your eyes.

Place wings in **CROCK-POT®** slow cooker. Combine soy sauce, sherry, honey, hoisin sauce, orange juice, garlic and chile pepper, if desired, in medium bowl; pour over wings. Cover; cook on LOW 3 to 3½ hours or on HIGH 1½ to 2 hours.

Makes 6 to 8 servings

Parmesan Ranch Snack Mix

- 3 cups corn or rice cereal squares
- 2 cups oyster crackers
- 1 package (5 ounces) bagel chips, broken in half
- 1½ cups mini pretzel twists
- 1 cup pistachio nuts
- 2 tablespoons grated Parmesan cheese
- ¼ cup (½ stick) butter, melted
- 1 package (1 ounce) dry ranch salad dressing mix
- ½ teaspoon garlic powder

1. Combine cereal, oyster crackers, bagel chips, pretzels, nuts and cheese in **CROCK-POT®** slow cooker; mix gently.

2. Combine butter, salad dressing mix and garlic powder in small bowl. Pour over cereal mixture; toss lightly to coat. Cover; cook on LOW 3 hours.

3. Stir gently. Cook, uncovered, on LOW 30 minutes.

Makes about 9½ cups

Chicken and Asiago Stuffed Mushrooms

20 large white mushrooms, stems removed and reserved

3 tablespoons extra virgin olive oil, divided

¼ cup finely chopped onion

2 cloves garlic, minced

¼ cup Madeira wine

½ pound uncooked chicken sausage, casings removed or ground chicken

1 cup grated Asiago cheese

¼ cup Italian-style seasoned dry bread crumbs

3 tablespoons chopped fresh parsley

½ teaspoon salt

¼ teaspoon black pepper

1. Lightly brush mushroom caps with 1 tablespoon oil; set aside. Finely chop mushroom stems.

2. Heat remaining 2 tablespoons oil in large nonstick skillet over medium-high heat. Add onion; cook about 1 minute or until just beginning to soften. Add mushroom stems; cook 5 to 6 minutes or until beginning to brown. Stir in garlic; cook 1 minute.

3. Pour in wine; cook 1 minute. Add sausage; cook 3 to 4 minutes or until no longer pink, stirring to break into small pieces. Remove from heat; cool 5 minutes. Stir in cheese, bread crumbs, parsley, salt and pepper.

4. Divide mushroom-sausage mixture among mushroom caps, pressing slightly to compress. Place stuffed mushroom caps in single layer in **CROCK-POT®** slow cooker. Cover; cook on LOW 4 hours or on HIGH 2 hours or until mushrooms are tender and filling is cooked through.

Makes 4 to 5 servings

Tip: Stuffed mushrooms are a great way to impress guests with your gourmet home-cooking skills. These appetizers appear time-intensive and fancy, but they are actually simple with the help of a **CROCK-POT®** slow cooker.

Asian Chicken Fondue

2 cups chicken broth

1 cup shiitake mushrooms, stems removed

1 leek, chopped

1 head baby bok choy, coarsely chopped

2 tablespoons oyster sauce

1 tablespoon mirin

1 tablespoon teriyaki sauce

2 pounds boneless, skinless chicken breasts, cut into 1-inch cubes

Salt and black pepper

1 tablespoon canola oil

1 cup cubed butternut squash

2 tablespoons cold water

1 tablespoon cornstarch

1 can (8 ounces) baby corn, drained

1 can (8 ounces) water chestnuts, drained

1. Combine broth, mushrooms, leek, bok choy, oyster sauce, mirin and teriyaki sauce in **CROCK-POT®** slow cooker. Cover; cook on LOW while following remaining instructions.

2. Season chicken with salt and pepper. Heat oil in large skillet over medium-high heat. Add chicken; cook and stir about 8 minutes or until lightly browned. Stir into **CROCK-POT®** slow cooker. Stir in butternut squash. Cover; cook on LOW 4 to 4½ hours.

3. Stir water into cornstarch in small bowl until smooth. Stir baby corn and water chestnuts into **CROCK-POT®** slow cooker. Whisk in cornstarch mixture. Cover; cook on LOW 20 to 30 minutes.

4. Serve with bamboo skewers, fondue forks or tongs. Broth may also be served in small soup bowls.

Makes 6 to 8 servings

CHICKEN
AND ASIAGO
STUFFED
MUSHROOMS

Thai Coconut Chicken Meatballs

1 pound ground chicken

2 green onions, chopped

1 clove garlic, minced

2 teaspoons toasted sesame oil

2 teaspoons mirin

1 teaspoon fish sauce

½ cup unsweetened canned coconut milk

¼ cup chicken broth

2 teaspoons packed brown sugar

1 teaspoon Thai red curry paste

1 tablespoon canola oil

2 teaspoons lime juice

2 tablespoons water

1 tablespoon cornstarch

1. Combine chicken, green onions, garlic, sesame oil, mirin and fish sauce in large bowl. Shape into 1½-inch meatballs. Combine coconut milk, broth, brown sugar and curry paste in small bowl.

2. Heat canola oil in large skillet over medium-high heat. Working in batches, brown meatballs on all sides. Transfer to **CROCK-POT®** slow cooker. Add coconut milk mixture. Cover; cook on HIGH 3½ to 4 hours. Stir in lime juice.

3. Stir water into cornstarch in small bowl until smooth. Whisk into sauce in **CROCK-POT®** slow cooker. Cook, uncovered, on HIGH 10 to 15 minutes or until sauce is slightly thickened.

Makes 4 to 5 servings

Tip: Meatballs that are of equal size will be done at the same time. To ensure your meatballs are the same size, pat seasoned ground meat into an even rectangle and then slice into even rows and columns. Roll each portion into a smooth ball.

Asian-Spiced Chicken Wings

3 pounds chicken wings, tips removed

1 cup packed brown sugar

1 cup soy sauce

½ cup ketchup

¼ cup dry sherry

2 teaspoons fresh ginger, minced

2 cloves garlic, minced

½ cup hoisin sauce

1 tablespoon fresh lime juice

3 tablespoons sesame seeds, toasted*

¼ cup thinly sliced green onions

To toast sesame seeds, spread in small skillet. Shake skillet over medium heat 2 minutes or until seeds begin to pop or turn golden brown.

1. Preheat broiler. Place wings on broiler pan. Broil chicken wings 4 to 5 inches from heat 10 minutes or until browned. Transfer wings to **CROCK-POT®** slow cooker. Stir in brown sugar, soy sauce, ketchup, sherry, ginger and garlic. Cover; cook on LOW 5 to 6 hours or on HIGH 2 to 3 hours, stirring halfway through cooking time.

2. Remove wings with slotted spoon to serving platter. Remove ¼ cup of cooking liquid; discard remaining liquid. Combine reserved liquid with hoisin sauce and lime juice in medium bowl. Drizzle mixture over wings; sprinkle with sesame seeds and green onions.

Makes 10 to 16 servings

Note: For 5-, 6- or 7-quart **CROCK-POT®** slow cooker, increase chicken wings to 5 pounds.

Tip: Chicken wings are always crowd pleasers. Garnishing them with toasted sesame seeds and green onions gives these appetizers added crunch and contrasting color.

THAI COCONUT
CHICKEN MEATBALLS

ORIENTAL
CHICKEN
WINGS

Oriental Chicken Wings

32 chicken wings, tips removed
    and split at joints
 1 cup chopped red onion
 1 cup soy sauce
¾ cup packed light brown sugar
¼ cup dry sherry
 2 tablespoons chopped fresh ginger
 2 cloves garlic, minced
    Chopped fresh chives (optional)

1. Preheat broiler. Broil wings about 5 minutes per side; transfer to **CROCK-POT®** slow cooker.

2. Combine red onion, soy sauce, brown sugar, sherry, ginger and garlic in large bowl. Add to **CROCK-POT®** slow cooker; stir to blend well. Cover; cook on LOW 5 to 6 hours or on HIGH 2 to 3 hours. Sprinkle with chives.

Makes 32 appetizers

Pizza Fondue

½ pound bulk Italian sausage
 1 cup chopped onion
 2 jars (26 ounces each) meatless pasta
    sauce
 4 ounces thinly sliced ham, finely chopped
 1 package (3 ounces) sliced pepperoni,
    finely chopped
¼ teaspoon red pepper flakes
 1 pound mozzarella cheese, cut into
    ¾-inch cubes
 1 loaf Italian or French bread, cut into
    1-inch cubes

1. Brown sausage and onion 6 to 8 minutes in large skillet over medium-high, stirring to break up meat. Drain fat. Transfer to **CROCK-POT®** slow cooker.

2. Stir in pasta sauce, ham, pepperoni and red pepper flakes. Cover; cook on LOW 3 to 4 hours. Serve warm fondue with cheese and bread cubes.

Makes 20 to 25 servings

BRATS
IN BEER

Brats in Beer

1½ pounds bratwurst (5 to 6 links)
1 can (12 ounces) amber ale or beer
1 onion, thinly sliced
2 tablespoons packed brown sugar
2 tablespoons dry red wine or cider
  vinegar
  Spicy brown mustard
  Cocktail rye bread

1. Combine bratwurst, ale, onion, brown sugar and wine in **CROCK-POT®** slow cooker. Cover; cook on LOW 4 to 5 hours.

2. Remove bratwurst from cooking liquid. Cut into ½-inch-thick slices.

3. To make mini open-faced sandwiches, spread mustard on cocktail rye bread. Top with bratwurst slices and onion, if desired. (Or serve whole bratwurst on toasted split French or Italian rolls.)

Makes 30 to 36 appetizers

Tip: Choose a light-colored beer when cooking brats. Hearty ales can leave the meat tasting slightly bitter.

Maple-Glazed Meatballs

1½ cups ketchup
1 cup maple syrup
⅓ cup soy sauce
1 tablespoon quick-cooking tapioca
1½ teaspoons ground allspice
1 teaspoon dry mustard
2 packages (about 16 ounces each) frozen
  fully cooked meatballs, partially thawed
  and separated
1 can (20 ounces) pineapple chunks in
  juice, drained

1. Combine ketchup, maple syrup, soy sauce, tapioca, allspice and mustard in **CROCK-POT®** slow cooker.

2. Carefully stir meatballs and pineapple chunks into ketchup mixture.

3. Cover; cook on LOW 5 to 6 hours. Stir before serving. Serve warm; insert cocktail picks, if desired.

Makes about 48 meatballs

CEREAL
SNACK MIX

Cereal Snack Mix

- 6 tablespoons unsalted butter, melted
- 2 tablespoons curry powder
- 2 tablespoons soy sauce
- 1 tablespoon sugar
- 1 tablespoon paprika
- 2 teaspoons ground cumin
- ½ teaspoon salt
- 5 cups rice squares cereal
- 5 cups corn squares cereal
- 1 cup tiny pretzels
- ⅓ cup lightly salted peanuts

1. Pour butter into **CROCK-POT®** slow cooker. Stir in curry powder, soy sauce, sugar, paprika, cumin and salt. Stir in cereals, pretzels and peanuts. Cook, uncovered, on HIGH 45 minutes, stirring often to avoid scorching.

2. Turn **CROCK-POT®** slow cooker to LOW. Cook, uncovered, on LOW 3 to 4 hours, stirring often. Turn off heat. Let cool completely.

Makes 20 servings

Artichoke and Nacho Cheese Dip

- 2 cans (10¾ ounces each) condensed nacho cheese soup, undiluted
- 1 can (14 ounces) quartered artichoke hearts, drained and coarsely chopped
- 1 cup (4 ounces) shredded pepper jack cheese
- 1 can (4 ounces) evaporated milk
- 2 tablespoons snipped fresh chives, divided
- ½ teaspoon paprika
  Crackers or chips

Combine soup, artichokes, cheese, evaporated milk, 1 tablespoon chives and paprika in **CROCK-POT®** slow cooker. Cover; cook on LOW 2 hours. Stir well; sprinkle with remaining 1 tablespoon chives. Serve with crackers.

Makes about 1 quart

THAI CHICKEN WINGS

Thai Chicken Wings

1 tablespoon peanut oil

5 pounds chicken wings, tips removed and split at joints

½ cup unsweetened canned coconut milk

1 tablespoon sugar

1 tablespoon Thai green curry paste

1 tablespoon fish sauce

¾ cup prepared spicy peanut sauce

Chopped green onions (optional)

1. Heat oil in large nonstick skillet over medium-high heat. Working in batches, brown wings on all sides. Transfer to **CROCK-POT**® slow cooker.

2. Stir coconut milk, sugar, curry paste and fish sauce into **CROCK-POT**® slow cooker. Cover; cook on LOW 6 to 7 hours or on HIGH 3 to 3½ hours. Remove wings with slotted spoon to large bowl; stir in peanut sauce. Garnish with green onions.

Makes 8 servings

Creamy Seafood Dip

1 package (8 ounces) shredded pepper jack cheese

1 can (6 ounces) lump crabmeat, drained

1 pound cooked shrimp, peeled, deveined and chopped

1 cup heavy cream, divided

1 round sourdough bread loaf (about 1 pound)

1. Place cheese in **CROCK-POT**® slow cooker. Add crabmeat, shrimp and ¾ cup cream. Stir well to combine. Cover; cook on HIGH 10 to 15 minutes or until cheese is melted.

2. Meanwhile, cut off top of bread and hollow out to create bowl. Cut extra bread into large pieces. Place bread bowl on serving plate. Place extra bread around bowl.

3. Check consistency of dip. Stir in up to ¼ cup additional cream, as needed. Pour into bread bowl.

Makes 6 to 8 servings

Sun-Dried Tomato Appetizer Spread

3 cups chopped onion

3 jars (about 7 ounces each) sun-dried tomatoes, packed in oil, drained and finely chopped

½ cup red wine vinegar

3 tablespoons sugar

1 tablespoon minced garlic

1 piece (2 inches) fresh ginger, peeled and grated

1 teaspoon herbes de Provence

½ teaspoon salt

1 package (8 ounces) cream cheese

Sprigs fresh basil (optional)

Assorted crackers

1. Combine onion, sun-dried tomatoes, vinegar, sugar, garlic, ginger, herbes de Provence and salt in 2-quart **CROCK-POT®** slow cooker; stir gently to mix. Cover; cook on LOW 4 to 5 hours or on HIGH 3 hours, stirring occasionally. Turn off heat. Let mixture cool before using.

2. To serve, slice cream cheese in half horizontally (use dental floss for clean cut) and separate pieces. Spread ⅓ cup tomato mixture onto 1 cream cheese half. Top with remaining cream cheese half and spread ⅓ cup tomato mixture on top. Garnish with basil sprigs and serve with crackers. Refrigerate or freeze remaining tomato mixture for another use.

Makes 3 cups

Tip: This tomato and cream cheese appetizer may be assembled in advance. Refrigerate in airtight container until serving.

"Melt Your Mouth" Hot Wings

40 chicken wing drumettes

2 teaspoons creole seasoning

⅛ teaspoon black pepper

2½ cups hot pepper sauce

4 tablespoons vegetable oil

4 tablespoons vinegar

4 teaspoons honey

1 teaspoon red pepper flakes

1 cup blue cheese dressing (optional)

1. Preheat broiler. Coat broiler pan with nonstick cooking spray. Rinse wings and pat dry. Sprinkle both sides with creole seasoning and black pepper. Broil 6 inches from heat 10 minutes. Turn wings over and broil 10 minutes or until browned and cooked through. Transfer to **CROCK-POT®** slow cooker.

2. Combine hot pepper sauce, oil, vinegar, honey and red pepper flakes in medium bowl; pour over wings. Cover; cook on LOW 5 to 6 hours, stirring every hour. Serve with dressing, if desired.

Makes 10 to 12 servings

SUN-DRIED TOMATO
APPETIZER SPREAD

Chicken Liver Pâté

PÂTÉ

1½ pounds chicken livers, trimmed of fat and membrane

1 small onion, thinly sliced

3 sprigs fresh thyme

2 cloves garlic, crushed

¼ teaspoon salt

1 tablespoon water

3 tablespoons cold butter, cut into 4 pieces

2 tablespoons heavy cream

2 tablespoons dry sherry

GARNISH

½ shallot, minced

2 tablespoons chopped fresh parsley

1 tablespoon sherry vinegar

⅛ teaspoon sugar

Salt and black pepper

Melba toast or toast points

1. Rinse chicken livers and pat dry. Place in **CROCK-POT**® slow cooker. Add onion, thyme, garlic, salt and water. Cover; cook on LOW 2 hours.

2. Remove and discard thyme sprigs. Pour remaining ingredients from **CROCK-POT**® slow cooker into strainer and cool until just warm to the touch. Transfer to food processor or blender; pulse to coarsely chop livers. Add butter, one piece at a time, pulsing after each addition just to combine.

3. Add cream and sherry; pulse to combine. Transfer to small loaf pan, pressing plastic wrap to surface of pâté. Refrigerate overnight, tightly wrapped in additional plastic wrap. Unmold pâté and slice to serve.

4. To garnish pâté, stir together shallot, parsley, vinegar, sugar, salt and pepper in small bowl. Set aside 5 minutes, then spoon over pâté. Serve with Melba toast.

Makes 8 to 10 servings

Tomato Topping for Bruschetta

6 medium tomatoes, peeled, seeded and diced

2 stalks celery, chopped

2 shallots, chopped

4 pepperoncini peppers, chopped*

2 tablespoons olive oil

2 teaspoons tomato paste

1 teaspoon salt

½ teaspoon black pepper

8 slices country bread or other large round bread

2 cloves garlic, cut in half

Pepperoncini peppers are pickled peppers sold in jars with brine. They are available in the condiment aisle of large supermarkets.

1. Drain tomatoes in fine mesh strainer. Combine tomatoes, celery, shallots, pepperoncini peppers, oil, tomato paste, salt and black pepper in **CROCK-POT**® slow cooker. Cover; cook on LOW 45 minutes to 1 hour.

2. Toast bread; immediately rub with garlic. Spread tomato topping on bread. Serve immediately.

Makes 8 servings

Variation: To serve as a main dish, omit bread and garlic and toss tomato topping with cooked penne pasta. You may also spoon the topping over roasted chicken breasts as a flavorful sauce.

CHICKEN LIVER PÂTÉ

Stuffed Baby Bell Peppers

1 tablespoon olive oil

½ onion, chopped

½ pound ground beef, chicken or turkey

½ cup cooked rice

3 tablespoons chopped fresh parsley

2 tablespoons lemon juice

1 tablespoon dried dill weed

1 tablespoon tomato paste, divided

½ teaspoon salt

⅛ teaspoon black pepper

¼ cup chicken or beef broth

1 bag yellow and red baby bell peppers (about 2 dozen)

1. Heat oil in medium skillet over medium heat. Add onion; cook and stir 5 minutes or until translucent.

2. Add beef; brown 6 to 8 minutes, stirring to break up meat. Drain fat. Transfer to large bowl. Add rice, parsley, lemon juice, dill, 1½ teaspoons tomato paste, salt and black pepper; mix well. Whisk broth and remaining 1½ teaspoons tomato paste in small bowl.

3. Cut lengthwise slit down side of each bell pepper; run under cold water to wash out seeds. Fill each bell pepper with 2 to 3 teaspoons meat mixture. Place filled bell peppers in **CROCK-POT**® slow cooker, filling side up. Add broth mixture. Cover; cook on LOW 5 hours or on HIGH 2½ hours.

Makes 16 to 18 servings

Bagna Cauda

¾ cup olive oil

6 tablespoons butter, softened

12 anchovy fillets, drained

6 cloves garlic

⅛ teaspoon red pepper flakes

Assorted foods for dipping such as endive spears, cauliflower florets, cucumber spears, carrot sticks, zucchini spears, red bell pepper pieces, sugar snap peas or crusty Italian or French bread slices

Place oil, butter, anchovies, garlic and red pepper flakes in food processor; process until smooth. Pour into 2½-quart or other small-sized **CROCK-POT**® slow cooker. Cover; cook on LOW 2 hours or until heated through. Serve with assorted dippers.

Makes 10 to 12 servings

Tip: Bagna Cauda is a warm Italian dip similar to the more famous fondue. The name is derived from "bagno caldo," meaning "warm bath" in Italian. This dip should be kept warm while serving, just like you would fondue.

Sweet and Spicy Sausage Rounds

1 pound kielbasa sausage, cut into ¼-inch-thick rounds

⅔ cup blackberry jam

⅓ cup steak sauce

1 tablespoon prepared mustard

½ teaspoon ground allspice

Place all ingredients in **CROCK-POT**® slow cooker; mix well. Cover; cook on HIGH 3 hours or until sausage is glazed.

Makes about 16 servings

STUFFED BABY BELL PEPPERS

FALL BEEF AND
BEER CASSEROLE

Beefy Main Dishes

Fall Beef and Beer Casserole

2 tablespoons oil
1½ pounds cubed beef stew meat
2 tablespoons all-purpose flour
1 cup beef broth
2 cups brown ale or beer
1 cup water
1 onion, sliced
2 carrots, sliced
1 leek, sliced
2 stalks celery, sliced
1 cup mushrooms, sliced
1 turnip, cubed
1 teaspoon mixed herbs

1. Heat oil in large skillet over medium-high heat. Cook beef until browned on all sides. Transfer to **CROCK-POT**® slow cooker.

2. Sprinkle flour over contents of skillet. Cook and stir 2 minutes. Gradually stir in broth, ale and water (adding liquid ingredients too fast could create lumps in the sauce). Bring to a boil and then pour over beef.

3. Add onion, carrots, leek, celery, mushrooms, turnip and herbs to **CROCK-POT**® slow cooker. Cover; cook on LOW 8 to 10 hours or on HIGH 4 to 6 hours.

Makes 4 to 6 servings

Sloppy Sloppy Joes

4 pounds ground beef
1 cup chopped onion
1 cup chopped green bell pepper
1 can (about 28 ounces) tomato sauce
2 cans (10¾ ounces each) condensed tomato soup, undiluted
1 cup packed brown sugar
¼ cup ketchup
3 tablespoons Worcestershire sauce
1 tablespoon ground mustard
1 tablespoon prepared mustard
1½ teaspoons chili powder
1 teaspoon garlic powder
   Toasted hamburger buns

1. Brown beef 6 to 8 minutes in large skillet over medium-high heat, stirring to break up meat. Drain fat.

2. Add onion and bell pepper; cook and stir 5 to 10 minutes or until onion is translucent.

3. Transfer mixture to **CROCK-POT**® slow cooker. Add tomato sauce, tomato soup, brown sugar, ketchup, Worcestershire sauce, ground mustard, prepared mustard, chili powder and garlic powder; stir until well blended. Cover; cook on LOW 4 to 6 hours. Serve on buns.

Makes 20 to 25 servings

Italian-Style Pot Roast

  2 teaspoons minced garlic
  1 teaspoon salt
  1 teaspoon dried basil
  1 teaspoon dried oregano
  ¼ teaspoon red pepper flakes
  1 boneless beef bottom round rump roast or chuck shoulder roast (about 2½ to 3 pounds)*
  1 large onion, quartered and thinly sliced
  1½ cups tomato-basil or marinara pasta sauce
  2 cans (about 15 ounces each) cannellini or Great Northern beans, rinsed and drained
  ¼ cup shredded fresh basil (optional)

Unless you have a 5-, 6- or 7-quart CROCK-POT® slow cooker, cut any roast larger than 2½ pounds in half so it cooks completely.

1. Combine garlic, salt, dried basil, oregano and red pepper flakes in small bowl; rub over roast.

2. Place onion slices in **CROCK-POT®** slow cooker. Place roast over onion slices in **CROCK-POT®** slow cooker, cutting in half if necessary. Pour pasta sauce over roast. Cover; cook on LOW 8 to 9 hours or until roast is fork-tender.

3. Remove roast to cutting board. Cover loosely with foil; let stand 10 to 15 minutes. Turn off heat. Let liquid in **CROCK-POT®** slow cooker stand 5 minutes to allow fat to rise. Skim off fat.

4. Stir beans into liquid. Cover; cook on LOW 15 to 30 minutes or until beans are heated through. Slice roast across the grain into thin slices. Serve with bean mixture. Garnish with fresh basil.

Makes 6 to 8 servings

Slow Cooker Brisket of Beef

  1 whole beef brisket (about 5 pounds)
  2 teaspoons minced garlic
  ½ teaspoon black pepper
  2 large onions, cut into ¼-inch slices and separated into rings
  1 bottle (12 ounces) chili sauce
  12 ounces beef broth, dark ale or water
  2 tablespoons Worcestershire sauce
  1 tablespoon packed brown sugar

1. Place brisket, fat side down, in **CROCK-POT®** slow cooker. Spread garlic evenly over brisket; sprinkle with pepper. Arrange onions over brisket. Combine chili sauce, broth, Worcestershire sauce and brown sugar in medium bowl; pour over brisket and onions. Cover; cook on LOW 8 hours.

2. Turn brisket over; stir onions into sauce and spoon over brisket. Cover; cook on LOW 1 to 2 hours or until brisket is fork-tender. Remove brisket to cutting board. Cover loosely with foil; let stand 10 minutes.

3. Turn off heat. Stir cooking liquid; let stand 5 minutes. Skim off fat. Carve brisket across the grain into thin slices. Spoon cooking liquid over brisket.

Makes 10 to 12 servings

Tip: Cooking liquid may be thinned to desired consistency with water or thickened by simmering, uncovered, in saucepan over medium-high heat.

ITALIAN-STYLE POT ROAST

Asian Beef with Mandarin Oranges

2 tablespoons vegetable oil

2 pounds boneless beef chuck roast, cut into ½-inch strips

1 onion, thinly sliced

1 head bok choy, chopped

1 green bell pepper, sliced

1 can (5 ounces) sliced water chestnuts, drained

1 package (about 3 ounces) shiitake mushrooms, sliced

⅓ cup soy sauce

2 teaspoons minced fresh ginger

¼ teaspoon salt

1 can (11 ounces) mandarin oranges, drained and syrup reserved

2 tablespoons cornstarch

2 cups beef broth

6 cups steamed rice

1. Heat oil in large skillet over medium-high heat. Working in batches, brown beef on all sides. Transfer to **CROCK-POT®** slow cooker.

2. Add onion to skillet; cook and stir over medium heat until softened. Add bok choy, bell pepper, water chestnuts, mushrooms, soy sauce, ginger and salt; cook and stir 5 minutes or until bok choy is wilted. Transfer to **CROCK-POT®** slow cooker.

3. Stir reserved mandarin orange syrup into cornstarch in medium bowl until smooth. Whisk into broth in large bowl; pour into **CROCK-POT®** slow cooker. Cover; cook on LOW 10 hours or on HIGH 5 to 6 hours or until beef is tender.

4. Stir in mandarin oranges. Spoon over rice in shallow serving bowls.

Makes 6 servings

Sicilian Steak Pinwheels

¾ pound mild or hot Italian sausage, casings removed

1¾ cups fresh bread crumbs

¾ cup grated Parmesan cheese

2 eggs

3 tablespoons minced fresh parsley, plus additional for garnish

1½ to 2 pounds round steak

1 cup frozen peas

Kitchen string, cut into 15-inch lengths

1 cup pasta sauce

1 cup beef broth

1. Coat **CROCK-POT®** slow cooker with nonstick cooking spray. Mix sausage, bread crumbs, cheese, eggs and 3 tablespoons parsley in large bowl until well blended; set aside.

2. Place round steak between two large sheets of plastic wrap. Using tenderizer mallet or back of skillet, pound steak until meat is about ⅜ inch thick. Remove top layer of plastic wrap. Spread sausage mixture over steak. Press peas into sausage mixture. Lift edge of plastic wrap at short end; roll up steak completely. Tie at 2-inch intervals with kitchen string. Transfer to **CROCK-POT®** slow cooker.

3. Combine pasta sauce and broth in medium bowl. Pour over meat. Cover; cook on LOW 6 hours or until meat is tender and sausage is cooked through.

4. Remove steak to serving platter; cover with foil to keep warm. Let stand 20 minutes before removing string and slicing. Meanwhile, skim and discard excess fat from sauce. Serve steak slices with sauce.

Makes 4 to 6 servings

ASIAN BEEF WITH
MANDARIN ORANGES

Merlot Beef and Sun-Dried Tomato Portobello Ragoût

1 jar (7 ounces) sun-dried tomatoes, packed in oil, drained and 3 tablespoons oil reserved

1 boneless beef chuck roast (about 3 pounds), cut into 1½-inch pieces

1 can (10½ ounces) beef consommé, undiluted

6 ounces sliced portobello mushrooms

1 medium green bell pepper, cut into thin strips

1 medium orange or yellow bell pepper, cut into thin strips

1 medium onion, cut into 8 wedges

2 teaspoons dried oregano

½ teaspoon salt plus additional for seasoning

¼ teaspoon garlic powder

½ cup Merlot or other dry red wine

2 tablespoons Worcestershire sauce

1 tablespoon balsamic vinegar

1 tablespoon cornstarch

Black pepper

Mashed potatoes, rice or egg noodles

1. Heat 1 tablespoon reserved oil from sun-dried tomatoes in large skillet over medium-high heat. Add one third of beef and brown on all sides. Transfer to **CROCK-POT®** slow cooker. Repeat with remaining oil and beef.

2. Add consommé to skillet; cook and stir to scrape up any browned bits. Pour mixture over beef. Add sun-dried tomatoes, mushrooms, bell peppers, onion, oregano, salt and garlic powder to **CROCK-POT®** slow cooker.

3. Combine Merlot and Worcestershire sauce in small bowl; reserve ¼ cup. Gently stir remaining Merlot mixture into **CROCK-POT®** slow cooker. Cover; cook on LOW 8 to 9 hours or on HIGH 4 to 5 hours or until beef is tender.

4. Stir vinegar and cornstarch into reserved ¼ cup Merlot mixture until cornstarch is dissolved. Add to **CROCK-POT®** slow cooker. Stir until well blended. Cover; cook on HIGH 15 minutes or until thickened slightly. Add additional salt and black pepper. Serve over mashed potatoes.

Makes 8 servings

Tip: Consommé is just clarified broth. If you can't find canned beef consommé, you may substitute beef broth.

Hot and Juicy Reuben Sandwiches

1 corned beef, trimmed (about 1½ pounds)

2 cups sauerkraut, drained

½ cup beef broth

1 small onion, sliced

1 clove garlic, minced

¼ teaspoon caraway seeds

4 to 6 black peppercorns

8 slices pumpernickel or rye bread

4 slices Swiss cheese

Prepared mustard

1. Place corned beef in **CROCK-POT®** slow cooker. Add sauerkraut, broth, onion, garlic, caraway seeds and peppercorns. Cover; cook on LOW 7 to 9 hours.

2. Remove beef to cutting board. Cut beef across grain into 16 (½-inch-thick) slices. Divide evenly among 4 slices of bread. Top each slice with ½ cup drained sauerkraut mixture and 1 slice cheese. Spread mustard on remaining 4 bread slices; place on sandwiches.

Makes 4 servings

**MERLOT BEEF AND SUN-DRIED
TOMATO PORTOBELLO RAGOÛT**

EASY FAMILY BURRITOS

Easy Family Burritos

1 **boneless beef chuck shoulder roast (2 to 3 pounds)***

1 **jar (24 ounces) *or* 2 jars (16 ounces each) salsa**

Flour tortillas, warmed

Optional Toppings: shredded cheese, sour cream, salsa, shredded lettuce, diced tomato, diced onion or guacamole

*Unless you have a 5-, 6- or 7-quart CROCK-POT® slow cooker, cut any roast larger than 2½ pounds in half so it cooks completely.

1. Place roast in **CROCK-POT**® slow cooker; top with salsa. Cover; cook on LOW 8 to 10 hours.

2. Remove beef to cutting board; shred beef with two forks. Return to cooking liquid; mix well. Cover; cook on LOW 1 to 2 hours or until heated through.

3. Serve shredded beef wrapped in warm tortillas. Top as desired.

Makes 8 servings

Easy Beef Stroganoff

3 **cans (10¾ ounces each) condensed cream of mushroom soup, undiluted**

1 **cup sour cream**

½ **cup water**

1 **package (1 ounce) dry onion soup mix**

2 **pounds cubed beef stew meat**

Combine soup, sour cream, water and soup mix in **CROCK-POT**® slow cooker. Add beef; stir until well coated. Cover; cook on LOW 6 hours or on HIGH 3 hours.

Makes 4 to 6 servings

Beef with Apples and Sweet Potatoes

1 **boneless beef chuck shoulder roast (about 2 pounds), trimmed and cut into 2-inch cubes**

1 **can (40 ounces) sweet potatoes, drained**

2 **small onions, sliced**

2 **apples, peeled, cored and sliced**

½ **cup beef broth**

2 **cloves garlic, minced**

1 **teaspoon salt**

1 **teaspoon dried thyme, divided**

¾ **teaspoon black pepper, divided**

2 **tablespoons cold water**

1 **tablespoon cornstarch**

¼ **teaspoon ground cinnamon**

1. Place beef, sweet potatoes, onions, apples, broth, garlic, salt, ½ teaspoon thyme and ½ teaspoon pepper in **CROCK-POT**® slow cooker. Cover; cook on LOW 8 to 9 hours.

2. Remove beef, sweet potatoes, onions and apples to platter; cover with foil to keep warm. Turn off heat. Let cooking liquid stand 5 minutes to allow fat to rise. Skim off fat and discard.

3. Stir water, cornstarch, remaining ½ teaspoon thyme, ¼ teaspoon pepper and cinnamon in small bowl until smooth. Whisk into cooking liquid. Turn **CROCK-POT**® slow cooker to HIGH. Cover; cook on HIGH 15 minutes or until cooking liquid is thickened. Serve sauce over beef, sweet potatoes, onions and apples.

Makes 6 servings

Tip: CROCK-POT® slow cookers cook at a low heat for a long time. Therefore, they are a great way to cook dishes calling for less tender cuts of meat, because long, slow cooking helps tenderize these cuts.

Hearty Beef Short Ribs

2½ pounds flanken-style beef short ribs, bone-in

1 to 2 tablespoons coarse salt

1 to 2 tablespoons black pepper

2 tablespoons olive oil, divided

2 carrots, diced

2 celery stalks, diced

1 large yellow onion, diced

3 cloves garlic, minced

3 whole bay leaves

⅓ cup dry red wine

⅓ cup crushed tomatoes

⅓ cup balsamic vinegar

Carrot slices, cooked (optional)

Hot cooked noodles (optional)

1. Season ribs with salt and black pepper. Drizzle with 1 tablespoon oil. Heat remaining 1 tablespoon oil in large skillet. Cook ribs 2 to 3 minutes per side or until just browned. Transfer ribs to **CROCK-POT**® slow cooker. Add diced carrots, celery, onion, garlic and bay leaves.

2. Combine wine, tomatoes and vinegar in small bowl. Season with salt and black pepper, if desired. Pour mixture into **CROCK-POT**® slow cooker. Cover; cook on LOW 8 to 9 hours or on HIGH 5½ to 6 hours, turning once or twice, until meat is tender and falling off the bone.

3. Remove ribs to serving platter. Remove and discard bay leaves. Place sauce in food processor or blender; process to desired consistency. Pour sauce over ribs. Serve with sliced carrots and noodles, if desired.

Makes 6 to 8 servings

Tip: For a change of pace from ordinary short rib recipes, ask your butcher for flanken-style beef short ribs. Flanken-style ribs are cut across the bones into wide, flat portions. They provide all the meaty flavor of the more common English-style short ribs with smaller, more manageable bones.

Round Steak

1 boneless beef round steak (1½ pounds), trimmed and cut into 4 pieces

¼ cup all-purpose flour

1 teaspoon black pepper

½ teaspoon salt

1 tablespoon vegetable oil

1 can (10¾ ounces) condensed cream of mushroom soup, undiluted

¾ cup water

1 medium onion, quartered

1 can (4 ounces) sliced mushrooms, drained

¼ cup milk

1 package (1 ounce) dry onion soup mix

1 whole bay leaf

1. Place steak in large resealable food storage bag. Close bag and pound with meat mallet to tenderize steak. Combine flour, 1 teaspoon pepper and ½ teaspoon salt in small bowl; add to bag with steak. Shake to coat meat evenly.

2. Heat oil in large skillet over medium-high heat. Remove steak from bag; shake off excess flour. Add steak to skillet; brown on both sides. Transfer steak and pan juices to **CROCK-POT**® slow cooker.

3. Add soup, water, onion, mushrooms, milk, soup mix, bay leaf and seasonings to **CROCK-POT**® slow cooker; mix well. Cover; cook on LOW 5 to 6 hours or until steak is tender. Remove and discard bay leaf.

Makes 4 servings

Tip: Browning meat before cooking it in the **CROCK-POT**® slow cooker isn't necessary but helps to enhance the flavor and appearance of the finished dish.

HEARTY BEEF
SHORT RIBS

Slow Cooker Pepper Steak

2 **tablespoons vegetable oil**

3 **pounds boneless beef top sirloin steak, cut into strips**

1 **tablespoon minced garlic (5 to 6 cloves)**

1 **medium onion, chopped**

½ **cup soy sauce**

2 **teaspoons sugar**

1 **teaspoon salt**

½ **teaspoon ground ginger**

½ **teaspoon black pepper**

3 **green bell peppers, cut into strips**

¼ **cup cold water**

1 **tablespoon cornstarch**

Hot cooked rice

1. Heat oil in large skillet over medium heat. Brown steak strips in batches. Add garlic; cook and stir 2 minutes. Transfer steak strips, garlic and pan juices to **CROCK-POT®** slow cooker.

2. Add onion, soy sauce, sugar, salt, ginger and black pepper to **CROCK-POT®** slow cooker; mix well. Cover; cook on LOW 6 to 8 hours or until meat is tender (up to 10 hours). Add bell pepper strips during final hour of cooking.

3. Stir water into cornstarch in small bowl until smooth. Whisk into **CROCK-POT®** slow cooker. Turn **CROCK-POT®** slow cooker to HIGH. Cook, uncovered, on HIGH 15 minutes or until thickened. Serve with rice.

Makes 6 to 8 servings

Tip: Cooking times are guidelines. **CROCK-POT®** slow cookers, just like ovens, cook differently depending on a variety of factors. For example, cooking times will be longer at higher altitudes. You may need to slightly adjust cooking times.

EASY BEEF
BURGUNDY

Easy Beef Burgundy

1½ pounds boneless beef round steak, cut into 1-inch pieces

1 can (10¾ ounces) condensed cream of mushroom soup, undiluted

1 cup dry red wine

1 onion, chopped

1 can (4 ounces) sliced mushrooms, drained

1 package (about 1 ounce) dry onion soup mix

1 tablespoon minced garlic

Combine all ingredients in **CROCK-POT®** slow cooker. Cover; cook on LOW 6 to 8 hours or until beef is tender.

Makes 4 to 6 servings

Smothered Beef Patties

Worcestershire sauce

Garlic powder

Salt and black pepper

1 can (about 14 ounces) Mexican-style diced tomatoes with mild green chiles, undrained and divided

8 frozen beef patties, unthawed

1 onion, cut into 8 slices

Sprinkle bottom of **CROCK-POT®** slow cooker with small amount of Worcestershire sauce, garlic powder, salt, pepper and 2 tablespoons tomatoes. Add 1 frozen beef patty. Top with small amount of Worcestershire, garlic powder, salt, pepper, 2 tablespoons tomatoes and 1 onion slice. Repeat layers 7 times. Cover; cook on LOW 8 hours.

Makes 8 servings

Campfired-Up Sloppy Joes

1½ pounds lean ground beef

½ cup chopped sweet onion

1 medium red bell pepper, chopped

1 large clove garlic, crushed

½ cup ketchup

½ cup barbecue sauce

2 tablespoons cider vinegar

1 tablespoon Worcestershire sauce

1 tablespoon packed brown sugar

1 teaspoon chili powder

1 can (about 8 ounces) baked beans

6 kaiser rolls, split and warmed

Shredded sharp Cheddar cheese (optional)

1. Brown ground beef, onion, bell pepper and garlic 6 to 8 minutes in large skillet over medium-high heat, stirring to break up meat. Drain and discard excess fat. Transfer beef mixture to **CROCK-POT®** slow cooker.

2. Combine ketchup, barbecue sauce, vinegar, Worcestershire sauce, brown sugar and chili powder in small bowl. Transfer to **CROCK-POT®** slow cooker.

3. Add beans. Stir well to combine. Cover; cook on HIGH 3 hours.

4. To serve, fill split rolls with ½ cup sloppy joe mixture. Sprinkle with cheese, if desired, before topping sandwich with roll top.

Makes 6 servings

Serving Suggestion: Serve with a side of coleslaw.

Beefy Tostada Pie

2 teaspoons olive oil

1½ cups chopped onion

2 pounds ground beef

1 teaspoon chili powder

1 teaspoon ground cumin

1 teaspoon salt

2 cloves garlic, minced

1 can (15 ounces) tomato sauce

1 cup sliced black olives

8 flour tortillas

4 cups (16 ounces) shredded Cheddar cheese

Sour cream, salsa and chopped green onion (optional)

1. Heat oil in large skillet over medium heat. Add onion; cook and stir until tender. Add ground beef, chili powder, cumin, salt and garlic; cook and stir 6 to 8 minutes or until beef is browned. Drain fat. Add tomato sauce; cook and stir until heated through. Stir in olives.

2. Make foil handles using three 18×3-inch strips of heavy-duty foil or use regular foil folded to double thickness. Crisscross foil in spoke design; place across bottom and up side of stoneware. Lay 1 tortilla on foil strips. Spread with meat sauce and ½ cup cheese. Top with another tortilla, meat sauce and cheese. Repeat layers, ending with cheese. Cover; cook on HIGH 1½ hours.

3. To serve, lift out of **CROCK-POT®** slow cooker using foil handles and transfer to serving platter. Discard foil. Cut into wedges. Serve with sour cream, salsa and chopped green onion, if desired.

Makes 4 to 6 servings

CAMPFIRED-UP SLOPPY JOES

Classic Beef and Noodles

1 tablespoon vegetable oil

2 pounds cubed beef stew meat

¼ pound mushrooms, cut into halves

2 tablespoons chopped onion

2 cloves garlic, minced

1 teaspoon salt

1 teaspoon dried oregano

½ teaspoon black pepper

¼ teaspoon dried marjoram

1 whole bay leaf

1½ cups beef broth

⅓ cup dry sherry

1 container (8 ounces) sour cream

½ cup all-purpose flour

¼ cup water

4 cups hot cooked noodles

1. Heat oil in large skillet over medium heat. Brown beef in batches on all sides. Drain fat.

2. Combine beef, mushrooms, onion, garlic, salt, oregano, pepper, marjoram and bay leaf in **CROCK-POT**® slow cooker. Pour in broth and sherry. Cover; cook on LOW 8 to 10 hours or on HIGH 4 to 5 hours. Remove and discard bay leaf.

3. Combine sour cream, flour and water in small bowl. Stir about 1 cup cooking liquid from **CROCK-POT**® slow cooker into sour cream mixture. Add mixture to **CROCK-POT**® slow cooker; mix well. Cook, uncovered, on HIGH 30 minutes or until thickened and bubbly. Serve over noodles.

Makes 8 servings

Slow Cooker Steak Fajitas

1 beef flank steak (about 1 pound)

1 medium onion, cut into strips

½ cup medium salsa, plus additional for garnish

2 tablespoons chopped fresh cilantro

2 tablespoons fresh lime juice

2 cloves garlic, minced

1 tablespoon chili powder

1 teaspoon ground cumin

½ teaspoon salt

1 small green bell pepper, cut into strips

1 small red bell pepper, cut into strips

Flour tortillas, warmed

1. Cut flank steak lengthwise in half, then crosswise into thin strips; place meat in **CROCK-POT**® slow cooker. Combine onion, ½ cup salsa, cilantro, lime juice, garlic, chili powder, cumin and salt in **CROCK-POT**® slow cooker. Cover; cook on LOW 5 to 6 hours.

2. Add bell peppers. Cover; cook on LOW 1 hour.

3. Serve with flour tortillas and additional salsa, if desired.

Makes 4 servings

Tip: CROCK-POT® slow cooker recipes calling for raw meats should cook a minimum of 3 hours on LOW for food safety reasons. When in doubt, use an instant-read thermometer to ensure the meat has reached the recommended internal temperature for safe consumption.

CLASSIC BEEF AND NOODLES

Roast Beef Burritos

1 boneless beef bottom round roast (3 to 5 pounds)*

¼ cup water

½ to 1 teaspoon garlic powder

½ to 1 teaspoon black pepper

1 whole bay leaf

2 jars (16 ounces each) salsa

2 cans (4 ounces each) diced mild green chiles, undrained

½ large yellow onion, diced

8 to 10 burrito-size flour tortillas

1 cup (4 ounces) shredded Cheddar cheese

Unless you have a 5-, 6- or 7-quart CROCK-POT® slow cooker, cut any roast larger than 2½ pounds in half so it cooks completely.

1. Place roast in **CROCK-POT®** slow cooker; add water. Season with garlic powder and black pepper. Add bay leaf. Cover; cook on HIGH 6 hours or until beef is tender. Remove and discard bay leaf.

2. Remove beef to cutting board. Trim fat and discard. Shred beef with two forks. Let cooking liquid stand 5 minutes to allow fat to rise. Skim off fat and discard. Add shredded beef, salsa, chiles and onion to **CROCK-POT®** slow cooker; stir to mix. Cover; cook on HIGH 1 hour or until onion is tender.

3. To serve, place about 3 tablespoons beef onto each tortilla. Top with cheese and fold into burritos. Place burritos, seam sides down, on plates. Microwave on HIGH 30 seconds to melt cheese.

Makes 8 to 10 servings

Brisket with Bacon, Blue Cheese & Onions

2 large sweet onions, cut into ½-inch slices*

6 slices bacon

1 flat-cut boneless beef brisket (about 3½ pounds)
Salt and black pepper

2 cans (10½ ounces each) condensed beef consommé, undiluted

1 teaspoon cracked black peppercorns

¾ cup crumbled blue cheese

Preferably Maui, Vidalia or Walla Walla onions.

1. Coat inside of **CROCK-POT®** slow cooker with nonstick cooking spray. Line bottom with onion slices.

2. Heat large skillet over medium heat. Add bacon; cook and stir until chewy. Remove to paper towel-lined plate using slotted spoon; chop.

3. Season brisket with salt and pepper. Place in skillet. Brown brisket on all sides. Transfer to **CROCK-POT®** slow cooker.

4. Pour consommé into **CROCK-POT®** slow cooker. Sprinkle brisket with peppercorns and half of bacon. Cover; cook on HIGH 5 to 7 hours or until meat is tender.

5. Remove brisket to cutting board. Cover loosely with foil; let stand 10 to 15 minutes. Slice against the grain into ¾-inch slices. To serve, arrange onions on serving platter and spread slices of brisket on top. Sprinkle with blue cheese and remaining bacon. Add salt and pepper to cooking liquid, if desired, and serve with brisket.

Makes 6 to 8 servings

Tip: Use black pepper as a quick and simple flavor enhancer for **CROCK-POT®** slow cooker dishes.

ROAST BEEF BURRITOS

Yankee Pot Roast and Vegetables

1   beef chuck pot roast (about 2½ pounds), trimmed and cut into bite-size pieces
    Salt and black pepper
3   unpeeled medium baking potatoes (about 1 pound), cut into quarters
2   large carrots, cut into ¾-inch slices
2   stalks celery, cut into ¾-inch slices
1   medium onion, sliced
1   large parsnip, cut into ¾-inch slices
2   whole bay leaves
1   teaspoon dried rosemary
½   teaspoon dried thyme
½   cup beef broth

1. Season beef with salt and pepper. Combine potatoes, carrots, celery, onion, parsnip, bay leaves, rosemary and thyme in **CROCK-POT**® slow cooker. Place beef over vegetables. Pour broth over beef. Cover; cook on LOW 8½ to 9 hours or until beef is fork-tender.

2. Remove beef to serving platter. Arrange vegetables around beef. Remove and discard bay leaves before serving.

Makes 10 to 12 servings

Tip: To make gravy, ladle cooking liquid into 2-cup measure; let stand 5 minutes. Skim off fat and discard. Bring cooking liquid to a boil in small saucepan over medium-high heat. For each cup, stir ¼ cup cold water into 2 tablespoons all-purpose flour in small bowl until smooth. Add to boiling cooking liquid. Cook and stir 1 minute or until thickened.

Classic Spaghetti

2   tablespoons olive oil
2   onions, chopped
2   green bell peppers, sliced
2   stalks celery, sliced
4   teaspoons minced garlic
3   pounds lean ground beef
2   carrots, diced
1   cup sliced mushrooms
1   can (28 ounces) tomato sauce
1   can (28 ounces) stewed tomatoes, undrained
3   cups water
2   tablespoons minced fresh parsley
1   tablespoon sugar
1   tablespoon dried oregano
2   teaspoons salt
2   teaspoons black pepper
1   pound hot cooked spaghetti

1. Heat oil in large skillet over medium-high heat. Add onions, bell peppers, celery and garlic; cook and stir until tender. Transfer to **CROCK-POT**® slow cooker. Brown beef 6 to 8 minutes in same skillet, stirring to break up meat. Drain fat. Transfer to **CROCK-POT**® slow cooker.

2. Add carrots, mushrooms, tomato sauce, tomatoes, water, parsley, sugar, oregano, salt and black pepper to **CROCK-POT**® slow cooker. Cover; cook on LOW 6 to 8 hours or on HIGH 3 to 5 hours or until done. Serve sauce over spaghetti.

Makes 6 to 8 servings

**YANKEE POT ROAST
AND VEGETABLES**

Asian Ginger Beef over Bok Choy

2 tablespoons peanut oil

1½ pounds boneless beef chuck roast, cut into 1-inch pieces

3 green onions, cut into ½-inch slices

6 cloves garlic

1 cup chicken broth

½ cup water

¼ cup soy sauce

2 teaspoons ground ginger

1 teaspoon Asian chili paste

9 ounces fresh udon noodles or vermicelli, cooked and drained

3 cups bok choy, trimmed, washed and cut into 1-inch pieces

½ cup minced fresh cilantro

1. Heat oil in large skillet over medium-high heat. Working in batches, brown beef on all sides. Brown last batch of beef with green onions and garlic.

2. Transfer to **CROCK-POT**® slow cooker. Add broth, water, soy sauce, ginger and chili paste. Stir well to combine. Cover; cook on LOW 7 to 8 hours or on HIGH 3 to 4 hours or until beef is very tender.

3. Just before serving, add noodles to **CROCK-POT**® slow cooker; stir well. Add bok choy and stir again. Cook on HIGH 15 minutes or until bok choy is tender-crisp. Garnish with cilantro.

Makes 6 to 8 servings

Best Beef Brisket Sandwich Ever

1 beef brisket (about 3 pounds)*

2 cups apple cider, divided

1 head garlic, cloves separated, crushed and peeled

⅓ cup chopped fresh thyme *or* 2 tablespoons dried thyme

2 tablespoons whole black peppercorns

1 tablespoon mustard seeds

1 tablespoon Cajun seasoning

1 teaspoon ground allspice

1 teaspoon ground cumin

1 teaspoon celery seeds

2 to 4 whole cloves

1 can (12 ounces) dark beer

10 to 12 sourdough sandwich rolls, split

*Unless you have a 5-, 6- or 7-quart CROCK-POT® slow cooker, cut any roast larger than 2½ pounds in half so it cooks completely.

1. Place brisket, ½ cup cider, garlic, thyme, peppercorns, mustard seeds, Cajun seasoning, allspice, cumin, celery seeds and cloves in large resealable food storage bag. Seal bag; turn to coat. Marinate in refrigerator overnight.

2. Place brisket and marinade in **CROCK-POT**® slow cooker. Add remaining 1½ cups cider and beer. Cover; cook on LOW 10 hours or until brisket is tender.

3. Slice brisket and place on sandwich rolls. Strain sauce; drizzle over meat.

Makes 10 to 12 servings

ASIAN GINGER BEEF OVER BOK CHOY

ASIAN BEEF WITH BROCCOLI

Asian Beef with Broccoli

1½ pounds boneless beef chuck roast (about 1½ inches thick), sliced into thin strips*

1 can (10½ ounces) condensed beef consommé, undiluted

½ cup oyster sauce

2 tablespoons cornstarch

1 bag (16 ounces) fresh broccoli florets

Hot cooked rice

Sesame seeds (optional)

Freeze steak 30 minutes to make slicing easier.

1. Place beef in **CROCK-POT®** slow cooker. Pour consommé and oyster sauce over beef. Cover; cook on HIGH 3 hours.

2. Stir 2 tablespoons cooking liquid into cornstarch in small bowl until smooth. Add to **CROCK-POT®** slow cooker. Stir well to combine. Cover; cook on HIGH 15 minutes or until thickened.

3. Cook broccoli according to package directions. Add to **CROCK-POT®** slow cooker; toss gently to mix. Serve with rice and garnish with sesame seeds.

Makes 4 to 6 servings

Spicy Italian Beef

1 boneless beef chuck roast (3 to 4 pounds)*

1 jar (12 ounces) pepperoncini peppers**

1 can (about 14 ounces) beef broth

1 can (12 ounces) beer

1 onion, minced

2 tablespoons Italian seasoning

1 loaf French bread, cut into thick slices

8 to 10 slices provolone cheese (optional)

Unless you have a 5-, 6- or 7-quart CROCK-POT® slow cooker, cut any roast larger than 2½ pounds in half so it cooks completely.

**Pepperoncini peppers are pickled peppers sold in jars with brine. They are available in the condiment aisle of large supermarkets.*

1. Place roast in **CROCK-POT®** slow cooker; cutting into large pieces to fit, if necessary.

2. Drain pepperoncini peppers. Pull off stem ends and discard. Add pepperoncini peppers, broth, beer, onion and Italian seasoning to **CROCK-POT®** slow cooker; do not stir. Cover; cook on LOW 8 to 10 hours.

3. Remove beef to cutting board; shred with two forks. Return beef to cooking liquid; mix well. Serve on French bread. Top with cheese, if desired.

Makes 8 to 10 servings

HOT BEEF SANDWICHES AU JUS

Hot Beef Sandwiches au Jus

4 pounds beef bottom round roast, trimmed*

2 cans (about 10 ounces each) condensed beef broth, undiluted

1 can (12 ounces) beer

2 envelopes (1 ounce each) dried onion-flavor soup mix

1 tablespoon minced garlic

2 teaspoons sugar

1 teaspoon dried oregano

Crusty French rolls, sliced in half

Unless you have a 5-, 6- or 7-quart CROCK-POT® slow cooker, cut any roast larger than 2½ pounds in half so it cooks completely.

1. Place beef in **CROCK-POT®** slow cooker. Combine broth, beer, soup mix, garlic, sugar and oregano in large bowl. Pour mixture over beef. Cover; cook on HIGH 6 to 8 hours or until beef is fork-tender.

2. Remove beef to cutting board; shred with two forks. Return beef to cooking liquid; mix well. Serve on crusty rolls with extra cooking liquid for dipping.

Makes 8 to 10 servings

Slow-Cooked Beef Brisket Dinner

1 beef brisket (4 pounds), cut in half

4 to 6 medium potatoes, cut into 1-inch cubes

6 carrots, cut into 1-inch pieces

8 ounces mushrooms, sliced

½ large onion, sliced

1 stalk celery, cut into 1-inch pieces

3 beef bouillon cubes

5 cloves garlic, crushed

1 teaspoon black peppercorns

2 whole bay leaves

Salt and black pepper

Chopped fresh parsley (optional)

1. Place brisket, potatoes, carrots, mushrooms, onion, celery, bouillon cubes, garlic, peppercorns and bay leaves in **CROCK-POT®** slow cooker. Add enough water to cover ingredients. Cover; cook on LOW 6 to 8 hours.

2. Remove and discard bay leaves. Remove brisket to cutting board. Season with salt and black pepper. Slice meat across grain. Serve with vegetables. Garnish with parsley.

Makes 8 to 10 servings

**HARVEST BISTRO
PORK POT ROAST**

Pork-Packed Favorites

Harvest Bistro Pork Pot Roast

2 large onions, peeled and quartered

3 stalks celery, cut into 1- to 2-inch pieces

1 cup fresh whole cranberries

1 large pear, cored and cut into 8 wedges

1 large red cooking apple, cored and cut into 8 wedges

1 quince, peeled and chopped (optional)

⅔ cup packed dark brown sugar

2 tablespoons fresh thyme *or* 2 teaspoons dried thyme

2 teaspoons salt, divided

3 pounds lean pork butt roast, cut into 2- to 3-inch pieces

1 cup chicken broth

6 to 8 ounces Brie cheese, chopped

Fresh thyme (optional)

1. Combine onions, celery, cranberries, pear, apple and quince, if desired, in **CROCK-POT®** slow cooker. Sprinkle with brown suger, thyme, and 1 teaspoon salt. Place pork on top. Pour broth over pork. Sprinkle with ½ teaspoon salt. Cover; cook on LOW 7 hours.

2. Sprinkle cheese over pork. Cover; cook on LOW 1 hour. Remove pork to serving platter. Arrange vegetables and fruits around pork. Season with remaining 1½ teaspoons salt, if desired. Garnish with thyme.

Makes 6 to 8 servings

Vegetable-Stuffed Pork Chops

4 pork chops

Salt and black pepper

1 can (about 15 ounces) corn, drained

1 green bell pepper, chopped

1 cup Italian-style seasoned dry bread crumbs

1 small onion, chopped

½ cup uncooked converted long grain rice

1 can (8 ounces) tomato sauce

1. Cut pocket into each pork chop, cutting from edge to bone. Lightly season pockets with salt and black pepper. Combine corn, bell pepper, bread crumbs, onion and rice in large bowl. Stuff pork chops with rice mixture. Secure open side with toothpicks.

2. Place any remaining rice mixture in **CROCK-POT®** slow cooker; top with stuffed pork chops. Pour tomato sauce over pork chops. Cover; cook on LOW 8 to 10 hours.

3. Remove pork chops to serving platter. Remove and discard toothpicks. Serve with extra rice mixture.

Makes 4 servings

Tip: Your butcher can cut a pocket in the pork chops to save you time and to ensure even cooking.

Pork Loin with Sherry and Red Onions

3 large red onions, thinly sliced

1 cup pearl onions, blanched and peeled

2 tablespoons unsalted butter or margarine

2½ pounds boneless pork loin, tied

½ teaspoon salt

½ teaspoon black pepper

½ cup dry sherry

2 tablespoons chopped fresh Italian parsley

2 tablespoons water

1½ tablespoons cornstarch

1. Cook red and pearl onions in butter in medium skillet over medium heat until soft.

2. Rub pork loin with salt and pepper; place in **CROCK-POT®** slow cooker. Add onions, sherry and parsley. Cover; cook on LOW 8 to 10 hours or on HIGH 5 to 6 hours.

3. Remove pork loin to cutting board. Cover loosely with foil; let stand 10 to 15 minutes before slicing.

4. Stir water into cornstarch in small bowl until smooth. Whisk into cooking liquid in **CROCK-POT®** slow cooker. Cook on HIGH 15 minutes or until sauce has thickened. Serve sliced pork loin with onions and sherry sauce.

Makes 8 servings

Note: The mild flavor of pork is awakened by this rich, delectable sauce.

Tip: Double all ingredients except for the sherry, water and cornstarch if using a 5-, 6- or 7-quart **CROCK-POT®** slow cooker.

Cajun-Style Country Ribs

2 cups baby carrots

1 large onion, chopped

1 large green bell pepper, cut into 1-inch pieces

1 large red bell pepper, cut into 1-inch pieces

2 teaspoons minced garlic

2 tablespoons Cajun or Creole seasoning, divided

3½ to 4 pounds country-style pork ribs

1 can (about 14 ounces) stewed tomatoes, undrained

2 tablespoons water

1 tablespoon cornstarch

Hot cooked rice

1. Combine carrots, onion, bell peppers, garlic and 2 teaspoons Cajun seasoning in **CROCK-POT®** slow cooker; mix well.

2. Trim excess fat from ribs. Cut into individual ribs. Sprinkle 1 tablespoon Cajun seasoning over ribs; place in **CROCK-POT®** slow cooker over vegetables. Pour tomatoes over ribs. Cover; cook on LOW 6 to 8 hours or until ribs are fork-tender.

3. Remove ribs and vegetables from cooking liquid to serving platter. Cover with foil to keep warm. Let liquid stand 5 minutes to allow fat to rise. Skim off fat. Stir water into cornstarch and remaining 1 teaspoon Cajun seasoning in small bowl until smooth. Stir into **CROCK-POT®** slow cooker. Turn **CROCK-POT®** slow cooker to HIGH. Cook, uncovered, on HIGH 15 to 30 minutes or until sauce is thickened. Return ribs and vegetables to sauce; carefully stir to coat. Serve over rice.

Makes 6 to 8 servings

PORK LOIN WITH SHERRY AND RED ONIONS

Pork Loin Stuffed with Stone Fruits

1 boneless pork loin roast (about 4 pounds)*
  Salt and black pepper
2 tablespoons vegetable oil
2 tablespoons butter
1 onion, chopped
½ cup Madeira or sherry wine
1½ cups dried stone fruits (½ cup *each* plums, peaches and apricots)
2 cloves garlic, minced
¾ teaspoon salt
½ teaspoon black pepper
¼ teaspoon dried thyme
  Kitchen string, cut into 15-inch lengths
1 tablespoon olive oil

Unless you have a 5-, 6- or 7-quart CROCK-POT® slow cooker, cut any roast larger than 2½ pounds in half so it cooks completely.

1. Coat **CROCK-POT®** slow cooker with nonstick cooking spray. Season pork with salt and pepper. Heat vegetable oil in large skillet over medium-high heat. Brown pork on all sides. Remove pork to cutting board. Cover loosely with foil; let stand 10 to 15 minutes.

2. Melt butter in same skillet over medium heat. Add onion; cook and stir until translucent. Add Madeira; cook 2 to 3 minutes until mixture reduces slightly. Stir in dried fruit, garlic, ¾ teaspoon salt, ½ teaspoon black pepper and thyme; cook 1 minute. Remove from heat.

3. Cut strings from roast, if any. Butterfly roast lengthwise (use sharp knife to cut meat; cut to within 1½ inches of edge). Spread roast flat on cutting board, browned side down. Spoon fruit mixture onto pork roast. Bring sides together to close roast. Slide kitchen string under roast and tie roast shut, allowing 2 inches between ties. If any fruit escapes, push back gently. Place roast in **CROCK-POT®** slow cooker. Pour olive oil over roast. Cover; cook on LOW 5 to 6 hours or on HIGH 2 to 3 hours or until roast is tender.

4. Remove roast to cutting board. Cover loosely with foil; and let stand 10 to 15 minutes. Pour cooking liquid into small saucepan (strain through fine-mesh sieve first, if desired). Cook over high heat about 3 minutes to reduce sauce. Add salt and black pepper to sauce, if desired. Slice roast and serve with sauce.

Makes 8 to 10 servings

Tip: To butterfly a roast means to split the meat down the center without cutting all the way through. This allows the meat to be spread open so a filling can be added.

Sweet 'n' Spicy Ribs

5 cups barbecue sauce
¾ cup packed dark brown sugar
¼ cup honey
2 tablespoons Cajun seasoning
1 tablespoon garlic powder
1 tablespoon onion powder
6 pounds baby back pork ribs or beef ribs, cut into 3-rib portions

1. Combine barbecue sauce, brown sugar, honey, Cajun seasoning, garlic powder and onion powder in medium bowl. Remove 1 cup mixture for dipping sauce; refrigerate until ready to serve.

2. Place ribs in large **CROCK-POT®** slow cooker. Pour barbecue sauce mixture over ribs. Cover; cook on LOW 8 hours or until meat is very tender.

3. Remove ribs to serving platter. Cover loosely with foil. Skim fat from sauce; spoon some of sauce over ribs. Serve ribs with reserved sauce.

Makes 10 servings

Tip: To remove a small amount of fat from dishes cooked in the **CROCK-POT®** slow cooker, lightly pull a sheet of clean paper towel over the surface, letting the paper towel absorb some of the grease. Repeat this process as necessary.

**PORK LOIN STUFFED
WITH STONE FRUITS**

Rosemary Pork with Red Wine Risotto

1 boneless pork loin (about 3 pounds)
1 teaspoon salt
1 teaspoon black pepper
2 tablespoons olive oil
6 sprigs fresh rosemary, divided
2 cups chicken broth, divided
½ cup minced onion
2 tablespoons butter, divided
3 cloves garlic, minced
1 cup uncooked Arborio rice
1 cup dry red wine
¾ cup grated Parmesan cheese

1. Season pork with salt and pepper. Heat oil in large skillet over medium-high heat. Add 3 sprigs rosemary; place pork roast on top. Brown pork roast 5 to 7 minutes on all sides. Transfer roast and rosemary to **CROCK-POT®** slow cooker.

2. Add ¼ cup broth to skillet, stirring to scrape up browned bits. Add onion, butter and garlic; cook and stir until onion is translucent.

3. Add rice to skillet. Cook and stir 2 minutes or until rice just begins to brown. Stir in wine and remaining 1¾ cups broth. Pour mixture around roast. Cover; cook on HIGH 3 to 4 hours, stirring occasionally, until roast reaches 160°F on thermometer inserted into center.

4. Remove and discard rosemary. Remove roast to cutting board. Cover loosely with foil; let stand 10 to 15 minutes before slicing.

5. Stir remaining 1 tablespoon butter and cheese into rice. Serve risotto with roast and garnish with remaining rosemary.

Makes 4 to 6 servings

Mediterranean Pepper Pot

1 pound mild Italian sausage, casings removed
1½ cups water
1 can (about 15 ounces) navy beans, rinsed and drained
¼ cup chopped pepperoncini peppers*
1 medium yellow bell pepper, cut into 1-inch pieces
1 medium green bell pepper, cut into 1-inch pieces
1 can (about 14 ounces) diced tomatoes
2 teaspoons dried basil
1 teaspoon dried oregano
¼ cup ketchup

***Pepperoncini peppers are pickled peppers sold in jars with brine. They are available in the condiment aisle of large supermarkets.**

1. Coat **CROCK-POT®** slow cooker with nonstick cooking spray. Heat large skillet over medium-high heat. Add sausage and brown well. Drain and discard excess fat. Transfer to **CROCK-POT®** slow cooker.

2. Add water, beans, pepperoncini and bell peppers, tomatoes, basil and oregano. Cover; cook on LOW 7 to 8 hours or on HIGH 3 to 4 hours.

3. Turn off heat. Add ketchup; stir well. Let stand, covered, 15 minutes before serving.

Makes 4 servings

Tip: For flavor in an instant, serve entrées and main dishes made in your **CROCK-POT®** slow cooker with a garnish of freshly grated cheese, such as Parmesan, Romano or Asiago.

**ROSEMARY PORK WITH
RED WINE RISOTTO**

Spicy Citrus Pork with Pineapple Salsa

1 tablespoon ground cumin

½ teaspoon salt

1 teaspoon black pepper

3 pounds center-cut pork loin, rinsed and patted dry

2 tablespoons vegetable oil

4 cans (8 ounces each) pineapple tidbits in own juice, drained and ½ cup juice reserved*

3 tablespoons lemon juice, divided

2 teaspoons grated lemon peel

1 cup finely chopped orange or red bell pepper

4 tablespoons finely chopped red onion

2 tablespoons chopped fresh cilantro or mint

1 teaspoon grated fresh ginger (optional)

¼ teaspoon red pepper flakes (optional)

If tidbits are unavailable, purchase pineapple chunks and coarsely chop.

1. Coat **CROCK-POT**® slow cooker with nonstick cooking spray. Combine cumin, salt and black pepper in small bowl. Rub evenly onto pork. Heat oil in medium skillet over medium-high heat. Brown pork loin on all sides 1 to 2 minutes per side. Transfer to **CROCK-POT**® slow cooker.

2. Spoon 4 tablespoons of reserved pineapple juice and 2 tablespoons lemon juice over pork. Cover; cook on LOW 2 to 2¼ hours or on HIGH 1 hour and 10 minutes or until meat is tender.

3. Meanwhile, combine pineapple, remaining 4 tablespoons pineapple juice, remaining 1 tablespoon lemon juice, lemon peel, bell pepper, red onion, cilantro, ginger, if desired, and red pepper flakes, if desired, in medium bowl. Toss gently and blend well; set aside.

4. Remove pork to cutting board. Cover loosely with foil; let stand 10 to 15 minutes before slicing. Arrange pork slices on serving platter. Pour sauce evenly over slices. Serve salsa on the side.

Makes 12 servings

Sauerkraut Pork Ribs

1 tablespoon vegetable oil

3 to 4 pounds country-style pork ribs

1 large onion, thinly sliced

1 teaspoon caraway seeds

½ teaspoon garlic powder

¼ to ½ teaspoon black pepper

¾ cup water

2 jars (about 28 ounces each) sauerkraut

12 medium red potatoes, quartered

1. Heat oil in large skillet over medium-low heat. Brown ribs on all sides. Transfer to **CROCK-POT**® slow cooker. Drain fat.

2. Add onion to skillet; cook until tender. Add caraway seeds, garlic powder and pepper; cook 15 minutes. Transfer onion mixture to **CROCK-POT**® slow cooker.

3. Add water to skillet, stirring to scrape up brown bits. Pour pan juices into **CROCK-POT**® slow cooker. Partially drain sauerkraut, leaving some liquid; pour over meat. Top with potatoes. Cover; cook on LOW 6 to 8 hours or until potatoes are tender, stirring once during cooking.

Makes 12 servings

**SPICY CITRUS PORK
WITH PINEAPPLE SALSA**

Ham with Fruited Bourbon Sauce

1 bone-in ham (about 6 pounds)
½ cup apple juice
¾ cup packed dark brown sugar
½ cup raisins
1 teaspoon ground cinnamon
¼ teaspoon red pepper flakes
⅓ cup dried cherries
¼ cup bourbon, rum or apple juice
¼ cup cornstarch

1. Coat **CROCK-POT®** slow cooker with nonstick cooking spray. Add ham, cut side up. Combine apple juice, brown sugar, raisins, cinnamon and red pepper flakes in small bowl; stir well. Pour mixture evenly over ham. Cover; cook on LOW 9 to 10 hours or on HIGH 4½ to 5 hours. Add cherries 30 minutes before end of cooking time.

2. Transfer ham to cutting board. Cover loosely with foil; let stand 10 to 15 minutes before slicing.

3. Pour cooking liquid into large measuring cup and let stand 5 minutes. Skim and discard excess fat. Return cooking liquid to **CROCK-POT®** slow cooker.

4. Stir bourbon into cornstarch in small bowl until smooth. Whisk into cooking liquid. Cover; cook on HIGH 15 to 20 minutes or until thickened. Serve sauce over sliced ham.

Makes 10 to 12 servings

South Pacific Pork Ribs

2 tablespoons canola oil, divided
3½ to 4 pounds pork loin riblets (about 20 riblets)
 Salt and black pepper
1 onion, chopped
1 can (20 ounces) pineapple chunks in 100% pineapple juice, drained and about 1 cup juice reserved
¼ cup all-purpose flour
¼ cup ketchup
¼ cup packed brown sugar
¼ cup vinegar
½ cup water
1 tablespoon soy sauce

1. Heat 1 tablespoon oil in large skillet over medium-high heat. Season riblets with salt and pepper. Working in batches, brown riblets in hot oil, turning to brown both sides. Transfer to **CROCK-POT®** slow cooker as ribs are done. Halfway through browning, add remaining tablespoon oil to skillet. When all riblets are finished browning, stir onion into skillet. Cook 3 to 5 minutes or until softened.

2. Meanwhile, whisk pineapple juice and flour in small bowl until well blended; set aside. Stir ketchup, brown sugar, vinegar, water and soy sauce into skillet. Stir in juice mixture until well combined. Simmer until thickened. Add pineapple chunks and pour sauce over ribs. Cover; cook on LOW 8 to 10 hours or on HIGH 5 to 6 hours or until tender.

Makes 4 to 6 servings

HAM WITH FRUITED
BOURBON SAUCE

BIG AL'S HOT AND SWEET SAUSAGE SANDWICHES

Big Al's Hot and Sweet Sausage Sandwiches

- 4 to 5 pounds hot Italian sausage links
- 1 jar (26 ounces) pasta sauce
- 1 large Vidalia onion (or other sweet onion), sliced
- 1 green bell pepper, sliced
- 1 red bell pepper, sliced
- ¼ cup packed dark brown sugar
  Italian rolls, cut in half
  Provolone cheese, sliced (optional)

1. Combine sausages, pasta sauce, onion, bell peppers and brown sugar in **CROCK-POT**® slow cooker. Cover; cook on LOW 8 to 10 hours or on HIGH 4 to 6 hours.

2. Place sausages on rolls. Top with vegetable mixture. Add provolone cheese, if desired.

Makes 8 to 10 servings

Mango Ginger Pork Roast

- 1 pork shoulder roast (about 4 pounds)*
- ½ to 1 teaspoon ground ginger
  Salt and black pepper
- 2 cups mango salsa
- 2 tablespoons honey
- ¼ cup apricot preserves
  Hot cooked rice

*Unless you have a 5-, 6- or 7-quart CROCK-POT® slow cooker, cut any roast larger than 2½ pounds in half so it cooks completely.

1. Season roast with ginger, salt and pepper. Transfer to **CROCK-POT**® slow cooker.

2. Combine salsa, honey and preserves in medium bowl. Pour over roast. Cover; cook on LOW 6 to 8 hours. Turn **CROCK-POT**® slow cooker to HIGH. Cover; cook on HIGH 3 to 4 hours or until roast is tender. Serve with rice.

Makes 4 to 6 servings

Pork Chops with Dried Fruit and Onions

6 **bone-in end-cut pork chops (about 2½ pounds)**

   Salt and black pepper

3 **tablespoons vegetable oil**

2 **onions, diced**

2 **cloves garlic, minced**

¼ **teaspoon dried sage**

¾ **cup quartered pitted dried plums**

¾ **cup chopped mixed dried fruit**

3 **cups unsweetened unfiltered apple juice**

1 **whole bay leaf**

1. Season pork chops with salt and pepper. Heat oil in large skillet over medium-high heat. Working in batches, brown pork on both sides. Transfer to **CROCK-POT®** slow cooker.

2. Add onions to hot skillet. Reduce heat to medium; cook and stir until softened. Add garlic and cook 30 seconds. Sprinkle sage over mixture. Add dried plums, mixed fruit and apple juice. Bring mixture to a boil. Reduce heat and simmer, uncovered, 3 minutes, stirring to scrape up browned bits. Ladle mixture over pork chops.

3. Add bay leaf. Cover; cook on LOW 3½ to 4 hours or until pork chops are tender. Remove and discard bay leaf. Season with salt and pepper, if desired. To serve, spoon fruit and cooking liquid over pork chops.

Makes 6 servings

ROAST HAM WITH TANGY MUSTARD GLAZE

Roast Ham with Tangy Mustard Glaze

- 1 **fully cooked boneless ham (about 3 pounds), trimmed**
- ¼ **cup packed dark brown sugar**
- 2 **tablespoons lemon juice, divided**
- 1 **tablespoon Dijon mustard**
- ½ **teaspoon ground allspice**
- ¼ **cup granulated sugar**
- 2 **tablespoons cornstarch**

1. Place ham in **CROCK-POT**® slow cooker. Combine brown sugar, 2 teaspoons lemon juice, mustard and allspice in small bowl. Spoon evenly over ham. Cover; cook on LOW 6 to 7 hours or until ham is heated through. Remove ham to warm serving platter. Cover loosely with foil.

2. Pour cooking liquid from **CROCK-POT**® slow cooker into small heavy saucepan. Add granulated sugar, cornstarch and remaining 4 teaspoons lemon juice. Bring to a boil over medium-high heat. Reduce to medium; cook and stir until sauce is thickened and glossy.

3. Carve ham into slices and spoon sauce evenly over individual servings.

Makes 12 to 15 servings

Barbecued Pulled Pork Sandwiches

- 1 **pork shoulder roast (2½ pounds)**
- 1 **bottle (14 ounces) barbecue sauce**
- 1 **tablespoon fresh lemon juice**
- 1 **teaspoon packed brown sugar**
- 1 **medium onion, chopped**
- 8 **sandwich rolls or hamburger buns**

1. Place pork roast in **CROCK-POT**® slow cooker. Cover; cook on LOW 10 to 12 hours or on HIGH 5 to 6 hours.

2. Remove pork roast from **CROCK-POT**® slow cooker. Shred with two forks. Discard cooking liquid. Return pork to **CROCK-POT**® slow cooker; add barbecue sauce, lemon juice, brown sugar and onion. Cover; cook on LOW 2 hours or on HIGH 1 hour. Serve pork on rolls.

Makes 8 servings

Tip: For a 5-, 6- or 7-quart **CROCK-POT**® slow cooker, double all ingredients except for the barbecue sauce. Increase the barbecue sauce to 1½ bottles (about 21 ounces total).

Pork and Tomato Ragoût

2 pounds cubed pork stew meat

¼ cup all-purpose flour

3 tablespoons vegetable oil

1¼ cups dry white wine

2 pounds red potatoes, unpeeled and cut into ½-inch pieces

1 can (about 14 ounces) diced tomatoes

1 cup finely chopped onion

1 cup water

½ cup finely chopped celery

2 cloves garlic, minced

½ teaspoon black pepper

1 cinnamon stick

3 tablespoons chopped fresh parsley

1. Toss pork with flour in large bowl. Heat oil in large skillet over medium-high heat. Add pork; brown on all sides. Transfer to **CROCK-POT**® slow cooker.

2. Add wine to skillet; bring to a boil, stirring to scrape up browned bits. Pour into **CROCK-POT**® slow cooker.

3. Add potatoes, tomatoes, onion, water, celery, garlic, pepper and cinnamon stick. Cover; cook on LOW 6 to 8 hours or until pork and potatoes are tender. Remove and discard cinnamon stick. Adjust seasonings, if desired. Sprinkle with parsley.

Makes 6 servings

Tip: Vegetables such as potatoes and carrots can sometimes take longer to cook in a **CROCK-POT**® slow cooker than meat. Place evenly cut vegetables along the sides of the **CROCK-POT**® slow cooker when possible.

Pork Chops with Jalapeño-Pecan Cornbread Stuffing

6 boneless pork loin chops, trimmed and cut 1 inch thick (about 1½ pounds total)

Nonstick cooking spray

¾ cup chopped onion

¾ cup chopped celery

½ cup coarsely chopped pecans

½ jalapeño pepper, seeded and chopped*

1 teaspoon rubbed sage

½ teaspoon dried rosemary

⅛ teaspoon black pepper

4 cups unseasoned cornbread stuffing mix

1¼ cups reduced-sodium chicken broth

1 egg, lightly beaten

*Jalapeño peppers can sting and irritate the skin, so wear rubber gloves when handling peppers and do not touch your eyes.

1. Spray large skillet with cooking spray; heat over medium heat. Add pork; cook 5 minutes per side or until browned. Remove pork to plate. Cover loosely with foil.

2. Add onion, celery, pecans, jalapeño pepper, sage, rosemary and black pepper to skillet; cook 5 minutes or until onion and celery are tender.

3. Combine stuffing mix, vegetable mixture and broth in medium bowl. Stir in egg. Spoon stuffing mixture into **CROCK-POT®** slow cooker. Arrange pork on top. Cover; cook on LOW 5 hours or until pork is tender.

Makes 6 servings

Note: For a moister dressing, increase chicken broth to 1½ cups.

Shredded Apricot Pork Sandwiches

2 onions, thinly sliced

1 cup apricot preserves

½ cup packed dark brown sugar

½ cup barbecue sauce

¼ cup cider vinegar

2 tablespoons Worcestershire sauce

½ teaspoon red pepper flakes

1 boneless pork top loin roast (4 pounds)*

¼ cup water

2 tablespoons cornstarch

1 tablespoon grated fresh ginger

1 teaspoon salt

1 teaspoon black pepper

10 to 12 sesame or onion rolls, toasted

*Unless you have a 5-, 6- or 7-quart CROCK-POT® slow cooker, cut any roast larger than 2½ pounds in half so it cooks completely.

1. Combine onions, preserves, brown sugar, barbecue sauce, vinegar, Worcestershire sauce and red pepper flakes in large bowl. Place pork in **CROCK-POT®** slow cooker. Pour apricot mixture over top. Cover; cook on LOW 8 to 9 hours.

2. Remove pork to cutting board; cool slightly. Shred pork with two forks. Skim fat from sauce in **CROCK-POT®** slow cooker.

3. Stir water into cornstarch in small bowl until smooth. Stir in ginger, salt and black pepper. Whisk cornstarch mixture into sauce. Turn **CROCK-POT®** slow cooker to HIGH. Cook, uncovered, on HIGH 15 to 30 minutes or until thickened. Return pork to **CROCK-POT®** slow cooker; mix well. Serve on rolls.

Makes 10 to 12 servings

PORK CHOPS WITH JALAPEÑO-PECAN CORNBREAD STUFFING

Spicy Asian Pork Filling

1 boneless pork sirloin roast (about 3 pounds)*

½ cup soy sauce

1 tablespoon chili garlic sauce or chili paste

2 teaspoons minced fresh ginger

2 tablespoons water

1 tablespoon cornstarch

2 teaspoons dark sesame oil

*Unless you have a 5-, 6- or 7-quart CROCK-POT® slow cooker, cut any roast larger than 2½ pounds in half so it cooks completely.

1. Cut roast into 2- to 3-inch pieces. Combine pork, soy sauce, chili garlic sauce and ginger in **CROCK-POT®** slow cooker; mix well. Cover; cook on LOW 8 to 10 hours or until pork is fork-tender.

2. Remove roast to cutting board; cool slightly. Trim and discard excess fat. Shred pork with two forks. Let cooking liquid stand 5 minutes to allow fat to rise. Skim off and discard fat.

3. Stir water, cornstarch and oil in small bowl until smooth; whisk into cooking liquid. Turn **CROCK-POT®** slow cooker to HIGH. Cook, uncovered, on HIGH 10 minutes or until thickened. Return pork to **CROCK-POT®** slow cooker; mix well. Cover; cook on HIGH 15 to 30 minutes or until heated through.

Makes 5½ cups

Spicy Asian Pork Bundles: Place ¼ cup pork filling into large lettuce leaves. Add shredded carrots, if desired. Wrap to enclose. Makes about 20 bundles.

Mu Shu Pork: Lightly spread prepared plum sauce over small warm flour tortillas. Spoon ¼ cup pork filling and ¼ cup stir-fried vegetables into flour tortillas. Wrap to enclose. Serve immediately. Makes about 20 wraps.

Pork Roast Landaise

2 tablespoons olive oil

2½ pounds boneless center-cut pork loin roast

Salt and black pepper

1 medium onion, diced

2 cloves garlic, minced

2 teaspoons dried thyme

2 parsnips, cut into ¾-inch slices

¼ cup sugar

¼ cup red wine vinegar

½ cup port or sherry wine

2 cups chicken broth, divided

2 tablespoons cornstarch

3 pears, cored and sliced ¾ inch thick

1½ cups pitted prunes

1. Heat oil in large saucepan over medium-high heat. Season pork roast with salt and pepper; brown roast on all sides. Transfer roast to **CROCK-POT®** slow cooker.

2. Add onion and garlic to saucepan. Reduce heat to medium; cook and stir 2 to 3 minutes. Stir in parsnips and thyme. Transfer to **CROCK-POT®** slow cooker.

3. Combine sugar and vinegar in same saucepan; cook and stir 5 minutes or until mixture thickens into syrup. Add port and cook 1 minute. Add 1¾ cups chicken broth.

4. Stir remaining ¼ cup broth into cornstarch in small bowl until smooth. Whisk into sauce and cook until smooth and slightly thickened. Pour into **CROCK-POT®** slow cooker. Cover; cook on LOW 8 hours or on HIGH 4 hours. Add pears and prunes during last 30 minutes of cooking time.

Makes 4 to 6 servings

SPICY ASIAN
PORK BUNDLES

Lemon Pork Chops

- 1 **tablespoon vegetable oil**
- 4 **boneless pork chops**
- 3 **cans (8 ounces each) tomato sauce**
- 1 **large onion, quartered and sliced**
- 1 **green bell pepper, cut into strips**
- 1 **tablespoon lemon-pepper seasoning**
- 1 **tablespoon Worcestershire sauce**
- 1 **lemon, quartered, plus additional for garnish**

1. Heat oil in large skillet over medium-low heat. Brown pork chops on both sides. Drain fat. Transfer to **CROCK-POT®** slow cooker.

2. Combine tomato sauce, onion, bell pepper, lemon-pepper seasoning and Worcestershire sauce in medium bowl. Add to **CROCK-POT®** slow cooker.

3. Squeeze juice from lemon quarters over mixture; drop squeezed lemons into **CROCK-POT®** slow cooker. Cover; cook on LOW 6 to 8 hours or until pork is tender. Remove squeezed lemons before serving. Serve with additional lemon quarters, if desired.

Makes 4 servings

Tip: Browning pork before adding it to the **CROCK-POT®** slow cooker helps reduce the fat. Just remember to drain the fat from the skillet before transferring the pork to the **CROCK-POT®** slow cooker.

HAM AND CHEESE
PASTA BAKE

Ham and Cheese Pasta Bake

12 ounces uncooked rigatoni pasta

1 ham steak, cubed

1 container (10 ounces) refrigerated light Alfredo sauce

2 cups (8 ounces) shredded mozzarella cheese, divided

2 cups half-and-half, warmed

1 tablespoon cornstarch

1. Fill large saucepan with salted water; bring to a boil over high heat. Add pasta; cook 7 minutes. Drain pasta; transfer to **CROCK-POT®** slow cooker.

2. Stir ham, Alfredo sauce and 1 cup cheese into pasta. Stir half-and-half into cornstarch in small bowl until smooth; pour over pasta. Sprinkle with remaining 1 cup cheese. Cover; cook on LOW 3½ to 4 hours or until pasta is tender and liquid is absorbed.

Makes 6 servings

Chinese Pork Tenderloin

2 pork tenderloins (about 2 pounds total), cut into 1-inch pieces

1 green bell pepper, cut into ½-inch pieces

1 red bell pepper, cut into ½-inch pieces

1 onion, thinly sliced

2 carrots, thinly sliced

1 jar (15 ounces) sweet and sour sauce

1 tablespoon soy sauce

½ teaspoon hot pepper sauce

Hot cooked rice

Fresh cilantro (optional)

Place pork in **CROCK-POT®** slow cooker. Stir bell peppers, onion, carrots, sweet and sour sauce, soy sauce and hot pepper sauce into **CROCK-POT®** slow cooker; mix well. Cover; cook on LOW 6 to 7 hours or on HIGH 4 to 5 hours. Stir just before serving. Serve over rice. Garnish with cilantro.

Makes 8 servings

Fall-off-the-Bone BBQ Ribs

½ **cup paprika**

¼ **cup sugar**

¼ **cup onion powder**

1½ **teaspoons salt**

1½ **teaspoons black pepper**

2½ **pounds baby back pork ribs, silver skin removed**

1 **can (20 ounces) beer or beef broth**

1 **quart barbecue sauce**

½ **cup honey**

Sesame seeds and fresh chopped chives (optional)

1. Preheat grill. Lightly oil grill grid.

2. Meanwhile, combine paprika, sugar, onion powder, salt and pepper in small bowl. Generously season ribs with dry rub mixture. Place ribs on grid. Cook 3 minutes on each side or until ribs have grill marks.

3. Portion ribs into sections of 3 to 4 bones. Place in **CROCK-POT**® slow cooker. Pour beer over ribs. Cover; cook on HIGH 2 hours. Combine barbecue sauce and honey in medium bowl; add to **CROCK-POT**® slow cooker. Cover; cook on HIGH 1½ hours. Sprinkle with sesame seeds and chives, if desired. Serve with extra sauce on the side.

Makes 6 to 8 servings

Cuban Pork Sandwiches

1 **pork loin roast (about 2 pounds)**
½ **cup orange juice**
2 **tablespoons lime juice**
1 **tablespoon minced garlic**
1½ **teaspoons salt**
½ **teaspoon red pepper flakes**
8 **crusty bread rolls, split in half (6 inches each)**
2 **tablespoons yellow mustard**
8 **slices Swiss cheese**
8 **thin ham slices**
4 **small dill pickles, thinly sliced lengthwise**

1. Coat inside of **CROCK-POT**® slow cooker with nonstick cooking spray. Add pork loin.

2. Combine orange juice, lime juice, garlic, salt and red pepper flakes in small bowl. Pour over pork. Cover; cook on LOW 7 to 8 hours or on HIGH 3½ to 4 hours. Remove pork to cutting board. Cover loosely with foil; let stand 10 to 15 minutes before slicing.

3. To serve, spread mustard on both sides of rolls. Divide pork slices among roll bottoms. Top with Swiss cheese slice, ham slice and pickle slices; cover with top of roll.

4. Spray large skillet with nonstick cooking spray; heat over medium heat. Working in batches, arrange sandwiches in skillet. Cover with foil and top with dinner plate to press down sandwiches. (If necessary, weigh down with 2 to 3 cans to compress sandwiches lightly.) Heat about 8 minutes or until cheese is slightly melted.*

*__*Or use table top grill to compress and heat sandwiches.__*

Makes 8 servings

ARTICHOKE AND
TOMATO PAELLA

Vegetarian Delights

Artichoke and Tomato Paella

- 4 cups vegetable broth
- 2 cups uncooked converted rice
- ½ (10-ounce) package frozen chopped spinach, thawed and drained
- 1 green bell pepper, chopped
- 1 medium tomato, sliced into wedges
- 1 medium yellow onion, chopped
- 1 medium carrot, diced
- 3 cloves garlic, minced
- 1 tablespoon minced fresh Italian parsley
- 1 teaspoon salt
- ½ teaspoon black pepper
- 1 can (13½ ounces) artichoke hearts, quartered, rinsed and well drained
- ½ cup frozen peas

1. Combine broth, rice, spinach, bell pepper, tomato, onion, carrot, garlic, parsley, salt and black pepper in **CROCK-POT**® slow cooker; mix well. Cover; cook on LOW 4 hours or on HIGH 2 hours.

2. Before serving, add artichoke hearts and peas. Cover; cook on HIGH 15 minutes. Mix well before serving.

Makes 8 servings

Caribbean Sweet Potato and Bean Stew

- 2 sweet potatoes (about 1 pound), cut into 1-inch cubes
- 2 cups frozen cut green beans
- 1 can (about 15 ounces) black beans, rinsed and drained
- 1 can (about 14 ounces) vegetable broth
- 1 onion, sliced
- 2 teaspoons Caribbean jerk seasoning
- ½ teaspoon dried thyme
- ¼ teaspoon salt
- ¼ teaspoon ground cinnamon
- ⅓ cup slivered almonds, toasted*

*To toast almonds, spread in single layer in heavy skillet. Cook over medium heat 1 to 2 minutes or until nuts are lightly browned, stirring frequently.

Combine sweet potatoes, green beans, black beans, broth, onion, Caribbean jerk seasoning, thyme, salt and cinnamon in **CROCK-POT**® slow cooker. Cover; cook on LOW 5 to 6 hours or until vegetables are tender. Sprinkle with almonds.

Makes 4 servings

Cornbread and Bean Casserole

FILLING

- 1 medium onion, chopped
- 1 medium green bell pepper, diced
- 2 cloves garlic, minced
- 1 can (about 15 ounces) red kidney beans, rinsed and drained
- 1 can (about 15 ounces) pinto beans, rinsed and drained
- 1 can (about 15 ounces) diced tomatoes with mild green chiles
- 1 can (8 ounces) tomato sauce
- 1 teaspoon chili powder
- ½ teaspoon ground cumin
- ½ teaspoon black pepper
- ¼ teaspoon hot pepper sauce

TOPPING

- 1 cup yellow cornmeal
- 1 cup all-purpose flour
- 2½ teaspoons baking powder
- 1 tablespoon sugar
- ½ teaspoon salt
- 1¼ cups milk
- 2 eggs
- 3 tablespoons vegetable oil
- 1 can (8½ ounces) cream-style corn

1. Coat inside of **CROCK-POT®** slow cooker with nonstick cooking spray. Place onion, bell pepper and garlic in large skillet over medium heat; cook and stir 5 minutes or until tender. Transfer to **CROCK-POT®** slow cooker.

2. Stir beans, diced tomatoes, tomato sauce, chili powder, cumin, black pepper and hot pepper sauce into **CROCK-POT®** slow cooker. Cover; cook on HIGH 1 hour.

3. Combine cornmeal, flour, baking powder, sugar and salt in large bowl. Stir in milk, eggs and oil; mix well. Stir in corn. Spoon evenly over bean mixture in **CROCK-POT®** slow cooker. Cover; cook on HIGH 1½ to 2 hours or until cornbread topping is golden brown.

Makes 8 servings

Tip: Spoon any remaining cornbread topping into greased muffin cups. Bake 30 minutes at 375°F or until golden brown.

Vegetarian Sausage Rice

2 cups chopped green bell peppers

1 can (about 15 ounces) dark kidney beans, rinsed and drained

1 can (about 14 ounces) diced tomatoes with bell peppers and onions

1 cup chopped onion

1 cup sliced celery

1 cup water, divided

½ cup uncooked converted long grain rice

1¼ teaspoons salt

1 teaspoon hot pepper sauce, plus additional for garnish

½ teaspoon dried thyme

½ teaspoon red pepper flakes

3 whole bay leaves

1 package (8 ounces) frozen meatless breakfast patties, thawed

2 tablespoons extra virgin olive oil

½ cup chopped fresh Italian parsley

1. Combine bell peppers, beans, tomatoes, onion, celery, ½ cup water, rice, salt, 1 teaspoon hot pepper sauce, thyme, red pepper flakes and bay leaves in **CROCK-POT**® slow cooker. Cover; cook on LOW 4 to 5 hours. Remove and discard bay leaves.

2. Dice meatless patties. Heat oil in large nonstick skillet over medium-high heat. Add patties; cook 2 minutes or until lightly browned, scraping bottom of skillet occasionally.

3. Place patties in **CROCK-POT**® slow cooker. Do not stir. Add remaining ½ cup water to skillet. Bring to a boil over high heat; cook 1 minute, scraping up browned bits on bottom of skillet. Stir liquid and parsley into **CROCK-POT**® slow cooker. Serve immediately with additional hot pepper sauce.

Makes 8 cups

Garden Potato Casserole

1¼ pounds baking potatoes, unpeeled and sliced

1 small green or red bell pepper, thinly sliced

¼ cup finely chopped yellow onion

2 tablespoons butter, divided

½ teaspoon salt

½ teaspoon dried thyme

Black pepper

1 small yellow squash, thinly sliced

1 cup (4 ounces) shredded sharp Cheddar cheese

Chopped fresh chives

1. Place potatoes, bell pepper, onion, 1 tablespoon butter, salt, thyme and black pepper in **CROCK-POT**® slow cooker; mix well. Evenly layer squash over potato mixture; add remaining 1 tablespoon butter. Cover; cook on LOW 7 hours or on HIGH 4 hours.

2. Remove potato mixture to serving bowl. Sprinkle with cheese; let stand 2 to 3 minutes or until cheese is melted. Sprinkle with chives.

Makes 5 servings

VEGETARIAN
SAUSAGE RICE

Vegetable Curry

- 4 baking potatoes, diced
- 1 large onion, chopped
- 1 red bell pepper, chopped
- 2 carrots, diced
- 2 tomatoes, chopped
- 1 can (6 ounces) tomato paste
- ½ cup water
- 2 teaspoons cumin seeds
- ½ teaspoon garlic powder
- ½ teaspoon salt
- 3 cups cauliflower florets
- 1 package (10 ounces) frozen peas, thawed

Combine potatoes, onion, bell pepper, carrots and tomatoes in **CROCK-POT®** slow cooker. Stir in tomato paste, water, cumin seeds, garlic powder and salt. Add cauliflower; stir well. Cover; cook on LOW 8 to 9 hours or until vegetables are tender. Stir in peas just before serving.

Makes 6 servings

Green Bean Casserole

- 2 packages (10 ounces each) frozen green beans, thawed
- 1 can (10½ ounces) condensed cream of mushroom soup, undiluted
- 1 tablespoon chopped fresh Italian parsley
- 1 tablespoon chopped roasted red peppers
- 1 teaspoon dried sage
- ½ teaspoon salt
- ½ teaspoon black pepper
- ¼ teaspoon ground nutmeg
- ½ cup toasted slivered almonds*

*To toast almonds, spread in single layer in heavy skillet. Cook over medium heat 1 to 2 minutes or until nuts are lightly browned, stirring frequently.

Combine all ingredients except almonds in **CROCK-POT®** slow cooker. Cover; cook on LOW 3 to 4 hours. Sprinkle with almonds before serving.

Makes 4 to 6 servings

Wild Rice and Dried Cherry Risotto

1 cup dry-roasted salted peanuts

2 tablespoons sesame oil, divided

1 cup chopped onion

6 ounces uncooked wild rice

1 cup diced carrots

1 cup chopped green or red bell pepper

½ cup dried cherries

⅛ to ¼ teaspoon red pepper flakes

4 cups hot water

¼ cup teriyaki or soy sauce

1 teaspoon salt

1. Coat **CROCK-POT**® slow cooker with nonstick cooking spray. Heat large skillet over medium-high heat. Add peanuts. Cook and stir 2 to 3 minutes or until nuts begin to brown. Remove nuts to plate; set aside.

2. Heat 2 teaspoons oil in skillet. Add onion; cook and stir 6 minutes or until browned. Transfer to **CROCK-POT**® slow cooker.

3. Stir in rice, carrots, bell pepper, cherries, red pepper flakes and water. Cover; cook on HIGH 3 hours.

4. Turn off heat. Let stand 15 minutes, uncovered, until rice absorbs liquid. Stir in teriyaki sauce, peanuts, remaining 4 teaspoons oil and salt.

Makes 8 to 10 servings

Wild Rice and Mushroom Casserole

2 tablespoons olive oil

½ medium red onion, finely diced

1 large green pepper, finely diced

8 ounces mushrooms, thinly sliced

2 cloves garlic, minced

1 can (about 14 ounces) diced tomatoes

1 teaspoon dried oregano

1 teaspoon paprika

2 tablespoons butter

2 tablespoons all-purpose flour

1½ cups milk

2 cups (8 ounces) shredded pepper jack, Cheddar or Swiss cheese

1 teaspoon salt

½ teaspoon black pepper

2 cups wild rice, cooked according to package instructions

1. Heat oil in large skillet over medium heat. Add onion, green pepper and mushrooms. Cook 5 to 6 minutes, stirring occasionally, until vegetables soften. Add garlic, tomatoes, oregano and paprika. Continue to cook until heated through. Remove to large bowl to cool.

2. Melt butter in same skillet over medium heat; whisk in flour. Cook and stir 4 to 5 minutes or until smooth and golden. Whisk in milk and bring to a boil. Whisk in cheese. Season with salt and black pepper.

3. Combine wild rice and vegetables in large bowl. Fold in cheese sauce; mix gently.

4. Coat inside of **CROCK-POT®** slow cooker with nonstick cooking spray. Pour wild rice mixture into **CROCK-POT®** slow cooker. Cover; cook on LOW 4 to 6 hours or on HIGH 2 to 3 hours.

Makes 4 to 6 servings

Arroz con Queso

1 can (16 ounces) crushed tomatoes, undrained

1 can (about 15 ounces) black beans, rinsed and drained

1½ cups uncooked converted long grain rice

1 onion, chopped

1 cup cottage cheese

1 can (4 ounces) chopped mild green chiles

2 tablespoons vegetable oil

3 teaspoons minced garlic

2 cups (8 ounces) shredded Monterey Jack cheese, divided

Combine tomatoes, beans, rice, onion, cottage cheese, chiles, oil, garlic and 1 cup Monterey Jack cheese in **CROCK-POT®** slow cooker; mix thoroughly. Cover; cook on LOW 6 to 9 hours or until liquid is absorbed. Sprinkle with remaining Monterey Jack cheese before serving.

Makes 8 to 10 servings

Bean and Vegetable Burritos

2 tablespoons chili powder

2 teaspoons dried oregano

1½ teaspoons ground cumin

1 sweet potato, diced

1 can (about 15 ounces) black beans, rinsed and drained

4 cloves garlic, minced

1 onion, halved and thinly sliced

1 jalapeño pepper, seeded and minced*

1 green bell pepper, chopped

1 cup frozen corn, thawed and drained

3 tablespoons lime juice

1 tablespoon chopped fresh cilantro

½ cup (3 ounces) shredded Monterey Jack cheese

4 (10-inch) flour tortillas

Jalapeño peppers can sting and irritate the skin, so wear rubber gloves when handling peppers and do not touch your eyes.

1. Combine chili powder, oregano and cumin in small bowl.

2. Layer sweet potato, beans, half of chili powder mixture, garlic, onion, jalapeño pepper, bell pepper, remaining half of chili powder mixture and corn in **CROCK-POT®** slow cooker. Cover; cook on LOW 5 hours or until sweet potato is tender. Stir in lime juice and cilantro.

3. Preheat oven to 350°F. Spoon 2 tablespoons cheese down center of each tortilla. Top with 1 cup filling. Fold up bottom edges of tortillas over filling; fold in sides and roll to enclose filling. Place burritos, seam side down, on baking sheet. Cover with foil; bake 20 minutes or until heated through.

Makes 4 servings

Southwestern Corn and Beans

1 tablespoon olive oil

1 large onion, diced

1 or 2 jalapeño peppers, diced*

1 clove garlic, minced

2 cans (about 15 ounces each) light red kidney beans, rinsed and drained

1 bag (16 ounces) frozen corn, thawed and drained

1 can (about 14 ounces) diced tomatoes

1 green bell pepper, cut into 1-inch pieces

2 teaspoons chili powder

½ teaspoon salt

½ teaspoon ground cumin

½ teaspoon black pepper

Sour cream or plain yogurt (optional)

Sliced black olives (optional)

Jalapeño peppers can sting and irritate the skin, so wear rubber gloves when handling peppers and do not touch your eyes.

1. Heat oil in medium skillet over medium heat. Add onion, jalapeño pepper and garlic; cook and stir 5 minutes. Combine onion mixture, beans, corn, tomatoes, bell pepper, chili powder, salt, cumin and black pepper in **CROCK-POT®** slow cooker; mix well. Cover; cook on LOW 7 to 8 hours or on HIGH 2 to 3 hours.

2. Serve with sour cream and black olives, if desired.

Makes 6 servings

Tip: For a party, spoon this colorful vegetarian dish into hollowed-out bell peppers or bread bowls.

**BEAN AND VEGETABLE
BURRITOS**

MEXICAN-STYLE
RICE AND CHEESE

Mexican-Style
Rice and Cheese

- 1 **can (about 15 ounces) Mexican-style beans, rinsed and drained**
- 1 **can (about 14 ounces) diced tomatoes with mild green chiles**
- 2 **cups (8 ounces) shredded Monterey Jack or Colby cheese, divided**
- 1½ **cups uncooked converted long grain rice**
- 1 **large onion, finely chopped**
- ½ **(8-ounce) package cream cheese**
- 3 **cloves garlic, minced**

Coat inside of **CROCK-POT**® slow cooker with nonstick cooking spray. Combine beans, tomatoes, 1 cup Monterey Jack cheese, rice, onion, cream cheese and garlic in **CROCK-POT**® slow cooker; mix well. Cover; cook on LOW 6 to 8 hours or until rice is tender. Sprinkle with remaining 1 cup Monterey Jack cheese just before serving.

Makes 6 to 8 servings

Cheesy Slow Cooker
Potatoes

- 1 **bag (32 ounces) shredded hash brown potatoes**
- 2 **cans (10½ ounces each) condensed Cheddar cheese soup, undiluted**
- 1 **can (12 ounces) evaporated milk**
- 1 **cup chopped onion**

Combine all ingredients in **CROCK-POT**® slow cooker. Cover; cook on LOW 6 to 8 hours.

Makes 6 servings

Meatless Sloppy Joes

2 cups thinly sliced onions

2 cups chopped green bell peppers

1 can (about 15 ounces) kidney beans, drained and mashed

1 can (8 ounces) tomato sauce

2 tablespoons ketchup

1 tablespoon yellow mustard

2 cloves garlic, finely chopped

1 teaspoon chili powder

1 tablespoon cider vinegar (optional)

4 sandwich rolls

1. Combine onions, bell peppers, beans, tomato sauce, ketchup, mustard, garlic and chili powder in **CROCK-POT®** slow cooker. Cover; cook on LOW 5 to 5½ hours or until vegetables are tender.

2. Season to taste with cider vinegar, if desired. Serve on rolls.

Makes 4 servings

Open-Face Provençal Vegetable Sandwich

2 cups sliced shiitake mushroom caps

1 large zucchini, halved lengthwise and sliced ¼ inch thick

1 large red bell pepper, quartered lengthwise and thinly sliced

1 small onion, sliced lengthwise ¼ inch thick

1 small jalapeño pepper, seeded and minced*

¼ cup vegetable broth

¼ cup pitted kalamata olives

2 tablespoons capers

1 clove garlic, minced

1½ tablespoons olive oil, divided

½ teaspoon dried oregano
  Salt and black pepper

4 teaspoons white wine vinegar
  Crusty bread, cut into thick slices

½ cup (3 ounces) shredded mozzarella cheese (optional)

Jalapeño peppers can sting and irritate the skin, so wear rubber gloves when handling peppers and do not touch your eyes.

1. Combine mushrooms, zucchini, bell pepper, onion, jalapeño pepper, broth, olives, capers, garlic, 1 tablespoon oil, oregano, salt and black pepper in **CROCK-POT®** slow cooker. Cover; cook on LOW 5 to 6 hours.

2. Turn off heat. Stir in vinegar and remaining ½ tablespoon oil. Let stand, uncovered, 15 to 30 minutes or until vegetables absorb some of liquid. (Vegetable mixture should be lukewarm.) Season with additional salt and black pepper, if desired.

3. Spoon vegetables onto bread. Sprinkle each serving with 2 tablespoons cheese and broil 30 seconds or until cheese melts and browns, if desired.

Makes 6 servings

Cheesy Broccoli Casserole

2 packages (10 ounces each) frozen chopped broccoli, thawed

1 can (10½ ounces) condensed cream of celery soup, undiluted

1¼ cups (5 ounces) shredded sharp Cheddar cheese, divided

¼ cup minced onion

1 teaspoon paprika

1 teaspoon hot pepper sauce

½ teaspoon celery seeds

1 cup crushed potato chips or saltine crackers

1. Coat inside of **CROCK-POT®** slow cooker with nonstick cooking spray. Combine broccoli, soup, 1 cup cheese, onion, paprika, hot pepper sauce and celery seeds in **CROCK-POT®** slow cooker; mix well. Cover; cook on LOW 5 to 6 hours or on HIGH 2½ to 3 hours.

2. Uncover; sprinkle top with potato chips and remaining ¼ cup cheese. Cook, uncovered, on LOW 30 to 60 minutes or on HIGH 15 to 30 minutes or until cheese melts.

Makes 4 to 6 servings

Tip: Substitute thawed chopped spinach for the broccoli and top with crushed crackers or spicy croutons.

OPEN-FACE PROVENÇAL
VEGETABLE SANDWICH

Black Bean Stuffed Peppers

   Nonstick cooking spray
1 medium onion, finely chopped
¼ teaspoon ground red pepper
¼ teaspoon dried oregano
¼ teaspoon ground cumin
¼ teaspoon chili powder
1 can (about 15 ounces) black beans, rinsed and drained
6 tall green bell peppers, tops removed
1 cup (4 ounces) shredded reduced-fat Monterey Jack cheese
1 cup tomato salsa
½ cup fat-free sour cream

1. Spray medium skillet with cooking spray; add onion and cook until golden. Add ground red pepper, oregano, cumin and chili powder.

2. Mash half of black beans with cooked onion in medium bowl. Stir in remaining beans. Place bell peppers in **CROCK-POT®** slow cooker; spoon black bean mixture into bell peppers. Sprinkle with cheese. Pour salsa over cheese. Cover; cook on LOW 6 to 8 hours or on HIGH 3 to 4 hours. Serve each bell pepper with a dollop of sour cream, if desired.

Makes 6 servings

Tip: You may increase any of the recipe ingredients to taste except the tomato salsa, and use a 5-, 6- or 7-quart **CROCK-POT®** slow cooker. However, the peppers should fit comfortably in a single layer in your stoneware.

Jim's Mexican-Style Spinach

3 packages (10 ounces each) frozen chopped spinach
1 tablespoon canola oil
1 onion, chopped
1 clove garlic, minced
2 Anaheim peppers, roasted, peeled and minced*
3 fresh tomatillos, roasted, husks removed and chopped**
6 tablespoons fat-free sour cream (optional)

To roast peppers, heat heavy skillet over medium-high heat. Add peppers and cook, turning occasionally with tongs, until blackened all over. Place peppers in brown paper bag for 2 to 5 minutes. Remove peppers from bag and scrape off charred skin. Cut off top and pull out core. Slice lengthwise and scrape off veins and any remaining seeds with a knife.

**To roast tomatillos, heat skillet over medium heat. Add tomatillos and cook, turning often, until husks are brown and interior flesh is soft. Remove from skillet. Remove and discard husks when cool enough to handle.*

1. Place frozen spinach in **CROCK-POT®** slow cooker.

2. Heat oil in large skillet over medium heat. Cook and stir onion and garlic 5 minutes or until onion is soft but not browned. Add Anaheim peppers and tomatillos; cook 3 to 4 minutes.

3. Add mixture to **CROCK-POT®** slow cooker. Cover; cook on LOW 4 to 6 hours. Serve with sour cream, if desired.

Makes 6 servings

BLACK BEAN
STUFFED PEPPERS

Penne Pasta Zuppa

1 can (about 15 ounces) white beans, rinsed and drained

2 medium yellow squash, diced

2 tomatoes, diced

2 small red potatoes, cubed

2 leeks, sliced lengthwise into quarters then chopped

1 carrot, diced

¼ pound fresh green beans, washed, stemmed and diced

2 fresh sage leaves, minced

1 teaspoon salt

½ teaspoon black pepper

8 cups water

¼ pound uncooked penne pasta

Grated Romano cheese (optional)

1. Combine beans, squash, tomatoes, potatoes, leeks, carrot, green beans, sage, salt and pepper in **CROCK-POT®** slow cooker. Add water; stir well to combine. Cover; cook on HIGH 2 hours, stirring occasionally. Turn **CROCK-POT®** slow cooker to LOW. Cover; cook on LOW 8 hours, stirring occasionally.

2. Turn **CROCK-POT®** slow cooker to HIGH. Add pasta. Cover; cook on HIGH 30 minutes or until pasta is cooked through. Garnish with cheese.

Makes 6 servings

Southwestern Stuffed Peppers

4 green bell peppers

1 can (about 15 ounces) black beans, rinsed and drained

1 cup (4 ounces) shredded pepper jack cheese

½ cup medium salsa

½ cup frozen corn

½ cup chopped green onions

⅓ cup uncooked long grain rice

1 teaspoon chili powder

½ teaspoon ground cumin

Sour cream (optional)

1. Cut thin slice off top of each bell pepper. Combine beans, cheese, salsa, corn, green onions, rice, chili powder and cumin in medium bowl. Spoon filling evenly into each bell pepper.

2. Place bell peppers in **CROCK-POT®** slow cooker. Cover; cook on LOW 4 to 6 hours. Serve with sour cream, if desired.

Makes 4 servings

Tip: For firmer rice in the finished dish, substitute converted rice for regular long grain rice.

PENNE PASTA ZUPPA

Caponata

1 medium eggplant (about 1 pound), peeled and cut into ½-inch pieces

1 can (about 14 ounces) diced tomatoes

1 medium onion, chopped

1 red bell pepper, cut into ½-inch pieces

½ cup medium-hot salsa

¼ cup extra virgin olive oil

2 tablespoons capers, drained

2 tablespoons balsamic vinegar

3 cloves garlic, minced

1 teaspoon dried oregano

¼ teaspoon salt

⅓ cup packed fresh basil, cut into thin strips

Toasted sliced Italian or French bread

1. Mix eggplant, tomatoes, onion, bell pepper, salsa, oil, capers, vinegar, garlic, oregano and salt in **CROCK-POT®** slow cooker. Cover; cook on LOW 7 to 8 hours or until vegetables are crisp-tender.

2. Stir in basil. Serve at room temperature with toasted bread.

Makes about 5¼ cups

Broccoli and Cheese Strata

2 cups chopped broccoli florets

4 slices firm white bread (½ inch thick)

4 teaspoons butter

1½ cups (6 ounces) shredded Cheddar cheese

1½ cups milk

3 eggs

½ teaspoon salt

½ teaspoon hot pepper sauce

⅛ teaspoon black pepper

1 cup water

1. Spray 1-quart casserole dish that fits in **CROCK-POT**® slow cooker with nonstick cooking spray. Cook broccoli in boiling water 10 minutes or until tender. Drain. Spread one side of each bread slice with 1 teaspoon butter. Arrange 2 slices bread, buttered sides up, in prepared casserole dish. Layer with cheese, broccoli and remaining 2 bread slices, buttered sides down.

2. Beat milk, eggs, salt, hot pepper sauce and black pepper in medium bowl. Pour over bread.

3. Place small wire rack in **CROCK-POT**® slow cooker. Pour in water. Place casserole on rack. Cover; cook on HIGH 3 hours.

Makes 4 servings

Asian Golden Barley with Cashews

2 tablespoons unsalted butter

1 cup hulled barley, rinsed and sorted

3 cups vegetable broth

1 cup chopped celery

1 green bell pepper, chopped

1 yellow onion, minced

1 clove garlic, minced

¼ teaspoon black pepper

¼ cup cashews (optional)

1. Heat large skillet over medium heat. Add butter and barley. Cook and stir about 10 minutes or until barley is slightly browned. Transfer to **CROCK-POT®** slow cooker.

2. Add broth, celery, bell pepper, onion, garlic and black pepper. Stir well to combine. Cover; cook on LOW 4 to 5 hours or on HIGH 2 to 3 hours or until barley is tender and liquid is absorbed. Garnish with cashews.

Makes 4 servings

Vegetable and Red Lentil Soup

1 can (about 14 ounces) vegetable broth

1 can (about 14 ounces) diced tomatoes

2 medium zucchini or yellow summer squash, chopped

1 red or yellow bell pepper, chopped

½ cup thinly sliced carrot

½ cup dried red lentils, rinsed and sorted

½ teaspoon salt

½ teaspoon sugar

¼ teaspoon black pepper

2 tablespoons chopped fresh basil or thyme

½ cup croutons or shredded cheese (optional)

1. Combine broth, tomatoes, zucchini, bell pepper, carrot, lentils, salt, sugar and black pepper in **CROCK-POT®** slow cooker; mix well. Cover; cook on LOW 8 hours or on HIGH 4 hours or until lentils and vegetables are tender.

2. Ladle into shallow bowls. Sprinkle with basil and croutons, if desired.

Makes 6 servings

Tip: When adapting your favorite recipe for a **CROCK-POT®** slow cooker, reduce the liquid by as much as half, because foods don't lose as much moisture during slow cooking as during conventional cooking.

HERBED TURKEY BREAST
WITH ORANGE SAUCE

5 Ingredients or Less

Herbed Turkey Breast with Orange Sauce

- 1   large onion, chopped
- 3   cloves garlic, minced
- 1   teaspoon dried rosemary
- ½   teaspoon black pepper
- 1   boneless, skinless turkey breast (3 pounds)
- 1½ cups orange juice

1. Place onion in **CROCK-POT®** slow cooker. Combine garlic, rosemary and pepper in small bowl.

2. Cut slices about three fourths of the way through turkey at 2-inch intervals. Rub garlic mixture between slices. Place turkey, cut side up, in **CROCK-POT®** slow cooker. Pour orange juice over turkey. Cover; cook on LOW 7 to 8 hours.

3. Slice turkey. Serve with orange sauce.

Makes 4 to 6 servings

Tip: Don't peek! The **CROCK-POT®** slow cooker can take as long as 30 minutes to regain heat lost when the cover is removed. Only remove the cover when instructed to do so by the recipe.

Corned Beef and Cabbage

- 1   head cabbage (about 1½ pounds), cut into 6 wedges
- 4   ounces baby carrots
- 1   corned beef (about 3 pounds) with seasoning packet, (perforate packet with knife tip)
- 4   cups water
- ⅓   cup prepared mustard
- ⅓   cup honey

1. Place cabbage and carrots in **CROCK-POT®** slow cooker. Place seasoning packet on top. Add corned beef, fat side up. Pour in water. Cover; cook on LOW 10 hours.

2. Remove and discard seasoning packet. Combine mustard and honey in small bowl. Slice beef; serve with vegetables and mustard sauce.

Makes 6 servings

Garlic and Herb Polenta

3   tablespoons butter, divided
8   cups water
2   cups yellow cornmeal
2   teaspoons finely minced garlic
2   teaspoons salt
3   tablespoons chopped fresh herbs such
    as parsley, chives, thyme or chervil
    (or a combination)

Coat inside of **CROCK-POT**® slow cooker with
1 tablespoon butter. Add water, cornmeal, garlic,
salt and remaining 2 tablespoons butter; stir.
Cover; cook on LOW 4 hours or on HIGH
3 hours, stirring occasionally. Stir in chopped
herbs just before serving.

Makes 6 servings

Tip: Polenta may also be poured into a greased
13×9-inch pan and allowed to cool until set. Cut
into squares (or slice as desired) to serve. For
even more great flavor, chill polenta slices until
firm, then grill or fry until golden brown.

Knockwurst and Cabbage

    Olive oil
8 to 10 knockwurst sausage links
1   head red cabbage, cut into ¼-inch slices
½   cup thinly sliced white onion
2   teaspoons caraway seeds
1   teaspoon salt
4   cups chicken broth

1. Heat oil in skillet over medium heat. Brown
sausages on all sides, turning as they brown.
Transfer to **CROCK-POT**® slow cooker.

2. Add cabbage and onion to **CROCK-POT**®
slow cooker. Sprinkle with caraway seeds and
salt. Add broth. Cover; cook on LOW 4 hours or
on HIGH 2 hours or until sausages are cooked
through and cabbage and onion are soft.

Makes 8 to 10 servings

GARLIC AND HERB POLENTA

Simmered Napa Cabbage with Dried Apricots

4 cups napa cabbage or green cabbage, cored, cleaned and sliced thin

1 cup chopped dried apricots

¼ cup clover honey

2 tablespoons orange juice

½ cup dry red wine

   Salt and black pepper

   Grated orange peel (optional)

1. Combine cabbage and apricots in **CROCK-POT®** slow cooker; toss well.

2. Combine honey and orange juice in small bowl; stir until smooth. Drizzle over cabbage. Add wine. Cover; cook on LOW 5 to 6 hours or on HIGH 2 to 3 hours or until cabbage is tender.

3. Season with salt and pepper. Garnish with orange peel.

Makes 4 servings

Cheesy Slow Cooker Chicken

6 boneless, skinless chicken breasts (about 1½ pounds)

   Salt

   Black pepper

   Garlic powder

2 cans (10½ ounces each) condensed cream of chicken soup, undiluted

1 can (10½ ounces) condensed Cheddar cheese soup, undiluted

   Chopped fresh parsley (optional)

   Hot cooked pasta

1. Place 3 chicken breasts in **CROCK-POT®** slow cooker. Season with salt, pepper and garlic powder. Repeat with remaining 3 breasts and seasonings.

2. Combine soups in medium bowl; pour over chicken. Cover; cook on LOW 6 to 8 hours or until chicken is tender. Sprinkle with parsley, if desired. Serve over pasta.

Makes 6 servings

Tip: This sauce is also delicious over rice or mashed potatoes.

SIMMERED NAPA
CABBAGE WITH
DRIED APRICOTS

SCALLOPED
POTATOES
AND HAM

Scalloped Potatoes and Ham

- 6 large russet potatoes, unpeeled and sliced into ¼-inch rounds
- 1 ham steak (about 1½ pounds), cut into cubes
- 1 can (10½ ounces) condensed cream of mushroom soup, undiluted
- 1 soup can water
- 1 cup (4 ounces) shredded Cheddar cheese
  Grill seasoning

1. Coat inside of **CROCK-POT®** slow cooker with nonstick cooking spray. Arrange potatoes and ham in layers in **CROCK-POT®** slow cooker.

2. Combine soup, water, cheese and grill seasoning in medium bowl; pour over potatoes and ham. Cover; cook on HIGH 3½ hours or until potatoes are fork-tender. Turn **CROCK-POT®** slow cooker to LOW. Cover; cook on LOW 1 hour.

Makes 5 to 6 servings

Simply Delicious Pork Roast

- 1½ pounds boneless pork loin, cut into 6 pieces *or* 6 boneless pork loin chops
- 4 medium Golden Delicious apples, peeled and sliced
- 3 tablespoons packed brown sugar
- 1 teaspoon ground cinnamon
- ½ teaspoon salt

1. Place pork in **CROCK-POT®** slow cooker. Cover with apples.

2. Combine brown sugar, cinnamon and salt in small bowl; sprinkle over apples. Cover; cook on LOW 6 to 8 hours.

Makes 6 servings

Simple Shredded Pork Tacos

2 pounds boneless pork roast

1 cup salsa

1 can (4 ounces) chopped mild green chiles

½ teaspoon garlic salt

½ teaspoon black pepper

Flour or corn tortillas

Optional Toppings: salsa, sour cream, diced tomatoes, shredded cheese, shredded lettuce

1. Place roast, 1 cup salsa, chiles, garlic salt and pepper in **CROCK-POT**® slow cooker. Cover; cook on LOW 8 hours or until meat is tender.

2. Remove pork from **CROCK-POT**® slow cooker to cutting board; shred with two forks. Serve on tortillas with sauce and desired toppings.

Makes 6 servings

Tip: Cut the pork roast to fit in the bottom of your **CROCK-POT**® slow cooker in one or two layers.

MACARONI
AND CHEESE

Macaroni and Cheese

- 6 **cups cooked elbow macaroni**
- 2 **tablespoons butter**
- 6 **cups (24 ounces) shredded Cheddar cheese**
- 4 **cups evaporated milk**
- 2 **teaspoons salt**
- ½ **teaspoon black pepper**

Toss macaroni with butter in large bowl. Stir in cheese, evaporated milk, salt and pepper. Transfer to **CROCK-POT**® slow cooker. Cover; cook on HIGH 2 to 3 hours.

Makes 6 to 8 servings

Tip: Make this mac 'n' cheese recipe more fun by adding some tasty mix-ins. Diced green or red bell pepper, peas, hot dog slices, chopped tomato, browned ground beef or chopped onion are all great options. Be creative!

Harvest Ham Supper

- 6 **carrots, cut into 2-inch pieces**
- 3 **medium sweet potatoes, quartered**
- 1 **to 1½ pounds boneless ham**
- 1 **cup maple syrup**

1. Arrange carrots and potatoes in bottom of **CROCK-POT**® slow cooker.

2. Place ham on top of vegetables. Pour syrup over ham and vegetables. Cover; cook on LOW 6 to 8 hours.

Makes 6 servings

Pesto Rice and Beans

1 **can (about 15 ounces) Great Northern
   beans, rinsed and drained**
1 **can (about 14 ounces) vegetable broth**
½ **cup uncooked converted long grain rice**
1½ **cups frozen cut green beans, thawed and
   drained**
½ **cup prepared pesto**
   Grated Parmesan cheese (optional)

1. Combine Great Northern beans, broth and rice
in **CROCK-POT®** slow cooker. Cover; cook on
LOW 2 hours.

2. Stir in green beans. Cover; cook on LOW
1 hour or until rice and beans are tender.

3. Turn off heat. Transfer **CROCK-POT®**
stoneware to heatproof surface. Stir in pesto and
cheese, if desired. Let stand, covered, 5 minutes
or until cheese is melted. Serve immediately.

Makes 8 servings

Barbecue Roast Beef

2 **pounds boneless cooked roast beef**
1 **bottle (12 ounces) barbecue sauce**
1½ **cups water**
10 **to 12 sandwich rolls, halved**

1. Combine roast beef, barbecue sauce and
water in **CROCK-POT®** slow cooker. Cover; cook
on LOW 2 hours.

2. Remove beef from **CROCK-POT®** slow cooker
to cutting board; shred with two forks. Return
beef to sauce; mix well. Serve on rolls.

Makes 10 to 12 servings

Tip: To save time, freeze leftovers as individual
portions. Just reheat in a microwave for fast
meals!

PARMESAN POTATO
WEDGES

Parmesan Potato Wedges

- 2 pounds red potatoes, unpeeled and cut into ½-inch wedges
- ¼ cup finely chopped yellow onion
- 1½ teaspoons dried oregano
- ½ teaspoon salt
- ¼ teaspoon black pepper
- 2 tablespoons butter, cubed
- ¼ cup grated Parmesan cheese

1. Layer potatoes, onion, oregano, salt and pepper in **CROCK-POT®** slow cooker; dot with butter. Cover; cook on HIGH 4 hours.

2. Remove potatoes to serving platter; sprinkle with cheese.

Makes 6 servings

Creamy Chicken

- 3 boneless, skinless chicken breasts *or* 6 boneless, skinless chicken thighs
- 2 cans (10½ ounces each) condensed cream of chicken soup, undiluted
- 1 can (about 14 ounces) chicken broth
- 1 can (4 ounces) sliced mushrooms, drained
- ½ medium onion, diced
  Salt and black pepper

Place all ingredients except salt and pepper in **CROCK-POT®** slow cooker. Cover; cook on LOW 6 to 8 hours. Season with salt and pepper.

Makes 3 servings

Corn on the Cob with Garlic Herb Butter

½ cup (1 stick) unsalted butter, softened

3 to 4 cloves garlic, minced

2 tablespoons finely minced fresh parsley

4 to 5 ears of corn, husked

Salt and black pepper

1. Combine butter, garlic and parsley in small bowl.

2. Place each ear of corn on a piece of foil and generously spread with butter mixture. Season with salt and pepper and tightly seal foil. Place in **CROCK-POT®** slow cooker; overlapping ears, if necessary. Add enough water to come one fourth of the way up each ear. Cover; cook on LOW 4 to 5 hours or on HIGH 2 to 2½ hours.

Makes 4 to 5 servings

Bacon and Onion Brisket

6 slices bacon, cut crosswise into ½-inch pieces
1 flat-cut boneless brisket, seasoned with salt and black pepper (about 2½ pounds)
3 medium onions, sliced
2 cans (10½ ounces each) condensed beef consommé, undiluted
   Salt and black pepper

1. Heat large skillet over medium heat. Add bacon; cook and stir until crisp. Transfer to **CROCK-POT**® slow cooker using slotted spoon.

2. Add brisket to skillet; brown on all sides. Transfer to **CROCK-POT**® slow cooker.

3. Reduce heat to medium. Add onions; cook and stir 3 to 5 minutes or until softened. Add to **CROCK-POT**® slow cooker. Pour in consommé. Cover; cook on HIGH 6 to 8 hours or until meat is tender.

4. Remove brisket to cutting board. Cover loosely with foil; let stand 10 to 15 minutes. Slice brisket against the grain into thin slices; season with salt and pepper. Spoon bacon, onions and cooking liquid over brisket to serve.

Makes 6 servings

Slow Cooker Chicken Dinner

4 boneless, skinless chicken breasts (about 1 pound)
1 can (10½ ounces) condensed cream of chicken soup, undiluted
⅓ cup milk
1 package (6 ounces) stuffing mix
1⅔ cups water

1. Place chicken in **CROCK-POT**® slow cooker. Combine soup and milk in small bowl. Pour soup mixture over chicken.

2. Combine stuffing mix and water in large bowl. Spoon stuffing over chicken. Cover; cook on LOW 6 to 8 hours.

Makes 4 servings

BACON AND
ONION BRISKET

Peach Cobbler

2 packages (16 ounces each) frozen peaches, thawed and drained

½ cup plus 1 tablespoon sugar, divided

2 teaspoons ground cinnamon, divided

½ teaspoon ground nutmeg

½ cup all-purpose flour

6 tablespoons butter, cubed

Whipped cream (optional)

1. Combine peaches, ½ cup sugar, 1½ teaspoons cinnamon and nutmeg in medium bowl. Transfer to **CROCK-POT®** slow cooker.

2. Combine flour, remaining 1 tablespoon sugar and remaining ½ teaspoon cinnamon in small bowl. Cut in butter with pastry blender or two knives until mixture resembles coarse crumbs. Sprinkle over peach mixture. Cover; cook on HIGH 2 hours. Serve with whipped cream, if desired.

Makes 4 to 6 servings

Tip: To make cleanup easier when cooking sticky or sugary foods, spray the inside of the **CROCK-POT®** slow cooker with nonstick cooking spray before adding ingredients.

Apricot and Brie Dip

½ cup dried apricots, finely chopped

⅓ cup plus 1 tablespoon apricot preserves, divided

¼ cup apple juice

1 round wheel Brie cheese (2 pounds), rind removed and cut into cubes

Bread or crackers

1. Combine dried apricots, ⅓ cup apricot preserves and apple juice in **CROCK-POT®** slow cooker. Cover; cook on HIGH 40 minutes.

2. Stir in cheese. Cover; cook on HIGH 30 to 40 minutes or until cheese is melted. Stir in remaining 1 tablespoon preserves. Turn **CROCK-POT®** slow cooker to LOW; serve warm with bread or crackers.

Makes 3 cups

PEACH COBBLER

Bittersweet Chocolate-Espresso Crème Brûlée

½ cup chopped bittersweet chocolate

5 egg yolks

1½ cups heavy cream

½ cup granulated sugar

¼ cup espresso

¼ cup Demerara or raw sugar

1. Arrange 5 (6-ounce) ramekins or custard cups inside **CROCK-POT®** slow cooker. Pour enough water to come halfway up sides of ramekins (taking care to keep water out of ramekins). Divide chocolate among ramekins.

2. Whisk egg yolks in small bowl; set aside. Heat small saucepan over medium heat. Add cream, granulated sugar and espresso; cook and stir until mixture begins to boil. Pour hot cream in thin, steady stream into egg yolks, whisking constantly. Pour through fine mesh strainer into clean bowl.

3. Ladle into prepared ramekins in bottom of **CROCK-POT®** slow cooker. Cover; cook on HIGH 1 to 2 hours or until custard is set around edges but still soft in centers. Carefully remove ramekins; cool to room temperature. Cover and refrigerate until serving.

4. Spread tops of custards with Demerara sugar just before serving. Serve immediately.

Makes 5 servings

Fresh Herbed Turkey Breast

2 tablespoons butter, softened

¼ cup fresh sage leaves, minced

¼ cup fresh tarragon, minced

1 clove garlic, minced

1 teaspoon black pepper

½ teaspoon salt

1 (4-pound) split turkey breast

1 tablespoon plus 1½ teaspoons cornstarch

1. Combine butter, sage, tarragon, garlic, pepper and salt. Rub butter mixture all over turkey breast.

2. Place turkey breast in **CROCK-POT®** slow cooker. Cover; cook on LOW 8 to 10 hours or on HIGH 4 to 5 hours or until turkey is no longer pink in the center.

3. Remove turkey breast to serving platter; cover loosely with foil to keep warm. Slowly whisk cornstarch into cooking juices; cook on HIGH 10 minutes or until thickened and smooth. Slice turkey breast. Serve with sauce.

Makes 8 servings

Note: Recipe can be doubled for a 5-, 6- or 7-quart **CROCK-POT®** slow cooker.

Tip: Fresh herbs enliven this simple, excellent main dish.

BITTERSWEET CHOCOLATE-
ESPRESSO CRÈME BRÛLÉE

Easy Cheesy BBQ Chicken

6 **boneless, skinless chicken breasts (about 1½ pounds)**

1 **bottle (26 ounces) barbecue sauce**

6 **slices bacon, crisp-cooked and cut in half**

6 **slices Swiss cheese**

1. Place chicken in **CROCK-POT®** slow cooker. Cover with barbecue sauce. Cover; cook on LOW 8 to 9 hours. (If sauce becomes too thick during cooking, add a little water.)

2. Place 2 bacon halves and 1 cheese slice on each chicken breast in **CROCK-POT®** slow cooker. Turn **CROCK-POT®** slow cooker to HIGH. Cover; cook on HIGH until cheese melts.

Makes 6 servings

Tip: To make cleanup easier, coat the inside of the **CROCK-POT®** slow cooker with nonstick cooking spray before adding the ingredients. To remove any sticky barbecue sauce residue, soak the stoneware in hot sudsy water, then scrub it with a plastic or nylon scrubber. Don't use steel wool.

Glazed Pork Loin

1 **bag (1 pound) baby carrots**

4 **boneless pork loin chops**

1 **jar (8 ounces) apricot preserves**

Place carrots in **CROCK-POT®** slow cooker. Place pork on top; spread with preserves. Cover; cook on LOW 8 hours or on HIGH 4 hours.

Makes 4 servings

Posole

3 **pounds pork tenderloin, cubed**

3 **cans (about 14 ounces each) white hominy, rinsed and drained**

1 **cup chili sauce**

Combine all ingredients in **CROCK-POT®** slow cooker. Cover; cook on LOW 10 hours or on HIGH 5 hours.

Makes 8 servings

EASY CHEESY BBQ CHICKEN

CHUNKY RANCH
POTATOES

Chunky Ranch Potatoes

3 pounds unpeeled red potatoes,
  quartered
1 cup water
½ cup prepared ranch dressing
½ cup grated Parmesan or Cheddar cheese
  (optional)
¼ cup minced fresh chives

1. Place potatoes in **CROCK-POT®** slow cooker.
Add water. Cover; cook on LOW 7 to 9 hours or
on HIGH 4 to 6 hours or until potatoes are tender.

2. Stir in ranch dressing, cheese and chives.
Break up potatoes into chunks.

Makes 8 servings

Orange Chicken

1 can (12 ounces) orange soda
½ cup soy sauce
4 boneless, skinless chicken breasts
  (about 1 pound)
  Hot cooked rice

Pour soda and soy sauce into **CROCK-POT®**
slow cooker. Add chicken and turn to coat. Cover;
cook on LOW 5 to 6 hours. Serve over rice.

Makes 4 servings

Simple Slow Cooker Pork Roast

4 to 5 red potatoes, unpeeled and cut into bite-size pieces

4 carrots, cut into bite-size pieces

1 marinated pork loin roast (3 to 4 pounds)*

½ cup water

1 package (10 ounces) frozen baby peas

Salt and black pepper

If marinated roast is unavailable, combine ¼ cup olive oil, 1 tablespoon minced garlic and 1½ tablespoons Italian seasoning in large resealable food storage bag. Add pork; turn to coat. Marinate in refrigerator at least 2 hours or overnight.

1. Layer potatoes, carrots and pork roast in **CROCK-POT**® slow cooker. (If necessary, cut roast in half to fit.) Add water. Cover; cook on LOW 6 to 8 hours.

2. Add peas during last hour of cooking. Remove pork to serving platter. Season with salt and pepper. Slice and serve with vegetables.

Makes 6 servings

CHORIZO CHILI

Chorizo Chili

1 **pound ground beef**

8 **ounces bulk raw chorizo sausage** *or*
   **½ (15-ounce) package raw chorizo
   sausage**

1 **can (about 15 ounces) chili beans in chili
   sauce**

2 **cans (about 14 ounces each) chili-style
   diced tomatoes**

   **Sour cream, chives and shredded
   Cheddar cheese (optional)**

Place beef and chorizo in **CROCK-POT**® slow
cooker. Break up with fork to form small chunks.
Stir beans and tomatoes into **CROCK-POT**® slow
cooker. Cover; cook on LOW 7 hours. Skim off
and discard excess fat before serving.

Makes 6 servings

Italian Beef

1 **beef rump roast (3 to 5 pounds)***

1 **can (about 14 ounces) beef broth**

2 **cups mild giardiniera**

8 **crusty Italian bread rolls, split**

**Unless you have a 5-, 6- or 7-quart CROCK-POT®
slow cooker, cut any roast larger than 2½ pounds
in half so it cooks completely.*

1. Place roast in **CROCK-POT**® slow cooker;
add broth and giardiniera. Cover; cook on LOW
10 hours.

2. Remove beef from **CROCK-POT**® slow cooker
to cutting board; shred beef with two forks.
Return to cooking liquid; mix well. To serve,
spoon beef and sauce onto rolls.

Makes 8 servings

Chili and Cheese "Baked" Potato Supper

4 russet potatoes (about 2 pounds), unpeeled

2 cups prepared chili

½ cup (2 ounces) shredded Cheddar cheese

4 tablespoons sour cream (optional)

2 green onions, sliced

1. Prick potatoes in several places with fork. Wrap potatoes in foil. Place in **CROCK-POT**® slow cooker. Cover; cook on LOW 8 to 10 hours or on HIGH 4 to 5 hours. Carefully unwrap potatoes and place on serving dish.

2. Heat chili in microwave or on stovetop. Split hot potatoes and spoon chili on top. Sprinkle with cheese, sour cream, if desired, and green onions.

Makes 4 servings

Tequila-Poached Pears

4 **Anjou pears, peeled**
2 **cups water**
1 **can (11½ ounces) pear nectar**
1 **cup tequila**
½ **cup sugar**
   Grated peel and juice of 1 lime
   Vanilla ice cream (optional)

Place pears in **CROCK-POT®** slow cooker. Combine water, nectar, tequila, sugar, lime peel and lime juice in medium saucepan. Bring to a boil over medium-high heat, stirring frequently. Boil 1 minute; pour over pears. Cover; cook on LOW 4 to 6 hours or on HIGH 2 to 3 hours or until pears are tender. Serve warm with poaching liquid and vanilla ice cream, if desired.

Tip: Poaching fruit in a sugar, juice or alcohol syrup helps the fruit retain its shape and become more flavorful.

Makes 4 servings

SLOW-ROASTED POTATOES

Slow-Roasted Potatoes

16 small new red potatoes, unpeeled
3 tablespoons butter, cubed
1 teaspoon paprika
½ teaspoon salt
¼ teaspoon garlic powder
  Black pepper

Combine all ingredients in **CROCK-POT®** slow cooker; mix well. Cover; cook on LOW 7 hours or on HIGH 4 hours. Remove potatoes with slotted spoon to serving dish; keep warm. Add 1 to 2 tablespoons water to cooking liquid and stir until well blended. Pour over potatoes.

Makes 3 to 4 servings

Fantastic Pot Roast

1 can (12 ounces) cola
1 bottle (10 ounces) chili sauce
2 cloves garlic (optional)
2½ pounds boneless beef chuck roast

Combine cola, chili sauce and garlic, if desired, in **CROCK-POT®** slow cooker. Add beef; turn to coat. Cover; cook on LOW 6 to 8 hours. Serve with sauce.

Makes 6 servings

AUTUMN CHICKEN

Chicken and Turkey

Autumn Chicken

1 can (14 ounces) whole artichoke hearts, drained
1 can (14 ounces) whole mushrooms, divided
12 boneless, skinless chicken breasts
1 jar (6½ ounces) marinated artichoke hearts, undrained
½ cup dry white wine
½ cup balsamic vinaigrette
  Hot cooked egg noodles
  Paprika (optional)

Spread whole artichokes over bottom of **CROCK-POT®** slow cooker. Top with half of mushrooms. Layer chicken over mushrooms. Add marinated artichoke hearts with liquid. Add remaining mushrooms. Pour in wine and vinaigrette. Cover; cook on LOW 4 to 5 hours. Serve over noodles. Garnish with paprika.

Makes 10 to 12 servings

Tip: Don't add water to the **CROCK-POT®** slow cooker unless the recipe specifically says to do so. Foods don't lose as much moisture during slow cooking as they do during conventional cooking, so follow recipe guidelines for best results.

Turkey Piccata

2½ tablespoons all-purpose flour
¼ teaspoon salt
¼ teaspoon black pepper
1 pound turkey breast meat, cut into strips*
1 tablespoon butter
1 tablespoon olive oil
½ cup chicken broth
2 teaspoons lemon juice
  Grated peel of 1 lemon
2 cups hot cooked rice (optional)
2 tablespoons finely chopped fresh parsley

***You may substitute turkey tenderloins.**

1. Combine flour, salt and pepper in large resealable food storage bag. Add turkey. Seal bag; shake to coat. Heat butter and oil in large skillet over medium-high heat. Add turkey in single layer; brown on all sides. Transfer to **CROCK-POT®** slow cooker in single layer.

2. Pour broth into skillet, stirring to scrape up any browned bits. Pour into **CROCK-POT®** slow cooker. Add lemon juice and peel to **CROCK-POT®** slow cooker. Cover; cook on LOW 1 hour. Serve over rice, if desired. Garnish with parsley.

Makes 4 servings

Country Captain Chicken

4 boneless, skinless chicken thighs
2 tablespoons all-purpose flour
2 tablespoons vegetable oil, divided
1 cup chopped green bell pepper
1 large onion, chopped
1 stalk celery, chopped
1 clove garlic, minced
¼ cup chicken broth
2 cups canned crushed tomatoes or diced fresh tomatoes
½ cup golden raisins
1½ teaspoons curry powder
1 teaspoon salt
¼ teaspoon paprika
¼ teaspoon black pepper
  Hot cooked rice
  Sprigs fresh parsley (optional)

1. Coat chicken with flour; set aside. Heat 1 tablespoon oil in large skillet over medium-high heat. Add bell pepper, onion, celery and garlic. Cook and stir 5 minutes or until vegetables are tender. Place vegetables in **CROCK-POT**® slow cooker.

2. Heat remaining 1 tablespoon oil in same skillet over medium-high heat. Add chicken; cook 10 minutes or until browned on both sides. Place chicken in **CROCK-POT**® slow cooker.

3. Pour broth into skillet. Cook over medium-high heat, stirring to scrape up any browned bits from bottom of skillet. Pour broth mixture into **CROCK-POT**® slow cooker. Add tomatoes, raisins, curry powder, salt, paprika and black pepper to **CROCK-POT**® slow cooker. Cover; cook on LOW 3 hours. Serve chicken and sauce over rice. Garnish with parsley.

Makes 4 servings

Turkey with Chunky Cherry Relish

1 bag (16 ounces) frozen dark cherries, coarsely chopped
1 can (about 14 ounces) diced tomatoes with jalapeño peppers
1 package (6 ounces) dried cherry-flavored cranberries or dried cherries, coarsely chopped
2 small onions, thinly sliced
1 small green bell pepper, chopped
½ cup packed brown sugar
2 tablespoons quick-cooking tapioca
1½ tablespoons salt
½ teaspoon ground cinnamon
½ teaspoon black pepper
1 bone-in turkey breast (2½ to 3 pounds)
2 tablespoons water
1 tablespoon cornstarch

1. Place cherries, tomatoes, cranberries, onions, bell pepper, brown sugar, tapioca, salt, cinnamon and black pepper in **CROCK-POT**® slow cooker; mix well.

2. Place turkey on top of cherry mixture. Cover; cook on LOW 7 to 8 hours or until temperature registers 170°F on meat thermometer inserted into thickest part of breast, not touching bone. Remove turkey from **CROCK-POT**® slow cooker. Cover loosely with foil to keep warm.

3. Turn **CROCK-POT**® slow cooker to HIGH. Stir water into cornstarch in small bowl until smooth. Whisk cornstarch mixture into cherry mixture. Cook, uncovered, on HIGH 15 minutes or until sauce is thickened. Slice turkey; top with relish.

Makes 4 to 6 servings

COUNTRY CAPTAIN CHICKEN

Greek Chicken Pitas with Creamy Mustard Sauce

FILLING

1 medium green bell pepper, cut into ½-inch strips

1 medium onion, cut into 8 wedges

1 pound boneless, skinless chicken breasts, rinsed and patted dry

1 tablespoon extra virgin olive oil

2 teaspoons Greek seasoning

¼ teaspoon salt

SAUCE

¼ cup plain fat-free yogurt

¼ cup mayonnaise

1 tablespoon prepared mustard

¼ teaspoon salt

4 pita bread rounds

½ cup crumbled feta cheese

Optional toppings: sliced cucumbers, sliced tomatoes, kalamata olives

1. Coat inside of **CROCK-POT®** slow cooker with nonstick cooking spray. Place bell pepper and onion in bottom. Add chicken and drizzle with oil. Sprinkle evenly with Greek seasoning and ¼ teaspoon salt. Cover; cook on HIGH 1½ hours or until chicken is no longer pink in center (vegetables will be slightly tender-crisp).

2. Remove chicken to cutting board; slice. Remove vegetables to medium bowl using slotted spoon.

3. Combine yogurt, mayonnaise, mustard and ¼ teaspoon salt in small bowl; whisk until smooth.

4. Warm pita rounds according to package directions. Cut in half and layer with chicken, sauce, vegetables and feta cheese. Top as desired.

Makes 4 servings

Kat's Slow Chicken

4 to 6 boneless, skinless breasts *or* 1 cut-up whole chicken (3 pounds)

1 jar (26 ounces) pasta sauce

1 medium onion, sliced

1 medium green bell pepper, cut into strips

4 carrots, sliced

1 stalk celery, sliced

4 cloves garlic, minced

½ teaspoon salt

2 to 4 tablespoons water

1 to 2 tablespoons cornstarch

Prepared mashed potatoes or hot cooked egg noodles (optional)

1. Combine chicken, pasta sauce, onion, bell pepper, carrots, celery, garlic and salt in **CROCK-POT®** slow cooker. Cover; cook on LOW 6 to 8 hours.

2. Before serving, stir 2 tablespoons water into 1 tablespoon cornstarch in small bowl until smooth. Turn **CROCK-POT®** slow cooker to HIGH. Add to **CROCK-POT®** slow cooker. Cover; cook on HIGH 15 minutes or until mixture thickens. If mixture needs additional thickening, add remaining water and cornstarch. Serve chicken and vegetables over mashed potatoes, if desired.

Makes 4 to 6 servings

Tip: Vegetables such as potatoes and carrots can sometimes take longer to cook than meat. Place evenly cut vegetables along the sides of the **CROCK-POT®** slow cooker when possible.

GREEK CHICKEN PITAS WITH
CREAMY MUSTARD SAUCE

Stuffed Chicken Breasts

6 boneless, skinless chicken breasts

8 ounces feta cheese, crumbled

3 cups chopped fresh spinach leaves

⅓ cup sun-dried tomatoes, packed in oil, drained and chopped

1 teaspoon minced lemon peel

1 teaspoon dried basil, oregano or mint

½ teaspoon garlic powder

Black pepper

1 can (about 14 ounces) diced tomatoes

½ cup oil-cured olives*

Hot cooked polenta

Lemon peel twists (optional)

*If using pitted olives, add to CROCK-POT® slow cooker in the final hour of cooking.

1. Place 1 chicken breast between two pieces of plastic wrap. Using tenderizer mallet or back of skillet, pound until about ¼-inch thick. Repeat with remaining chicken.

2. Combine feta, spinach, sun-dried tomatoes, lemon peel, basil, garlic powder and pepper in medium bowl.

3. Place chicken breasts, smooth sides down, on work surface. Place 2 tablespoons feta mixture on wide end of each breast. Roll tightly.

4. Place rolled chicken, seam sides down, in **CROCK-POT®** slow cooker. Top with tomatoes and olives. Cover; cook on LOW 5½ to 6 hours or on HIGH 4 hours. Serve over polenta. Garnish with lemon peel.

Makes 6 servings

Easy Parmesan Chicken

8 ounces mushrooms, sliced

1 medium onion, cut into thin wedges

1 tablespoon olive oil

4 boneless, skinless chicken breasts

1 jar (26 ounces) pasta sauce

½ teaspoon dried basil

¼ teaspoon dried oregano

1 whole bay leaf

½ cup (2 ounces) shredded part-skim mozzarella cheese

¼ cup grated Parmesan cheese

Hot cooked spaghetti

1. Place mushrooms and onion in **CROCK-POT®** slow cooker.

2. Heat oil in large skillet over medium-high heat. Lightly brown chicken on both sides. Place chicken in **CROCK-POT®** slow cooker. Pour pasta sauce over chicken; add basil, oregano and bay leaf. Cover; cook on LOW 6 to 7 hours or on HIGH 3 to 4 hours or until chicken is tender. Remove and discard bay leaf.

3. Sprinkle chicken with cheeses. Cook, uncovered, on LOW 10 minutes or until cheeses melt. Serve over spaghetti.

Makes 4 servings

Tip: Dairy products should be added at the end of the cooking time because they will curdle if cooked in the **CROCK-POT®** slow cooker for a long time.

STUFFED CHICKEN BREASTS

SPICY ORANGE
CHICKEN NUGGETS

Spicy Orange Chicken Nuggets

 1   bag (28 ounces) frozen popcorn chicken bites
1½   cups prepared honey teriyaki marinade
 ½   cup orange juice concentrate
 ⅔   cup water
 1   tablespoon orange marmalade
 ½   teaspoon hot chile sauce or sriracha*
     Thinly sliced green onions
     Hot cooked rice

Sriracha is a Thai hot sauce and is available in Asian specialty markets and large supermarkets.

1. Preheat oven to 450°F. Spread chicken evenly on baking sheet. Bake 12 to 14 minutes or until crisp. (Do not brown.) Transfer to **CROCK-POT®** slow cooker.

2. Combine teriyaki marinade, juice concentrate, water, marmalade and chile sauce in medium bowl. Pour over chicken. Cover; cook on LOW 3 to 3½ hours.

3. Sprinkle with green onions and serve with rice.

Makes 8 or 9 servings

Greek-Style Chicken

 6   boneless, skinless chicken thighs, trimmed
 ½   teaspoon salt
 ½   teaspoon black pepper
 1   tablespoon olive oil
 ½   cup chicken broth
 1   lemon, thinly sliced
 ¼   cup pitted kalamata olives
 1   clove garlic, minced
 ½   teaspoon dried oregano
     Hot cooked orzo or rice

1. Season chicken with salt and pepper. Heat oil in large skillet over medium-high heat. Brown chicken on all sides. Transfer to **CROCK-POT®** slow cooker.

2. Add broth, lemon, olives, garlic and oregano. Cover; cook on LOW 5 to 6 hours or until chicken is tender. Serve with orzo.

Makes 4 to 6 servings

Tip: Freeze leftovers as individual portions; just reheat in a microwave for fast weeknight dinners!

Mexican Chicken and Black Bean Soup

4 bone-in chicken thighs, skin removed

1 cup finely chopped onion

1 can (about 14 ounces) chicken broth

1 can (about 14 ounces) diced tomatoes with Mexican seasoning or diced tomatoes with mild green chiles

1 can (about 15 ounces) black beans, rinsed and drained

1 cup frozen corn

1 can (4 ounces) chopped mild green chiles

1 tablespoon chili powder

1 teaspoon salt

1 teaspoon ground cumin

Optional toppings: sour cream, sliced avocado, shredded cheese, chopped fresh cilantro, fried tortilla strips

1. Coat inside of **CROCK-POT**® slow cooker with nonstick cooking spray. Add all ingredients except toppings. Cover; cook on HIGH 3 to 4 hours or until chicken is cooked through.

2. Remove chicken to cutting board with slotted spoon. Debone and chop chicken. Return to **CROCK-POT**® slow cooker; stir well. Serve in bowls. Top as desired.

Makes 4 servings

Chicken in Enchilada Sauce

- 1 **can (about 14 ounces) diced tomatoes with chipotle peppers***
- 1 **can (10 ounces) enchilada sauce**
- 1 **cup frozen or canned corn**
- ¼ **teaspoon ground cumin**
- ¼ **teaspoon black pepper**
- 1½ **pounds boneless, skinless chicken thighs, cut into bite-size pieces**
- 2 **tablespoons minced fresh cilantro**
- ½ **cup (2 ounces) shredded pepper jack cheese****

  Sliced green onions (optional)

*If tomatoes with chipotle peppers are not available, use diced tomatoes with green chiles or plain diced tomatoes plus ¼ teaspoon red pepper flakes.

**For a less spicy dish, use Monterey Jack cheese.

1. Combine tomatoes, enchilada sauce, corn, cumin and pepper in **CROCK-POT®** slow cooker. Add chicken; mix well. Cover; cook on LOW 6 to 7 hours.

2. Stir in cilantro. Sprinkle with cheese and garnish with green onions just before serving.

Makes 4 servings

Like Grandma's Chicken 'n' Dumplings

- 2 **cups cooked chicken**
- 1 **can (10½ ounces) condensed cream of mushroom soup, undiluted**
- 1 **can (10½ ounces) condensed cream of chicken soup, undiluted**
- 2 **soup cans water**
- 4 **teaspoons all-purpose flour**
- 2 **teaspoons chicken bouillon granules**
- ½ **teaspoon black pepper**
- 1 **can refrigerated buttermilk biscuits (8 biscuits)**

1. Mix all ingredients except biscuits in **CROCK-POT®** slow cooker.

2. Cut biscuits into quarters and gently stir into mixture. Cover; cook on LOW 4 to 6 hours.

Makes 4 to 6 servings

Sweet and Sour Chicken

¼ cup chicken broth

2 tablespoons reduced-sodium soy sauce

2 tablespoons hoisin sauce

1 tablespoon cider vinegar

1 tablespoon tomato paste

2 teaspoons packed brown sugar

1 clove garlic, minced

¼ teaspoon black pepper

1 pound boneless, skinless chicken thighs, cut into 1-inch pieces

2 teaspoons cornstarch

2 tablespoons snipped fresh chives

Hot cooked rice

1. Combine broth, soy sauce, hoisin sauce, vinegar, tomato paste, brown sugar, garlic and pepper in **CROCK-POT®** slow cooker; mix well.

2. Add chicken; stir to coat. Cover; cook on LOW 2½ to 3½ hours.

3. Remove chicken to cutting board with slotted spoon. Cover loosely with foil to keep warm. Stir 2 tablespoons cooking liquid into cornstarch in small bowl until smooth; add to **CROCK-POT®** slow cooker. Stir in chives. Turn **CROCK-POT®** slow cooker to HIGH. Stir 2 minutes or until sauce is slightly thickened. Serve chicken and sauce over rice.

Makes 4 servings

Mu Shu Turkey

1 can (16 ounces) plums, drained and pitted
½ cup orange juice
¼ cup finely chopped onion
1 tablespoon minced fresh ginger
¼ teaspoon ground cinnamon
1 pound boneless, skinless turkey breast, cut into thin strips
6 (7-inch) flour tortillas, warmed
3 cups coleslaw mix

1. Place plums in blender or food processor; blend until almost smooth. Combine plums, orange juice, onion, ginger and cinnamon in **CROCK-POT**® slow cooker; mix well. Place turkey over plum mixture. Cover; cook on LOW 3 to 4 hours.

2. Divide turkey evenly among tortillas. Spoon 2 tablespoons plum sauce over turkey; top with ½ cup coleslaw mix. Fold up bottom edges of tortillas over filling, fold in sides and roll up to enclose filling. Use remaining plum sauce for dipping.

Makes 6 servings

Tip: To thicken a sauce in the **CROCK-POT**® slow cooker, remove the solid foods using a slotted spoon and reserve the sauce in the **CROCK-POT**® slow cooker. Mix ¼ cup cold water into 1 to 2 tablespoons cornstarch in small bowl until smooth. Whisk cornstarch mixture into the sauce. Cover; cook on HIGH 15 minutes or until the sauce is thickened.

Slow-Simmered Curried Chicken

1½ cups chopped onions
1 medium green bell pepper, chopped
1 pound boneless, skinless chicken breasts or thighs, cut into bite-size pieces
1 cup medium salsa
2 teaspoons grated fresh ginger
½ teaspoon garlic powder
½ teaspoon red pepper flakes
¼ cup chopped fresh cilantro
1 teaspoon sugar
1 teaspoon curry powder
½ teaspoon salt
Hot cooked rice

1. Place onions and bell pepper in **CROCK-POT**® slow cooker. Top with chicken.

2. Combine salsa, ginger, garlic powder and red pepper flakes in small bowl; spoon over chicken. Cover; cook on LOW 5 to 6 hours or until chicken is tender.

3. Combine cilantro, sugar, curry powder and salt in small bowl; stir into **CROCK-POT**® slow cooker. Turn **CROCK-POT**® slow cooker to HIGH. Cover; cook on HIGH 15 minutes or until heated through. Serve over rice.

Makes 4 servings

MU SHU TURKEY

Chicken and Wild Rice Casserole

3 tablespoons olive oil

2 slices bacon, chopped

1½ pounds chicken thighs, trimmed

½ cup diced onion

½ cup diced celery

2 tablespoons Worcestershire sauce

½ teaspoon salt

¼ teaspoon black pepper

½ teaspoon dried sage

1 cup converted long grain white rice

1 package (4 ounces) wild rice

6 ounces brown mushrooms, wiped clean and quartered*

3 cups hot chicken broth**

2 tablespoons chopped fresh Italian parsley (optional)

Use "baby bellas" or cremini mushrooms. Or you may substitute white button mushrooms.

**Use enough broth to cover chicken.*

1. Spread oil on bottom of **CROCK-POT®** slow cooker. Microwave bacon on HIGH 1 minute. Transfer to **CROCK-POT®** slow cooker. Place chicken in **CROCK-POT®** slow cooker, skin side down. Add onion, celery, Worcestershire sauce, salt, pepper, sage, white rice, wild rice, mushrooms and broth. Cover; cook on LOW 3 to 4 hours or until rice is tender.

2. Turn off heat. Uncover; let stand 15 minutes before serving. Remove chicken skin, if desired. Garnish with chopped parsley.

Makes 4 to 6 servings

Saucy Tropical Turkey

3 to 4 turkey thighs (about 2½ pounds), skin removed

2 tablespoons vegetable oil

1 small onion, sliced

1 can (20 ounces) pineapple chunks, drained

1 red bell pepper, cut into ½-inch pieces

⅔ cup apricot preserves

3 tablespoons soy sauce

1 teaspoon grated lemon peel

1 teaspoon ground ginger

¼ cup cold water

2 tablespoons cornstarch

Hot cooked rice

1. Rinse turkey and pat dry. Heat oil in large skillet over medium-high heat. Brown turkey on all sides. Place onion in **CROCK-POT®** slow cooker. Transfer turkey to **CROCK-POT®** slow cooker; top with pineapple and bell pepper.

2. Combine preserves, soy sauce, lemon peel and ginger in small bowl; mix well. Spoon over turkey. Cover; cook on LOW 6 to 7 hours.

3. Remove turkey to serving platter; cover with foil to keep warm. Turn **CROCK-POT®** slow cooker to HIGH. Stir water into cornstarch in small bowl until smooth; whisk into cooking liquid. Cook, uncovered, on HIGH 15 minutes or until sauce is slightly thickened. Return turkey to **CROCK-POT®** slow cooker; cook until heated through. Serve with rice.

Makes 6 servings

CHICKEN AND WILD RICE CASSEROLE

Tarragon Turkey and Pasta

1½ to 2 pounds turkey tenderloins

½ cup thinly sliced celery

¼ cup thinly sliced green onions

4 tablespoons fresh tarragon, minced and divided

¼ cup dry white wine

1 teaspoon salt

1 teaspoon black pepper

½ cup plain yogurt

1 tablespoon fresh minced Italian parsley

1 tablespoon lemon juice

2 tablespoons water

1½ tablespoons cornstarch

4 cups hot cooked pasta

1. Combine turkey, celery, green onions, 2 tablespoons tarragon, wine, salt and pepper in **CROCK-POT®** slow cooker; mix well. Cover; cook on LOW 6 to 8 hours or on HIGH 3½ to 4 hours.

2. Remove turkey to cutting board; cut into ½-inch-thick medallions. Stir yogurt, remaining 2 tablespoons fresh tarragon, parsley and lemon juice into cooking liquid.

3. Stir water into cornstarch in small bowl until smooth. Whisk into cooking liquid and cook on HIGH until thickened. Serve turkey medallions over pasta. Drizzle with tarragon sauce.

Makes 4 servings

Note: Recipe can be doubled for a 5-, 6- or 7-quart **CROCK-POT®** slow cooker.

Tip: This easy dish is elegant enough to serve at a dinner party.

Spicy Grits with Chicken

4 cups chicken broth

1 cup grits*

1 jalapeño pepper, seeded and finely chopped**

½ teaspoon salt, plus additional for seasoning

¼ teaspoon paprika

¼ teaspoon black pepper, plus additional for seasoning

½ cup (3 ounces) shredded sharp Cheddar cheese

1½ cups chopped cooked chicken breast (about 12 ounces total)

½ cup half-and-half

2 tablespoons chopped fresh chives, plus additional for garnish

*Use coarse, instant, yellow or stone-ground grits.

**Jalapeño peppers can sting and irritate the skin, so wear rubber gloves when handling peppers and do not touch your eyes.

1. Combine broth, grits, jalapeño pepper, ½ teaspoon salt, paprika and ¼ teaspoon black pepper in **CROCK-POT®** slow cooker. Stir well. Cover; cook on LOW 4 hours.

2. Add cheese and stir until melted. Stir in chicken, half-and-half and 2 tablespoons chives. Season with additional salt and pepper. Cover; cook on LOW 15 minutes to blend flavors. Garnish with additional chives, if desired. Serve immediately.

Makes 6 servings

MEDITERRANEAN CHICKEN
BREASTS AND WILD RICE

Mediterranean Chicken Breasts and Wild Rice

1 pound boneless, skinless chicken breasts, lightly pounded

Salt and black pepper

1 cup wild rice blend

10 cloves garlic, crushed

½ cup sun-dried tomatoes, packed in oil or dried*

½ cup capers, drained

2 cups water

½ cup fresh-squeezed lemon juice

¼ cup extra virgin olive oil

If using dry sun-dried tomatoes, soak in boiling water to soften before chopping.

1. Season chicken with salt and pepper. Place chicken in **CROCK-POT**® slow cooker. Add rice, garlic, tomatoes and capers; stir well.

2. Combine water, lemon juice and oil in small bowl; pour mixture over rice and chicken. Stir once to coat chicken. Cover; cook on LOW 8 hours.

Makes 4 servings

Lemon and Herb Turkey Breast

1 split turkey breast (about 3 pounds)

½ cup lemon juice

½ cup dry white wine

6 cloves garlic, minced

¼ teaspoon salt

¼ teaspoon dried parsley

¼ teaspoon dried tarragon

¼ teaspoon dried rosemary

¼ teaspoon dried sage

¼ teaspoon black pepper

Place turkey in **CROCK-POT**® slow cooker, adjusting to fit as needed. Combine remaining ingredients in small bowl; pour over turkey. Cover; cook on LOW 8 to 10 hours or on HIGH 4 to 5 hours.

Makes 6 servings

Cream Cheese Chicken with Broccoli

4 pounds boneless, skinless chicken breasts, cut into ½-inch pieces

1 tablespoon olive oil

1 package (1 ounce) Italian salad dressing mix

Nonstick cooking spray

2 cups (about 8 ounces) sliced mushrooms

1 cup chopped onion

1 can (10½ ounces) condensed reduced-fat cream of chicken soup, undiluted

1 bag (10 ounces) frozen broccoli florets, thawed

1 package (8 ounces) low-fat cream cheese, cubed

¼ cup dry sherry

Hot cooked pasta

1. Toss chicken with oil in large bowl. Sprinkle with salad dressing mix. Transfer to **CROCK-POT®** slow cooker. Cover; cook on LOW 3 hours.

2. Coat large skillet with cooking spray; heat over medium heat. Add mushrooms and onion; cook 5 minutes or until onion is tender, stirring occasionally.

3. Add soup, broccoli, cream cheese and sherry to skillet; cook and stir until heated through. Transfer to **CROCK-POT®** slow cooker. Cover; cook on LOW 1 hour. Serve chicken and sauce over pasta.

Makes 10 to 12 servings

Tip: For easier preparation, cut up the chicken and vegetables for this recipe the night before. Wrap the chicken and vegetables separately, and store in the refrigerator. Don't place the **CROCK-POT®** stoneware in the refrigerator.

Turkey Paprikash

2 tablespoons all-purpose flour

¼ teaspoon salt

¼ teaspoon black pepper

¼ teaspoon sweet paprika

⅛ teaspoon red pepper flakes

1 pound turkey breast, cut into bite-size pieces

2 tablespoons olive oil

1 onion, chopped

1 clove garlic, minced

1 can (about 14 ounces) diced tomatoes

12 ounces uncooked wide egg noodles

¼ cup sour cream

Sliced pimiento-stuffed green olives

1. Combine flour, salt, black pepper, paprika and red pepper flakes in large resealable food storage bag. Add turkey; shake to coat. Heat oil in large skillet over medium-high heat. Add turkey in single layer; brown on all sides. Arrange turkey in single layer in **CROCK-POT**® slow cooker.

2. Add onion and garlic to skillet; cook and stir 2 minutes or until onion is browned. Transfer to **CROCK-POT**® slow cooker. Stir in tomatoes. Cover; cook on LOW 1 to 2 hours or until turkey is tender.

3. Meanwhile, cook noodles until tender. Drain and place in large shallow bowl. Spoon turkey and sauce over noodles. Top with sour cream and olives.

Makes 4 servings

Creamy Chicken and Spinach Lasagna

1¼ cups (5 ounces) shredded Swiss or mozzarella cheese, divided

1 cup ricotta cheese

1 teaspoon dried oregano

¼ teaspoon red pepper flakes, plus additional for garnish

1 container (10 ounces) refrigerated Alfredo pasta sauce

⅓ cup water

4 uncooked no-boil lasagna noodles

1 package (10 ounces) frozen chopped spinach, thawed and squeezed dry

1½ cups cooked diced chicken

¼ cup grated Parmesan cheese

1. Combine 1 cup Swiss cheese, ricotta cheese, oregano and ¼ teaspoon red pepper flakes in small bowl; set aside. Combine Alfredo sauce with water in small bowl.

2. Coat inside of **CROCK-POT**® slow cooker with nonstick cooking spray. Break 2 lasagna noodles in half and place on bottom. Spread half of ricotta mixture over noodles. Top with half of spinach. Arrange half of chicken and half of Parmesan cheese over spinach. Pour half of Alfredo mixture over top. Repeat layers, beginning with noodles and ending with Alfredo mixture. Cover; cook on LOW 3 hours.

3. Turn off heat. Sprinkle remaining ¼ cup Swiss cheese on top. Cover; let stand 5 minutes or until cheese is melted. To serve, cut into squares or wedges. Garnish with additional red pepper flakes.

Makes 4 servings

TURKEY PAPRIKASH

Chicken Provençal

2 pounds boneless, skinless chicken thighs, each cut into quarters

2 medium red bell peppers, cut into ¼-inch-thick slices

1 medium yellow pepper, cut into ¼-inch-thick slices

1 onion, thinly sliced

1 can (28 ounces) plum tomatoes, drained

3 cloves garlic, minced

¼ teaspoon salt

¼ teaspoon dried thyme

¼ teaspoon fennel seeds, crushed

3 strips orange peel

½ cup fresh basil leaves, chopped

1. Place chicken, bell peppers, onion, tomatoes, garlic, salt, thyme, fennel seeds and orange peel in **CROCK-POT**® slow cooker. Mix thoroughly.

2. Cover; cook on LOW 7 to 9 hours or on HIGH 3 to 4 hours. Sprinkle with basil just before serving.

Makes 8 servings

Note: Recipe can be doubled for a 5-, 6- or 7-quart **CROCK-POT**® slow cooker.

Serving Suggestion: This Southern French chicken dish contrasts the citrus with sweetness. Serve with a crusty French baguette and seasonal vegetables.

Spanish Chicken with Rice

2 tablespoons olive oil

11 ounces cooked linguiça or kielbasa sausage, sliced into ½-inch rounds

6 boneless, skinless chicken thighs (about 1 pound)

1 onion, chopped

5 cloves garlic, minced

2 cups converted long grain rice

½ cup diced carrots

1 red bell pepper, chopped

½ teaspoon salt

¼ teaspoon black pepper

¼ teaspoon saffron threads (optional)

3½ cups hot reduced-sodium chicken broth

½ cup peas

1. Heat oil in medium skillet over medium heat. Add sausage; cook and stir until browned. Transfer to **CROCK-POT**® slow cooker with slotted spoon.

2. Add chicken to skillet and brown on all sides. Transfer to **CROCK-POT**® slow cooker. Add onion to skillet; cook and stir 5 minutes or until soft. Stir in garlic and cook 30 seconds. Transfer to **CROCK-POT**® slow cooker.

3. Add rice, carrots, bell pepper, salt, black pepper and saffron, if desired, to **CROCK-POT**® slow cooker. Pour broth over mixture. Cover; cook on HIGH 3½ to 4 hours.

4. Stir in peas. Cover; cook on HIGH 15 minutes or until heated through.

Makes 6 servings

CHICKEN PROVENÇAL

CHICKEN PARISIENNE

Chicken Parisienne

6 boneless, skinless chicken breasts (about 1½ pounds), cut into bite-size pieces

½ teaspoon salt

½ teaspoon black pepper

½ teaspoon paprika

1 can (10½ ounces) condensed cream of mushroom or cream of chicken soup, undiluted

2 cans (4 ounces each) sliced mushrooms, drained

½ cup dry white wine

1 container (8 ounces) sour cream

Hot cooked egg noodles

1. Place chicken in **CROCK-POT**® slow cooker. Sprinkle with salt, pepper and paprika. Add soup, mushrooms and wine; mix well. Cover; cook on HIGH 2 to 3 hours.

2. Add sour cream during last 30 minutes of cooking. Serve over noodles.

Makes 6 servings

Zesty Chicken and Rice Supper

2 boneless, skinless chicken breasts, cut into 1-inch pieces

2 large green bell peppers, coarsely chopped

1 small onion, chopped

1 can (about 28 ounces) diced tomatoes

1 cup uncooked converted long grain rice

1 cup water

1 package (about 1 ounce) taco seasoning

1 teaspoon salt

1 teaspoon black pepper

1 teaspoon ground red pepper

Shredded Cheddar cheese (optional)

Place all ingredients except cheese in **CROCK-POT**® slow cooker; stir well. Cover; cook on LOW 6 to 8 hours or on HIGH 3 to 4 hours. Garnish with cheese.

Makes 3 to 4 servings

Cuban-Style Curried Turkey

4 tablespoons all-purpose flour

1 teaspoon salt

½ teaspoon black pepper

2 pounds turkey breast, cut into 1-inch cubes*

4 tablespoons vegetable oil, divided

2 small onions, chopped

2 cloves garlic, minced

2 cans (about 14 ounces each) diced tomatoes

2 cans (about 15 ounces each) black beans, rinsed and drained

1 cup chicken broth

⅔ cup raisins

½ teaspoon curry powder

¼ teaspoon red pepper flakes

Juice of 1 lime (2 tablespoons)

2 tablespoons minced fresh cilantro

2 tablespoons minced green onion

4 cups cooked rice

*You may substitute turkey tenderloins.

1. Combine flour, salt and pepper in large resealable food storage bag. Add turkey; shake well to coat. Heat 2 tablespoons oil in large skillet over medium heat. Add turkey; brown on all sides in batches, about 5 minutes per batch. Transfer to **CROCK-POT®** slow cooker.

2. Heat remaining 2 tablespoons oil in same skillet. Add onions; cook and stir over medium heat 3 minutes or until golden. Stir in garlic; cook 30 seconds. Transfer to **CROCK-POT®** slow cooker.

3. Stir tomatoes, beans, broth, raisins, curry powder and red pepper flakes into **CROCK-POT®** slow cooker. Cover; cook on LOW 1 hour. Stir in lime juice. Sprinkle with cilantro and green onion. Adjust seasonings, if desired. Serve over rice.

Makes 8 servings

Tip: Curry powder is a blend of different spices and can vary in spiciness from mild to quite hot. If you prefer a hotter flavor, look for Madras curry powder.

SWEET AND SOUR SHRIMP WITH PINEAPPLE

From the Sea

Sweet and Sour Shrimp with Pineapple

- 3 cans (8 ounces each) pineapple chunks
- 2 packages (6 ounces each) frozen snow peas, thawed
- ⅓ cup plus 2 teaspoons sugar
- ¼ cup cornstarch
- 2 chicken bouillon cubes
- 2 cups boiling water
- 4 teaspoons soy sauce
- 1 teaspoon ground ginger
- 1 pound medium raw shrimp, peeled and deveined (with tails on)*
- ¼ cup cider vinegar
  Hot cooked rice

Or 1 pound frozen medium raw shrimp, peeled, deveined and unthawed.

1. Drain pineapple chunks, reserving 1 cup juice. Place pineapple and snow peas in **CROCK-POT®** slow cooker.

2. Combine sugar and cornstarch in medium saucepan. Dissolve bouillon cubes in boiling water in small bowl; add to saucepan. Mix in reserved pineapple juice, soy sauce and ginger; bring to a boil and cook 1 minute. Pour mixture into **CROCK-POT®** slow cooker. Cover; cook on LOW 4½ to 5½ hours.

3. Add shrimp and vinegar. Cover; cook on LOW 30 minutes or until shrimp are cooked through. Serve over rice.

Makes 4 servings

Scallops in Fresh Tomato and Herb Sauce

- 2 tablespoons vegetable oil
- 1 medium red onion, peeled and diced
- 1 clove garlic, minced
- 3½ cups fresh tomatoes, peeled*
- 1 can (12 ounces) tomato pureé
- 1 can (6 ounces) tomato paste
- ¼ cup dry red wine
- 2 tablespoons chopped Italian parsley
- 1 tablespoon chopped fresh oregano
- ¼ teaspoon black pepper
- 1½ pounds fresh scallops
  Hot cooked pasta or rice

To peel tomatoes, place one at a time in simmering water 10 seconds. (Add 30 seconds if tomatoes are not fully ripened.) Immediately plunge into a bowl of cold water for another 10 seconds. Peel skin with a knife.

1. Heat oil in medium skillet over medium heat. Add onion and garlic; cook and stir 7 to 8 minutes, or until onions are soft and translucent. Transfer to **CROCK-POT®** slow cooker.

2. Add tomatoes, tomato purée, tomato paste, wine, parsley, oregano and pepper. Cover; cook on LOW 6 to 8 hours.

3. Turn **CROCK-POT®** slow cooker to HIGH. Add scallops. Cook on HIGH 15 minutes or until scallops are cooked through. Serve over pasta.

Makes 4 servings

Asian Lettuce Wraps

2 teaspoons canola oil

1½ pounds boneless, skinless chicken breasts or pork shoulder, chopped into ¼-inch pieces

2 leeks, trimmed, chopped into ¼-inch pieces

1 cup shiitake mushrooms, stems removed and caps chopped into ¼-inch pieces

1 stalk celery, chopped into ¼-inch pieces

1 tablespoon oyster sauce

1 tablespoon soy sauce

1 teaspoon dark sesame oil

¼ teaspoon black pepper

2 tablespoons water

1 bag (8 ounces) cole slaw or broccoli slaw mix

½ red bell pepper, cut into thin strips

½ pound large raw shrimp, peeled, deveined and cut into ¼-inch pieces

3 tablespoons salted dry roasted peanuts, coarsely chopped

Hoisin sauce

10 to 15 crisp romaine lettuce leaves, white rib removed and patted dry

Fresh whole chives

1. Heat canola oil in large skillet over medium-high heat. Add chicken; brown on all sides. Transfer to **CROCK-POT®** slow cooker. Add leeks, mushrooms, celery, oyster sauce, soy sauce, sesame oil, black pepper and water to **CROCK-POT®** slow cooker. Toss slaw and bell pepper in medium bowl; place in single layer on top of chicken.

2. Cover; cook on LOW 4 to 5 hours or on HIGH 2 to 2½ hours or until chicken is cooked through. Stir in shrimp during last 20 minutes of cooking. When shrimp are pink and opaque, transfer mixture to large bowl. Add peanuts; mix well.

3. To serve, spread 1 teaspoon hoisin sauce on lettuce leaf. Add 1 to 2 tablespoons meat mixture and tightly roll; secure by tying chives around rolled leaves.

Makes 5 to 6 servings

Cod Tapenade

4 cod fillets or other firm white fish
   (2 to 3 pounds total)
   Salt and black pepper
2 lemons, thinly sliced
   Tapenade (recipe follows)

1. Season cod with salt and pepper.

2. Arrange half of lemon slices on bottom of **CROCK-POT**® slow cooker. Top with cod; cover with remaining lemon slices. Cover; cook on HIGH 1 hour or just until fish is cooked through (actual time depends on thickness of fish).

3. Remove fish to serving plates; discard lemon. Top with Tapenade.

Makes 4 servings

Tapenade

½ pound pitted kalamata olives
2 tablespoons chopped fresh thyme
   or Italian parsley
2 tablespoons capers, drained
2 tablespoons anchovy paste
1 clove garlic
¼ teaspoon grated orange peel
⅛ teaspoon ground red pepper
½ cup olive oil

Place olives, thyme, capers, anchovy paste, garlic, orange peel and ground red pepper in food processor or blender; pulse to roughly chop. Add oil; pulse briefly to form a chunky paste.

Makes about 1 cup

Tip: In a hurry? Substitute store-brought tapenade for homemade!

Mom's Tuna Casserole

2 **cans (12 ounces each) solid albacore tuna, drained and flaked**

3 **cups diced celery**

3 **cups crushed potato chips, divided**

6 **hard-cooked eggs, chopped**

1 **can (10½ ounces) condensed cream of mushroom soup, undiluted**

1 **can (10½ ounces) condensed cream of celery soup, undiluted**

1 **cup mayonnaise**

1 **teaspoon dried tarragon**

1 **teaspoon black pepper**

1. Combine tuna, celery, 2½ cups potato chips, eggs, soups, mayonnaise, tarragon and pepper in **CROCK-POT®** slow cooker; stir well. Cover; cook on LOW 5 to 7 hours.

2. Sprinkle with remaining ½ cup potato chips before serving.

Makes 8 servings

Tip: Don't use your **CROCK-POT®** slow cooker to reheat leftover foods. Transfer cooled leftover food to a resealable food storage bag or storage container with a tight-fitting lid and refrigerate. Use a microwave oven, the stove top or the oven for reheating.

Caribbean Shrimp with Rice

1 package (12 ounces) frozen shrimp,
   thawed

½ cup chicken broth

1 clove garlic, minced

1 teaspoon chili powder

½ teaspoon salt

½ teaspoon dried oregano

1 cup frozen peas, thawed

½ cup diced tomatoes

2 cups cooked long grain white rice

1. Combine shrimp, broth, garlic, chili powder, salt and oregano in **CROCK-POT®** slow cooker. Cover; cook on LOW 2 hours.

2. Add peas and tomatoes. Cover; cook on LOW 5 minutes. Stir in rice. Cover; cook on LOW 5 minutes or until rice is heated through.

Makes 4 servings

Braised Sea Bass with Aromatic Vegetables

2 tablespoons butter or olive oil

2 bulbs fennel, thinly sliced

3 large carrots, julienned

3 large leeks, cleaned and thinly sliced

Kosher salt and black pepper

6 fillets sea bass or other firm-fleshed white fish (2 to 3 pounds total)

1. Melt butter in large skillet over medium-high heat. Add fennel, carrots and leeks; cook and stir until beginning to soften and lightly brown. Season with salt and pepper. Arrange half of vegetables in bottom of **CROCK-POT®** slow cooker.

2. Season bass with salt and pepper; place on top of vegetables in **CROCK-POT®** slow cooker. Top with remaining vegetables. Cover; cook on LOW 2 to 3 hours or on HIGH 1 to 1½ hours or until fish is cooked through.

Makes 6 servings

Shrimp Jambalaya

1 can (28 ounces) diced tomatoes

1 medium onion, chopped

1 medium red bell pepper, chopped

1 stalk celery, chopped

2 tablespoons minced garlic

2 teaspoons dried parsley

2 teaspoons dried oregano

1 teaspoon hot pepper sauce

½ teaspoon dried thyme

2 pounds large cooked shrimp, peeled and deveined

2 cups uncooked instant rice

2 cups chicken broth

1. Combine tomatoes, onion, bell pepper, celery, garlic, parsley, oregano, hot pepper sauce and thyme in **CROCK-POT®** slow cooker. Cover; cook on LOW 8 hours or on HIGH 4 hours.

2. Stir in shrimp. Cover; cook on LOW 20 minutes.

3. Meanwhile, prepare rice according to package directions, substituting broth for water. Serve jambalaya over rice.

Makes 6 servings

Cheesy Shrimp on Grits

1 cup finely chopped green bell pepper

1 cup finely chopped red bell pepper

½ cup thinly sliced celery

1 bunch green onions, chopped, divided

¼ cup (½ stick) butter, cubed

1¼ teaspoons seafood seasoning

2 whole bay leaves

¼ teaspoon ground red pepper

1 pound medium raw shrimp, peeled and deveined

5⅓ cups water

1⅓ cups quick-cooking grits

2 cups (8 ounces) shredded sharp Cheddar cheese

¼ cup whipping cream or half-and-half

1. Coat inside of **CROCK-POT®** slow cooker with nonstick cooking spray. Add bell peppers, celery, all but ½ cup green onions, butter, seafood seasoning, bay leaves and ground red pepper. Cover; cook on LOW 4 hours or on HIGH 2 hours.

2. Turn **CROCK-POT®** slow cooker to HIGH. Add shrimp. Cover; on HIGH cook 15 minutes.

3. Meanwhile, bring water to a boil in medium saucepan. Add grits; cook according to package directions.

4. Remove and discard bay leaves. Stir in cheese, cream and remaining ½ cup green onions. Cook on HIGH 5 minutes or until cheese melts. Serve over grits.

Makes 6 servings

Tip: This dish is also delicious served over polenta.

Tip: Seafood is delicate and should be added to the **CROCK-POT®** slow cooker during the last 15 to 30 minutes of the cooking time if you're cooking on HIGH, and during the last 30 to 45 minutes if you're cooking on LOW. This type of seafood overcooks easily, becoming tough and rubbery.

Cioppino

1 pound cod, halibut or any firm-fleshed white fish, cubed

1 cup sliced mushrooms

2 carrots, sliced

1 onion, chopped

1 green bell pepper, chopped

1 teaspoon minced garlic

1 can (15 ounces) tomato sauce

1 can (about 14 ounces) beef broth

1 teaspoon salt

½ teaspoon black pepper

½ teaspoon dried oregano

1 can (7 ounces) cooked clams

½ pound cooked shrimp

1 package (6 ounces) cooked crabmeat

Minced fresh parsley

1. Combine cod, mushrooms, carrots, onion, bell pepper, garlic, tomato sauce, broth, salt, black pepper and oregano in **CROCK-POT®** slow cooker. Cover; cook on LOW 10 to 12 hours.

2. Turn **CROCK-POT®** slow cooker to HIGH. Add clams, shrimp and crabmeat. Cover; cook on HIGH 30 minutes or until seafood is heated through. Garnish with parsley before serving.

Makes 6 servings

Shrimp Creole

¼ cup (½ stick) butter

1 onion, chopped

¼ cup biscuit baking mix

3 cups water

2 cans (6 ounces each) tomato paste

1 cup chopped celery

1 cup chopped green bell pepper

2 teaspoons salt

½ teaspoon sugar

2 whole bay leaves

   Black pepper

4 pounds shrimp, peeled and deveined

   Hot cooked rice

1. Cook and stir butter and onion in medium skillet over medium heat until onion is tender. Stir in biscuit mix. Place mixture in **CROCK-POT®** slow cooker.

2. Add water, tomato paste, celery, bell pepper, salt, sugar, bay leaves and black pepper. Cover; cook on LOW 6 to 8 hours.

3. Turn **CROCK-POT®** slow cooker to HIGH. Add shrimp. Cover; cook on HIGH 45 minutes to 1 hour or until shrimp are done. Remove and discard bay leaves. Serve over rice.

Makes 8 to 10 servings

Manhattan Clam Chowder

- 3 **slices bacon, diced**
- 2 **stalks celery, chopped**
- 3 **onions, chopped**
- 2 **cups water**
- 1 **can (about 14 ounces) stewed tomatoes, undrained and chopped**
- 4 **small red potatoes, diced**
- 2 **carrots, diced**
- ½ **teaspoon dried thyme**
- ½ **teaspoon black pepper**
- ½ **teaspoon Louisiana-style hot sauce**
- 1 **pound minced clams***

If fresh clams are unavailable, use canned clams; 6 (6½-ounce) cans yield about 1 pound of clams. Drain and discard liquid.

1. Heat skillet over medium heat. Add bacon; cook and stir until crisp. Transfer to **CROCK-POT®** slow cooker using slotted spoon.

2. Add celery and onions to skillet; cook and stir until tender. Place in **CROCK-POT®** slow cooker.

3. Mix in water, tomatoes, potatoes, carrots, thyme, pepper and hot sauce. Cover; cook on LOW 6 to 8 hours or HIGH 4 to 6 hours. Add clams during last half hour of cooking.

Makes 4 servings

Tip: Shellfish and mollusks are delicate and should be added to the **CROCK-POT®** slow cooker during the last 15 to 30 minutes of the cooking time if you're cooking on HIGH, and during the last 30 to 45 minutes if you're cooking on LOW. This type of seafood overcooks easily, becoming tough and rubbery. So watch your cooking times and cook only long enough for foods to be done.

Shrimp and Pepper Bisque

1 can (about 14 ounces) chicken broth

1 bag (12 ounces) frozen bell pepper stir-fry mix, thawed

½ pound frozen cauliflower florets, thawed

1 stalk celery, sliced

1 tablespoon seafood seasoning

½ teaspoon dried thyme

12 ounces medium raw shrimp, peeled and deveined

2 cups half-and-half

2 to 3 green onions, finely chopped

1. Combine broth, stir-fry mix, cauliflower, celery, seafood seasoning and thyme in **CROCK-POT®** slow cooker. Cover; cook on LOW 8 hours or on HIGH 4 hours.

2. Turn **CROCK-POT®** slow cooker to HIGH. Stir in shrimp. Cover; cook on HIGH 15 minutes or until shrimp are pink and opaque. Purée soup in batches in blender or food processor. Return to **CROCK-POT®** slow cooker. Stir in half-and-half. Ladle into bowls and sprinkle with green onions.

Makes 4 servings

Tip: For a creamier, smoother consistency, strain through several layers of damp cheesecloth.

New England Clam Chowder

- 6 slices bacon, diced
- 2 onions, chopped
- 5 cans (6½ ounces each) clams, drained and liquid reserved
- 6 medium red potatoes, cubed
- 2 tablespoons minced garlic
- 1 teaspoon black pepper
- 2 cans (12 ounces each) evaporated milk
  Salt (optional)
  Snipped fresh chives (optional)

1. Heat skillet over medium heat. Add bacon and onion; cook and stir until crisp. Transfer to **CROCK-POT®** slow cooker using slotted spoon.

2. Add enough water to reserved clam liquid to make 3 cups. Pour into **CROCK-POT®** slow cooker. Add potatoes, garlic and pepper. Cover; cook on LOW 5 to 8 hours or HIGH 1 to 3 hours.

3. Mix in clams and evaporated milk. Cover; cook on LOW 30 to 45 minutes. Add salt, if desired. Garnish with snipped fresh chives.

Makes 6 to 8 servings

Tip: Shellfish and mollusks are delicate and should be added to the **CROCK-POT®** slow cooker during the last 15 to 30 minutes of the cooking time if you're cooking on HIGH, and during the last 30 to 45 minutes if you're cooking on LOW. This type of seafood overcooks easily, becoming tough and rubbery. So watch your cooking times and cook only long enough for foods to be done.

Cajun Chicken and Shrimp Creole

- 1 pound skinless chicken thighs
- 1 red bell pepper, chopped
- 1 large onion, chopped
- 1 stalk celery, diced
- 1 can (about 14 ounces) diced tomatoes
- 1 clove garlic, minced
- 1 tablespoon sugar
- 1 teaspoon paprika
- 1 teaspoon Cajun seasoning
- 1 teaspoon salt
- 1 teaspoon black pepper
- 1 pound medium raw shrimp, peeled and deveined
- 1 tablespoon fresh lemon juice
  Hot pepper sauce
- 1 cup hot cooked rice

1. Place chicken thighs in **CROCK-POT®** slow cooker. Add the bell pepper, onion, celery, tomatoes, garlic, sugar, paprika, Cajun seasoning, salt and black pepper. Cover; cook on LOW 7 to 9 hours or on HIGH 3 to 4 hours.

2. Add shrimp, lemon juice and hot pepper sauce to **CROCK-POT®** slow cooker. Cover; cook on LOW 1 hour or on HIGH 30 minutes. Serve over rice.

Makes 6 servings

Tip: Recipe can be doubled for a 5-, 6- or 7-quart **CROCK-POT®** slow cooker.

NEW ENGLAND
CLAM CHOWDER

Saffron-Scented Shrimp Paella

3 tablespoons olive oil, divided

1½ cups chopped onions

4 cloves garlic, thinly sliced

Salt

1 cup roasted red bell pepper, diced

1 cup chopped tomato

1 whole bay leaf

1 large pinch saffron

1 cup dry white wine

8 cups chicken broth

4 cups uncooked rice

25 large raw shrimp, peeled and deveined (with tails on)

Salt and white pepper

1. Heat 2 tablespoons oil in large skillet over medium heat. Add onions, garlic and salt; cook and stir 5 minutes or until translucent. Add bell pepper, tomato, bay leaf and saffron; cook and stir until heated through. Add wine. Continue cooking until liquid is reduced by half. Add broth. Bring to a simmer. Adjust seasonings, if desired, and stir in rice. Transfer to **CROCK-POT®** slow cooker. Cover; cook on HIGH 30 minutes to 1 hour or until liquid is absorbed.

2. Toss shrimp in remaining 1 tablespoon oil in large bowl. Season with salt and white pepper. Place shrimp on rice in **CROCK-POT®** slow cooker. Cover; cook on HIGH 10 minutes or until shrimp are pink and opaque. Remove and discard bay leaf.

Makes 4 to 6 servings

Creamy Slow Cooker Seafood Chowder

1 quart (4 cups) half-and-half

2 cans (about 14 ounces each) whole white potatoes, drained and cubed

2 cans (10½ ounces each) condensed cream of mushroom soup, undiluted

1 bag (16 ounces) frozen hash brown potatoes

1 medium onion, minced

½ cup (1 stick) butter, cubed

1 teaspoon salt

1 teaspoon black pepper

5 cans (about 8 ounces each) whole oysters, rinsed and drained

2 cans (about 6 ounces each) whole baby clams, rinsed and drained

2 cans (about 4 ounces each) cocktail shrimp, rinsed and drained

1. Combine half-and-half, canned potatoes, soup, hash browns, onion, butter, salt and pepper in **CROCK-POT®** slow cooker. Mix well. Cover; cook on LOW 3½ to 4½ hours.

2. Add oysters, clams and shrimp; stir gently. Cover; cook on LOW 30 to 45 minutes.

Makes 8 to 10 servings

SAFFRON-SCENTED
SHRIMP PAELLA

Southwestern Salmon Po' Boys

1 red bell pepper, sliced

1 green bell pepper, sliced

1 onion, sliced

½ teaspoon Southwest chipotle seasoning

¼ teaspoon salt

¼ teaspoon black pepper

4 salmon fillets (about 6 ounces each), rinsed and patted dry

½ cup Italian dressing

¼ cup water

4 large French sandwich rolls *or* French bread, cut into 6-inch pieces and split

Chipotle mayonnaise*

Fresh cilantro (optional)

If unavailable, combine ¼ cup mayonnaise with ½ teaspoon adobo sauce or substitute regular mayonnaise.

1. Coat inside of **CROCK-POT®** slow cooker with nonstick cooking spray. Arrange half of sliced bell peppers and onion in bottom.

2. Combine seasoning, salt and black pepper in small bowl; rub over both sides of salmon. Place salmon on top of vegetables in **CROCK-POT®** slow cooker. Pour Italian dressing over salmon and top with remaining bell peppers and onions. Add water. Cover; cook on HIGH 1½ hours.

3. Toast rolls, if desired. Spread with chipotle mayonnaise and garnish with cilantro. Spoon 1 to 2 tablespoons cooking liquid onto rolls. Place salmon fillet on each roll (remove skin first, if desired). Top with vegetable mixture.

Makes 4 servings

Shrimp Louisiana-Style

1 pound medium raw shrimp, unpeeled (with tails on)

½ cup (1 stick) butter, cubed

⅓ cup lemon juice

1 tablespoon Worcestershire sauce

1 teaspoon seafood seasoning

1 teaspoon minced garlic

½ teaspoon salt

½ teaspoon black pepper

1½ teaspoons grated lemon peel, plus additional for garnish

Hot cooked rice

1. Coat inside of **CROCK-POT®** slow cooker with nonstick cooking spray. Add shrimp, butter, lemon juice, Worcestershire sauce, seafood seasoning, garlic, salt and pepper; mix well. Cover; cook on HIGH 1¼ hours.

2. Turn off heat. Stir in 1½ teaspoons lemon peel. Let stand, uncovered, 5 minutes. Serve in shallow soup bowls over rice. Garnish with grated lemon peel.

Makes 3 to 4 servings

Sweet and Sour Shrimp

1 can (16 ounces) sliced peaches in syrup, undrained

½ cup chopped green onions

½ cup chopped red bell pepper

½ cup chopped green bell pepper

½ cup chopped celery

⅓ cup vegetable broth

¼ cup light soy sauce

2 tablespoons rice wine vinegar

2 tablespoons dark sesame oil

1 teaspoon red pepper flakes

¼ cup water

2 tablespoons cornstarch

1 package (6 ounces) snow peas

1 pound cooked medium shrimp

1 cup cherry tomatoes, cut into halves

½ cup toasted walnut pieces*

Hot cooked rice

*To toast walnuts, spread in single layer in heavy skillet. Cook over medium heat 1 to 2 minutes or until nuts are lightly browned, stirring frequently.

1. Place peaches with syrup, green onions, bell peppers, celery, broth, soy sauce, vinegar, oil and red pepper flakes in **CROCK-POT**® slow cooker. Cover; cook on LOW 3 to 4 hours or on HIGH 2 to 3 hours or until vegetables are tender. Stir well.

2. Turn **CROCK-POT**® slow cooker to HIGH. Stir water into cornstarch in small bowl until smooth. Stir into vegetable mixture. Stir in snow peas. Cover; cook on HIGH 15 minutes or until thickened.

3. Add shrimp, tomatoes and walnuts to **CROCK-POT**® slow cooker. Cover; cook on HIGH 5 minutes or until shrimp are pink and opaque. Serve over rice.

Makes 4 to 6 servings

Creamy Crab Bisque

4 cups heavy cream

3 cups fresh crabmeat, flaked and picked over for shells

3 tablespoons unsalted butter

2 teaspoons grated lemon peel

1 teaspoon lemon juice

½ teaspoon ground nutmeg

¼ teaspoon ground allspice

3 tablespoons dry red wine

½ cup prepared mandlen (soup nuts), ground into crumbs*

Mandlen are small nugget-like crackers made from matzo meal, available in the supermarket ethnic foods aisle.

1. Combine cream, crabmeat, butter, lemon peel, lemon juice, nutmeg and allspice in **CROCK-POT®** slow cooker; stir well. Cover; cook on LOW 1 to 2 hours.

2. Stir in wine and mandlen crumbs. Cover; cook on LOW 10 minutes.

Makes 6 to 8 servings

SWISS CHEESE
SCALLOPED POTATOES

Spectacular Sides

Swiss Cheese Scalloped Potatoes

2 pounds baking potatoes, thinly sliced
½ cup finely chopped yellow onion
¼ teaspoon salt
¼ teaspoon ground nutmeg
2 tablespoons butter, cut into small pieces
½ cup milk
2 tablespoons all-purpose flour
½ cup (3 ounces) shredded Swiss cheese
¼ cup finely chopped green onions

1. Layer half of potatoes, ¼ cup onion, ⅛ teaspoon salt, ⅛ teaspoon nutmeg and 1 tablespoon butter in **CROCK-POT**® slow cooker. Repeat layers. Cover; cook on LOW 7 hours or on HIGH 4 hours.

2. Remove potatoes with slotted spoon to serving dish; keep warm.

3. Whisk milk into flour in small bowl until smooth; stir into cooking liquid. Stir in cheese. Cover; cook on HIGH 10 minutes or until slightly thickened. Stir; pour cheese mixture over potatoes. Sprinkle with green onions.

Makes 5 to 6 servings

Supper Squash Medley

2 butternut squash, peeled, seeded and diced
1 can (28 ounces) diced tomatoes
1 can (15 ounces) corn, drained
2 onions, chopped
2 green bell peppers, chopped
2 teaspoons minced garlic
2 mild fresh green chiles, chopped
1 cup chicken broth
1 teaspoon salt
½ teaspoon black pepper
1 can (6 ounces) tomato paste

1. Combine squash, diced tomatoes, corn, onions, bell peppers, garlic, chiles, broth, salt and black pepper in **CROCK-POT**® slow cooker. Cover; cook on LOW 6 hours.

2. Remove about ½ cup cooking liquid and blend with tomato paste. Retune to **CROCK-POT**® slow cooker; stir well. Cover; cook on LOW 30 minutes or until mixture is slightly thickened and heated through.

Makes 8 to 10 servings

Asiago and Asparagus Risotto-Style Rice

2 cups chopped onion
1 can (about 14 ounces) vegetable broth
1 cup uncooked converted rice
2 cloves garlic, minced
½ pound asparagus spears, trimmed and broken into 1-inch pieces
1 cup half-and-half, divided
½ cup (about 4 ounces) grated Asiago cheese, plus additional for garnish
¼ cup (½ stick) butter, cubed
½ (2 ounces) pine nuts or slivered almonds, toasted*
1 teaspoon salt

To toast pine nuts, spread in single layer in heavy skillet. Cook over medium heat 1 to 2 minutes or until nuts are lightly browned, stirring frequently.

1. Place onion, broth, rice and garlic in **CROCK-POT**® slow cooker; stir until well blended. Cover; cook on HIGH 2 hours or until rice is tender.

2. Stir in asparagus and ½ cup half-and-half. Cover; cook on HIGH 20 minutes or until asparagus is crisp-tender.

3. Stir in remaining ½ cup half-and-half, ½ cup cheese, butter, pine nuts and salt. Turn off heat. Cover; let stand 5 minutes or until cheese is slightly melted. Fluff with fork. Garnish with additional cheese.

Makes 4 servings

Tip: Risotto is a classic creamy rice dish of northern Italy and can be made with a wide variety of ingredients. Fresh vegetables and cheeses such as Asiago work especially well in risotto. Parmesan cheese, shellfish, white wine and herbs are also popular additions.

Herbed Fall Vegetables

2 medium Yukon Gold potatoes, peeled and cut into ½-inch cubes
2 medium sweet potatoes, peeled and cut into ½-inch cubes
3 parsnips, cut into ½-inch cubes
1 fennel bulb, sliced and cut into ½-inch cubes
½ to ¾ cup chopped fresh herbs, such as tarragon, parsley, sage or thyme
¼ cup (½ stick) butter, cut into small pieces
1 cup chicken broth
1 tablespoon Dijon mustard
1 tablespoon salt
Black pepper

1. Combine potatoes, parsnips, fennel, herbs and butter in **CROCK-POT**® slow cooker.

2. Whisk broth, mustard, salt and pepper in small bowl. Pour mixture over vegetables. Cover; cook on LOW 4½ hours or on HIGH 3 hours or until vegetables are tender, stirring occasionally.

Makes 6 servings

ASIAGO AND ASPARAGUS
RISOTTO-STYLE RICE

Spicy Beans Tex-Mex

⅓ cup lentils

1⅓ cups water

5 slices bacon

1 onion, chopped

1 can (about 15 ounces) pinto beans, rinsed and drained

1 can (about 15 ounces) red kidney beans, rinsed and drained

1 can (about 14 ounces) diced tomatoes

3 tablespoons ketchup

3 cloves garlic, minced

1 teaspoon chili powder

½ teaspoon ground cumin

¼ teaspoon red pepper flakes

1 whole bay leaf

1. Combine lentils and water in large saucepan. Bring to a boil over medium-high heat. Boil 20 to 30 minutes; drain.

2. Heat skillet over medium heat. Add bacon; cook and stir until crisp. Transfer to paper towels; crumble when cool enough to handle. Add onion to same skillet; cook and stir 5 minutes or until tender.

3. Combine lentils, bacon, onion, beans, tomatoes, ketchup, garlic, chili powder, cumin, red pepper flakes and bay leaf in **CROCK-POT®** slow cooker. Cover; cook on LOW 5 to 6 hours or on HIGH 3 to 4 hours. Remove and discard bay leaf.

Makes 8 to 10 servings

Spinach Spoon Bread

1 package (10 ounces) frozen chopped spinach, thawed and squeezed dry

1 red bell pepper, diced

4 eggs, lightly beaten

1 cup cottage cheese

1 package (5½ ounces) corn bread mix

6 green onions, sliced

½ cup (1 stick) butter, melted

1¼ teaspoons seasoned salt

1. Coat **CROCK-POT®** slow cooker with nonstick cooking spray.

2. Combine all ingredients in large bowl; mix well. Pour into **CROCK-POT®** slow cooker. Cook, uncovered, with lid slightly ajar to allow excess moisture to escape, on LOW 3 to 4 hours or on HIGH 1½ to 2 hours or until edges are golden and knife inserted into center comes out clean.

3. Loosen edges and bottom of bread with knife and invert onto plate. Cut into wedges or serve bread spooned from **CROCK-POT®** slow cooker.

Makes 8 servings

SPICY BEANS
TEX-MEX

Lemon-Mint Red Potatoes

2 pounds new red potatoes

3 tablespoons extra virgin olive oil

1 teaspoon salt

½ teaspoon Greek seasoning or dried oregano

¼ teaspoon garlic powder

¼ teaspoon black pepper

4 tablespoons chopped fresh mint, divided

2 tablespoons butter

2 tablespoons lemon juice

1 teaspoon grated lemon peel

1. Coat inside of **CROCK-POT®** slow cooker with nonstick cooking spray. Add potatoes and oil, stirring gently to coat. Sprinkle with salt, Greek seasoning, garlic powder and pepper. Cover; cook on LOW 7 hours or on HIGH 4 hours.

2. Stir in 2 tablespoons mint, butter, lemon juice and lemon peel until butter is completely melted. Cover; cook on HIGH 15 minutes to allow flavors to blend. Sprinkle with remaining 2 tablespoons mint.

Makes 4 servings

Tip: It's easy to prepare these potatoes ahead of time. Simply follow the recipe and then turn off the heat. Let it stand at room temperature for up to 2 hours. You may reheat or serve the potatoes at room temperature.

No-Fuss Macaroni & Cheese

2 cups (about 8 ounces) uncooked elbow macaroni

4 ounces pasteurized process cheese product, cut into cubes

1 cup (4 ounces) shredded mild Cheddar cheese

½ teaspoon salt

⅛ teaspoon black pepper

1½ cups milk

Combine macaroni, cheeses, salt and pepper in **CROCK-POT®** slow cooker. Pour in milk. Cover; cook on LOW 2 to 3 hours, stirring after 20 to 30 minutes.

Makes 6 to 8 servings

Gratin Potatoes with Asiago Cheese

6 slices bacon, cut into 1-inch pieces

6 medium baking potatoes, peeled and thinly sliced

½ cup grated Asiago cheese

Salt and black pepper

1½ cups heavy cream

1. Heat large skillet over medium heat. Add bacon; cook and stir until crisp. Transfer to paper towel-lined plate with slotted spoon.

2. Pour bacon drippings into **CROCK-POT®** slow cooker. Layer one fourth of potatoes on bottom of **CROCK-POT®** slow cooker. Sprinkle one fourth of bacon over potatoes and top with one fourth of cheese. Add salt and pepper. Repeat layers additional three times. Pour cream over all. Cover; cook on LOW 7 to 9 hours or on HIGH 5 to 6 hours.

Makes 4 to 6 servings

LEMON-MINT RED POTATOES

Lentils with Walnuts

1 cup brown lentils

1 very small onion or large shallot, chopped

1 stalk celery, trimmed and chopped

1 large carrot, chopped

¼ teaspoon crushed dried thyme

3 cups chicken broth

Salt and black pepper

¼ cup chopped walnuts

1. Combine lentils, onion, celery, carrot, thyme and broth in **CROCK-POT®** slow cooker. Cover; cook on HIGH 3 hours. Do not overcook. (Lentils should absorb most or all of broth. Slightly tilt **CROCK-POT®** slow cooker to check.)

2. Season with salt and pepper. Spoon lentils into serving bowl and sprinkle with walnuts.

Makes 4 to 6 servings

Tip: Top dish with 4 cooked bacon strips cut into bite-size pieces, if desired. To serve as a main dish, stir in 1 cup diced cooked ham.

BLUE CHEESE POTATOES

Blue Cheese Potatoes

    2 pounds red potatoes, peeled and cut into
       ½-inch pieces
 1¼ cups chopped green onions, divided
    2 tablespoons olive oil, divided
    1 teaspoon dried basil
    ½ teaspoon salt
    ¼ teaspoon black pepper
    ½ cup crumbled blue cheese

1. Layer potatoes, 1 cup green onions,
1 tablespoon oil, basil, salt and pepper in
CROCK-POT® slow cooker. Cover; cook on
LOW 7 hours or on HIGH 4 hours.

2. Gently stir in cheese and remaining
1 tablespoon oil. Cover; cook on HIGH 5 minutes
to allow flavors to blend. Transfer potatoes to
serving platter and top with remaining ¼ cup
green onions.

Makes 5 servings

Spiced Sweet Potatoes

    2 pounds sweet potatoes, cut into ½-inch
       pieces
    ¼ cup packed dark brown sugar
    1 teaspoon ground cinnamon
    ½ teaspoon ground nutmeg
    ⅛ teaspoon salt
    2 tablespoons butter, cubed
    1 teaspoon vanilla

1. Combine potatoes, brown sugar, cinnamon,
nutmeg and salt in **CROCK-POT**® slow cooker;
mix well. Cover; cook on LOW 7 hours or on
HIGH 4 hours.

2. Add butter and vanilla; gently stir to blend.

Makes 4 servings

EASY
DIRTY
RICE

Easy Dirty Rice

½ pound bulk Italian sausage

2 cups water

1 cup uncooked long grain rice

1 large onion, finely chopped

1 large green bell pepper, finely chopped

½ cup finely chopped celery

1½ teaspoons salt

½ teaspoon ground red pepper

½ cup chopped fresh parsley

1. Brown sausage 6 to 8 minutes in large skillet over medium-high heat, stirring to break up meat. Drain fat. Place sausage in **CROCK-POT**® slow cooker.

2. Stir in all remaining ingredients except parsley. Cover; cook on LOW 2 hours. Stir in parsley.

Makes 4 servings

Creamy Curried Spinach

3 packages (10 ounces each) frozen spinach, thawed

1 onion, chopped

4 teaspoons minced garlic

2 tablespoons curry powder

2 tablespoons butter, melted

¼ cup chicken broth

¼ cup heavy cream

1 teaspoon lemon juice

Combine spinach, onion, garlic, curry powder, butter and broth in **CROCK-POT**® slow cooker. Cover; cook on LOW 3 to 4 hours or on HIGH 2 hours. Stir in cream and lemon juice during last 30 minutes of cooking time.

Makes 6 to 8 servings

Mediterranean Red Potatoes

- 3 medium red potatoes, cut into cubes
- ⅔ cup fresh or frozen pearl onions
  Garlic-flavored cooking spray
- ½ teaspoon Italian seasoning
- ¼ teaspoon black pepper
- 1 small tomato, seeded and chopped
- ½ cup (2 ounces) feta cheese, crumbled
- 2 tablespoons chopped black olives

1. Place potatoes and onions in 1½-quart soufflé dish that fits inside **CROCK-POT®** slow cooker. Spray with garlic-flavored cooking spray; toss to coat. Add Italian seasoning and pepper; mix well. Cover dish tightly with foil.

2. Make foil handles using three 18 × 3-inch strips of heavy-duty foil or use regular foil folded to double thickness. Crisscross foil in spoke design; place across bottom and up side of stoneware. Place soufflé dish in center of strips in **CROCK-POT®** slow cooker. Pull foil strips up and over dish.

3. Pour hot water into **CROCK-POT®** slow cooker to about 1½ inches from top of soufflé dish. Cover; cook on LOW 7 to 8 hours.

4. Use foil handles to lift dish out of **CROCK-POT®** slow cooker. Stir tomato, cheese and olives into potato mixture.

Makes 4 servings

Skinny Corn Bread

1¼ cups all-purpose flour

½ cup yellow cornmeal

¼ cup sugar

1 teaspoon baking powder

1 teaspoon baking soda

1 teaspoon seasoned salt

1 cup fat-free buttermilk

¼ cup cholesterol-free egg substitute

¼ cup canola oil

1. Coat 3-quart **CROCK-POT®** slow cooker with nonstick cooking spray.

2. Sift together flour, cornmeal, sugar, baking powder, baking soda and seasoned salt in large bowl. Make well in center of dry mixture. Pour in buttermilk, egg substitute and oil. Mix in dry ingredients just until moistened. Pour mixture into **CROCK-POT®** slow cooker.

3. Cook, covered, with lid slightly ajar to allow excess moisture to escape, on LOW 3 to 4 hours or on HIGH 45 minutes to 1½ hours, or until edges are golden and knife inserted into center comes out clean. Remove stoneware from **CROCK-POT®** slow cooker. Cool on wire rack 10 minutes. Remove bread from stoneware and cool completely.

Makes 8 servings

Tip: This recipe works best in round **CROCK-POT®** slow cookers.

Wild Rice with Fruit & Nuts

2 cups wild rice or wild rice blend*

½ cup dried cranberries

½ cup chopped raisins

½ cup chopped dried apricots

½ cup almond slivers, toasted**

5 to 6 cups chicken broth

1 cup orange juice

2 tablespoons butter, melted

1 teaspoon ground cumin

2 green onions, thinly sliced

2 to 3 tablespoons chopped fresh parsley

Salt and black pepper

*Do not use parboiled rice or a blend containing parboiled rice.

**To toast almonds, spread in single layer in heavy skillet. Cook over medium heat 1 to 2 minutes or until nuts are lightly browned, stirring frequently.

1. Combine wild rice, cranberries, raisins, apricots and almonds in **CROCK-POT®** slow cooker.

2. Combine broth, orange juice, butter and cumin in medium bowl. Pour mixture over rice and stir to mix. Cover; cook on LOW 7 hours or on HIGH 2½ to 3 hours. Stir once, adding more hot broth if necessary.

3. Stir in green onions and parsley. Cover; cook on LOW 10 minutes.

Makes 6 to 8 servings

SKINNY CORN BREAD

Lemon Dilled Parsnips and Turnips

2 cups chicken broth

¼ cup chopped green onions

¼ cup lemon juice

¼ cup dried dill

1 teaspoon minced garlic

4 turnips, peeled and cut into ½-inch pieces

3 parsnips, cut into ½-inch pieces

¼ cup cold water

¼ cup cornstarch

1. Combine broth, green onions, lemon juice, dill and garlic in **CROCK-POT®** slow cooker.

2. Add turnips and parsnips; stir. Cover; cook on LOW 3 to 4 hours or on HIGH 1 to 3 hours.

3. Stir water into cornstarch in small bowl until smooth. Whisk into **CROCK-POT®** slow cooker. Stir well to combine. Cover; cook on HIGH 15 minutes or until thickened.

Makes 8 to 10 servings

Scalloped Potatoes and Parsnips

6 tablespoons butter

3 tablespoons all-purpose flour

1½ cups whipping cream

2 teaspoons ground mustard

1½ teaspoons salt

1 teaspoon dried thyme

½ teaspoon black pepper

2 baking potatoes, cut in half lengthwise, then crosswise into ¼-inch slices

2 parsnips, cut into ¼-inch slices

1 onion, chopped

2 cups (8 ounces) shredded sharp Cheddar cheese

1. Melt butter in medium saucepan over medium-high heat. Whisk in flour; cook 1 to 2 minutes. Gradually whisk in cream until smooth. Stir in mustard, salt, thyme and pepper.

2. Place potatoes, parsnips and onion in **CROCK-POT®** slow cooker. Add cream sauce. Cover; cook on LOW 7 hours or on HIGH 3½ hours or until potatoes are tender.

3. Turn off heat. Stir in cheese. Cover; let stand 5 minutes or until cheese melts.

Makes 4 to 6 servings

LEMON DILLED PARSNIPS AND TURNIPS

Tarragon Carrots
in White Wine

½ cup chicken broth

½ cup dry white wine

1 tablespoon lemon juice

1 tablespoon minced fresh tarragon

2 teaspoons finely chopped green onions

1½ teaspoons chopped fresh Italian parsley

1 clove garlic, minced

1 teaspoon salt

8 medium carrots, cut into matchsticks

2 tablespoons melba toast, crushed

2 tablespoons cold water

1. Combine broth, wine, lemon juice, tarragon, green onions, parsley, garlic and salt in **CROCK-POT®** slow cooker. Add carrots; stir well to combine. Cover; cook on LOW 2½ to 3 hours or on HIGH 1½ to 2 hours.

2. Dissolve toast crumbs in water and add to carrots. Cover; cook on LOW 10 minutes or until thickened.

Makes 6 to 8 servings

Polenta-Style
Corn Casserole

1 can (about 14 ounces) vegetable broth

½ cup cornmeal

1 can (7 ounces) corn, drained

1 can (4 ounces) diced mild green chiles, drained

¼ cup diced red bell pepper

½ teaspoon salt

¼ teaspoon black pepper

1 cup (4 ounces) shredded Cheddar cheese

1. Pour broth into **CROCK-POT®** slow cooker. Whisk in cornmeal. Add corn, chiles, bell pepper, salt and black pepper. Cover; cook on LOW 4 to 5 hours or on HIGH 2 to 3 hours.

2. Turn **CROCK-POT®** slow cooker to LOW. Stir in cheese. Cook, uncovered, on LOW 15 to 30 minutes or until cheese melts.

Makes 6 servings

Tip: For firmer polenta, divide cooked corn mixture among lightly greased individual ramekins or spread in pie plate. Cover and refrigerate until firm. Serve cold or at room temperature.

TARRAGON CARROTS
IN WHITE WINE

New England Baked Beans

4 slices bacon, chopped

3 cans (about 15 ounces each) Great Northern beans, rinsed and drained

½ cup water

1 small onion, chopped

⅓ cup canned diced tomatoes

3 tablespoons packed light brown sugar

3 tablespoons maple syrup

3 tablespoons molasses

2 cloves garlic, minced

½ teaspoon salt

½ teaspoon dry mustard

⅛ teaspoon black pepper

½ whole bay leaf

1. Heat skillet over medium heat. Add bacon; cook and stir until crisp. Transfer to **CROCK-POT®** slow cooker using slotted spoon.

2. Combine all remaining ingredients in **CROCK-POT®** slow cooker. Cover; cook on LOW 6 to 8 hours or until mixture is thickened. Remove and discard bay leaf.

Makes 4 to 6 servings

WINTER SQUASH AND APPLES

Winter Squash and Apples

1 teaspoon salt, plus additional for seasoning

½ teaspoon black pepper, plus additional for seasoning

1 butternut squash (about 2 pounds)

2 apples, sliced

1 medium onion, quartered and sliced

1½ tablespoons butter

1. Combine 1 teaspoon salt and ½ teaspoon pepper in small bowl.

2. Cut squash into 2-inch pieces; place in **CROCK-POT®** slow cooker. Add apples and onion. Sprinkle with salt and pepper mixture; stir well. Cover; cook on LOW 6 to 7 hours or until vegetables are tender.

3. Stir in butter and season to taste with additional salt and pepper.

Makes 4 to 6 servings

Cran-Orange Acorn Squash

5 tablespoons instant brown rice

3 tablespoons minced onion

3 tablespoons diced celery

3 tablespoons dried cranberries

Pinch ground sage

3 small acorn or carnival squash, cut in half

1 teaspoon butter, cubed

3 tablespoons orange juice

½ cup warm water

1. Combine rice, onion, celery, cranberries and sage in small bowl. Stuff each squash with rice mixture; dot with butter. Pour ½ tablespoon orange juice into each squash half over stuffing.

2. Stand squash in **CROCK-POT®** slow cooker. Pour water into **CROCK-POT®** slow cooker. Cover; cook on LOW 2½ hours or until squash are tender.

Makes 6 servings

Lemon and Tangerine Glazed Carrots

 6 cups sliced carrots
 1½ cups apple juice
 6 tablespoons butter
 ¼ cup packed brown sugar
 2 tablespoons grated lemon peel
 2 tablespoons grated tangerine peel
 ½ teaspoon salt
    Fresh parsley, chopped

Combine all ingredients except parsley in **CROCK-POT**® slow cooker. Cover; cook on LOW 4 to 5 hours or on HIGH 1 to 3 hours. Garnish with parsley.

Makes 10 to 12 servings

Creamy Red Pepper Polenta

 ¼ cup (½ stick) butter, melted
 ¼ teaspoon paprika, plus additional for garnish
 ⅛ teaspoon ground red pepper
 ⅛ teaspoon ground cumin
 6 cups boiling water
 2 cups yellow cornmeal
 1 small red bell pepper, finely chopped
 2 teaspoons salt

Combine butter, ¼ teaspoon paprika, ground red pepper and cumin in **CROCK-POT**® slow cooker. Add water, cornmeal, bell pepper and salt; stir well to combine. Cover; cook on LOW 3 to 4 hours or on HIGH 1 to 2 hours, stirring occasionally. Garnish with additional paprika.

Makes 4 to 6 servings

Braised Sweet and Sour Cabbage and Apples

2 tablespoons unsalted butter

6 cups coarsely shredded red cabbage

1 large sweet apple, peeled and cut into bite-size pieces

3 whole cloves

½ cup raisins

½ cup apple cider

3 tablespoons cider vinegar, divided

2 tablespoons packed dark brown sugar

½ teaspoon salt

¼ teaspoon black pepper

1. Melt butter in large skillet or saucepan over medium heat. Add cabbage; cook and stir 3 minutes or until glossy. Transfer to **CROCK-POT®** slow cooker.

2. Add apple, cloves, raisins, apple cider, 2 tablespoons vinegar, brown sugar, salt and pepper. Cover; cook on LOW 2½ to 3 hours.

3. To serve, remove and discard cloves. Stir in remaining 1 tablespoon vinegar.

Makes 4 to 6 servings

Cheesy Corn and Peppers

2 **pounds frozen corn**

2 **poblano peppers, chopped**

2 **tablespoons butter, cubed**

1 **teaspoon salt**

½ **teaspoon ground cumin**

¼ **teaspoon black pepper**

3 **ounces cream cheese, cut into cubes**

1 **cup (4 ounces) shredded sharp Cheddar cheese**

1. Coat inside of **CROCK-POT®** slow cooker with nonstick cooking spray. Combine corn, poblano peppers, butter, salt, cumin and black pepper in **CROCK-POT®** slow cooker. Cover; cook on HIGH 2 hours.

2. Stir in cheeses. Cover; cook on HIGH 15 minutes or until cheeses melt.

Makes 8 servings

MEXICAN CORNBREAD PUDDING

Mexican Cornbread Pudding

- 1 can (14½ ounces) cream-style corn
- ½ cup yellow cornmeal
- 1 can (4 ounces) diced mild green chiles
- 2 eggs
- 2 tablespoons sugar
- 2 tablespoons vegetable oil
- 2 teaspoons baking powder
- ½ teaspoon salt
- ½ cup (2 ounces) shredded Cheddar cheese

Coat inside of 2-quart **CROCK-POT**® slow cooker with nonstick cooking spray. Combine corn, cornmeal, chiles, eggs, sugar, oil, baking powder and salt in medium bowl. Stir well to blend. Pour into **CROCK-POT**® slow cooker. Cover; cook on LOW 2 to 2½ hours or until center is set. Turn off heat. Sprinkle cheese over top. Cover; let stand 5 minutes or until cheese is melted.

Makes 8 servings

Mama's Best Baked Beans

- 1 bag (1 pound) dried Great Northern beans
- 1 pound bacon
- 5 hot dogs, cut into ½-inch pieces
- 1 cup chopped onion
- 1 bottle (24 ounces) ketchup
- 2 cups packed dark brown sugar

1. Soak and cook beans according to package directions. Drain and refrigerate until ready to use.

2. Heat skillet over medium heat. Add bacon; cook and stir until crisp. Remove to paper towel-lined plate using slotted spoon. Crumble bacon; set aside. Discard all but 3 tablespoons drippings. Add hot dogs and onion to skillet; cook and stir over medium heat until onion is tender. Transfer to **CROCK-POT**® slow cooker.

3. Place cooked beans, bacon, ketchup and brown sugar to **CROCK-POT**® slow cooker; mix well. Cover; cook on LOW 2 to 4 hours.

Makes 4 to 6 servings

CARAMELIZED
ONION SAUCE

Gourmet Cooking

Caramelized Onion Sauce

- ½ cup (1 stick) butter, cut into pieces
- 3 pounds onions
- 2 teaspoons balsamic vinegar
- 1 teaspoon salt
- ½ teaspoon black pepper
- ½ cup beef broth

1. Coat inside of **CROCK-POT**® slow cooker with nonstick cooking spray. Place butter in **CROCK-POT**® slow cooker. Cover; cook on HIGH until melted.

2. Meanwhile, slice onions in half through stem ends. Remove outer peels and place flat on cutting board. Slice onions thinly, holding knife at an angle, cutting through to center. Add to melted butter in **CROCK-POT**® slow cooker. Stir in vinegar, salt and pepper. Turn **CROCK-POT**® slow cooker to LOW. Cook, uncovered, on LOW 8 to 10 hours or until onions are brown, soft and reduced in volume to about 3 cups.

3. Stir in broth, stirring to scrape up browned bits. Serve immediately or cool to room temperature and refrigerate in airtight container until needed. Reheat before serving.

Makes about 3 cups

Tip: This onion sauce is fabulous served over your favorite roasted poultry or meat. For a thicker sauce, add broth and turn **CROCK-POT**® slow cooker to HIGH. Cook, uncovered, on HIGH until desired consistency.

Turkey with Pecan-Cherry Stuffing

- 1 fresh or thawed frozen boneless turkey breast (about 3 to 4 pounds), skin removed
- 2 cups cooked rice
- ⅓ cup chopped pecans
- ⅓ cup dried cherries or cranberries
- 1 teaspoon poultry seasoning
- ¼ cup peach, apricot or plum preserves
- 1 teaspoon Worcestershire sauce

1. Cut slices three-fourths of the way through turkey at 1-inch intervals.

2. Combine rice, pecans, cherries and poultry seasoning in large bowl. Stuff rice mixture between slices. If necessary, skewer turkey lengthwise to hold it together.

3. Place turkey in **CROCK-POT**® slow cooker. Cover; cook on LOW 5 to 6 hours or until turkey registers 170°F on meat thermometer inserted into thickest part of breast, not touching stuffing.

4. Combine preserves and Worcestershire sauce in small bowl. Spoon over turkey. Turn off heat. Cover; let stand 5 minutes. Remove skewer before serving.

Makes 8 servings

Herbed Artichoke Chicken

1½ pounds boneless, skinless chicken breasts

1 can (about 14 ounces) whole tomatoes, drained and diced

1 can (14 ounces) artichoke hearts in water, drained

1 small onion, chopped

½ cup kalamata olives, pitted and sliced

1 cup fat-free chicken broth

¼ cup dry white wine

3 tablespoons quick-cooking tapioca

2 teaspoons curry powder

1 tablespoon chopped fresh Italian parsley

1 teaspoon dried sweet basil

1 teaspoon dried thyme

½ teaspoon salt

½ teaspoon black pepper

1. Combine chicken, tomatoes, artichokes, onion, olives, broth, wine, tapioca, curry powder, parsley, basil, thyme, salt and pepper in **CROCK-POT**® slow cooker; mix well.

2. Cover; cook on LOW 6 to 8 hours or on HIGH 3½ to 4 hours or until chicken is no longer pink in center.

Makes 6 servings

Tip: For a 5-, 6- or 7-quart **CROCK-POT**® slow cooker, double all ingredients, except for the chicken broth and white wine. Increase the chicken broth and white wine by one half.

Moroccan Chicken Tagine

3 pounds bone-in chicken pieces, skin removed

2 cups chicken broth

1 can (about 14 ounces) diced tomatoes

2 onions, chopped

1 cup chopped dried apricots

4 cloves garlic, minced

2 teaspoons ground cumin

1 teaspoon ground ginger

1 teaspoon ground cinnamon

½ teaspoon ground coriander

½ teaspoon ground red pepper

6 sprigs fresh cilantro

1 tablespoon water

1 tablespoon cornstarch

1 can (15 ounces) chickpeas, rinsed and drained

2 tablespoons chopped fresh cilantro

¼ cup slivered almonds, toasted*

Hot cooked rice

*To toast almonds, spread in single layer in heavy skillet. Cook over medium heat 1 to 2 minutes or until nuts are lightly browned, stirring frequently.

1. Place chicken in **CROCK-POT**® slow cooker. Combine broth, tomatoes, onions, apricots, garlic, cumin, ginger, cinnamon, coriander, ground red pepper and cilantro sprigs in medium bowl; pour over chicken. Cover; cook on LOW 4 to 5 hours or until chicken is cooked through.

2. Remove chicken to serving platter; cover with foil to keep warm. Turn **CROCK-POT**® slow cooker to HIGH. Stir water into cornstarch in small bowl until smooth. Stir cornstarch mixture and chickpeas into **CROCK-POT**® slow cooker. Cover; cook on HIGH 15 minutes or until sauce has thickened. Pour sauce over chicken. Sprinkle with chopped cilantro and toasted almonds. Serve over rice.

Makes 4 to 6 servings

HERBED ARTICHOKE CHICKEN

Basil Chicken Merlot with Wild Mushrooms

- 3 tablespoons extra virgin olive oil, divided
- 1 roasting chicken (about 3 pounds), skinned and cut up
- 1½ cups thickly sliced cremini mushrooms
- 1 medium yellow onion, diced
- 2 cloves garlic, minced
- 1 cup chicken broth
- 1 can (6 ounces) tomato paste
- ⅓ cup Merlot or dry red wine
- 2 teaspoons sugar
- 1 teaspoon ground oregano
- ¼ teaspoon salt
- ¼ teaspoon black pepper
- 2 tablespoons minced fresh basil
- 3 cups hot cooked ziti pasta, drained
- Grated Romano cheese (optional)

1. Heat 1½ to 2 tablespoons oil in skillet over medium heat. Working in batches, brown chicken pieces on each side 3 to 5 minutes, turning once. Remove to plate with slotted spoon.

2. Heat remaining oil in skillet. Add mushrooms, onion and garlic; cook and stir 7 to 8 minutes or until onion is soft. Transfer to **CROCK-POT®** slow cooker. Top with chicken.

3. Combine broth, tomato paste, wine, sugar, oregano, salt and pepper in medium bowl. Pour sauce over chicken. Cover; cook on LOW 7 to 9 hours or on HIGH 3 to 4 hours.

4. Stir in basil. Place pasta in serving bowls. Ladle chicken, mushrooms and sauce evenly over pasta. Garnish with cheese.

Makes 4 to 6 servings

Mediterranean Lamb Shanks

- 3 pounds lamb shanks
- Salt and black pepper
- All-purpose flour
- 2 tablespoons olive oil
- 1 medium red onion, chopped
- 2 cloves garlic, minced
- 2 cups dry red wine
- 1 medium eggplant, cut into ½-inch cubes
- 1 large red bell pepper, sliced
- 1 large tomato, seeded and chopped
- 1 teaspoon dried thyme
- ½ teaspoon dried rosemary
- 2 cinnamon sticks
- ½ cup kalamata olives, pitted (optional)
- 2 tablespoons minced fresh Italian parsley (optional)

1. Season lamb on both sides with salt and black pepper; lightly coat with flour. Heat oil in large skillet over medium heat. Add lamb; brown on all sides. Transfer to **CROCK-POT®** slow cooker.

2. Add onion and garlic to skillet; cook and stir 3 to 4 minutes or until onion is softened. Transfer to **CROCK-POT®** slow cooker.

3. Add wine, eggplant, bell pepper, tomato, thyme, rosemary and cinnamon sticks to **CROCK-POT®** slow cooker; stir well to combine. Cover; cook on LOW 7½ to 9½ hours or on HIGH 4½ to 6½ hours or until meat is tender. Remove cinnamon sticks before serving. Garnish with olives and parsley.

Makes 6 servings

BASIL CHICKEN MERLOT
WITH WILD MUSHROOMS

HUNGARIAN
LAMB GOULASH

Hungarian Lamb Goulash

- 1 package (16 ounces) frozen cut green beans, thawed
- 1 cup chopped onion
- 1¼ pounds lean lamb for stew, cut into 1-inch cubes
- 1 can (15 ounces) chunky tomato sauce
- 1½ cups fat-free reduced-sodium chicken broth
- 1 can (6 ounces) tomato paste
- 4 teaspoons paprika
- 3 cups hot cooked egg noodles

1. Place green beans and onion in **CROCK-POT®** slow cooker. Top with lamb.

2. Combine tomato sauce, broth, tomato paste and paprika in large bowl; mix well. Pour over lamb mixture. Cover; cook on LOW 6 to 8 hours. Stir goulash; serve over noodles.

Makes 6 servings

Chicken Mozambique

- 2½ pounds boneless, skinless chicken breasts
- 1 cup dry white wine
- ½ cup (1 stick) butter, cut into small pieces
- 1 small onion, chopped
- 2 tablespoons minced garlic
- 2 tablespoons lemon juice
- 2 tablespoons hot pepper sauce
- 1 teaspoon salt
  Hot cooked rice
  Paprika (optional)

Place chicken, wine, butter, onion, garlic, lemon juice, hot pepper sauce and salt in **CROCK-POT®** slow cooker. Cover; cook on LOW 8 hours or on HIGH 6 hours. Serve over rice. Sprinkle with paprika, if desired.

Makes 10 servings

Chicken Croustade

2 tablespoons canola oil

1½ pounds boneless, skinless chicken breasts, cut into ¼-inch pieces

Salt and black pepper

1 large portobello mushroom cap

1 shallot, minced

¼ cup dry white wine

1 tablespoon chopped fresh thyme

¼ teaspoon sweet paprika

¼ teaspoon ground cumin

¼ cup chicken broth

1 package puff pastry shells

1 egg yolk

2 tablespoons cream

3 tablespoons freshly grated Parmesan cheese

Minced fresh chives (optional)

1. Heat oil in large skillet over medium-high heat. Season chicken with salt and pepper; add to skillet. Brown chicken about 4 minutes on each side.

2. Meanwhile, scrape gills from mushroom cap with spoon and discard. Chop mushroom cap into ¼-inch pieces.

3. Transfer chicken to **CROCK-POT®** slow cooker. Return skillet to medium-high heat. Add shallot; cook 1 to 2 minutes or until softened. Add wine, stirring to scrape up any browned bits. Cook until wine is reduced to about 2 tablespoons; pour over chicken. Stir chopped mushroom, thyme, paprika, cumin and broth into **CROCK-POT®** slow cooker. Season with salt and pepper. Cover; cook on LOW 3 hours.

4. Two hours after starting to cook chicken, cook puff pastry shells according to package directions. Cool completely.

5. Twenty minutes before end of cooking time, beat egg yolk and cream in small bowl. Stir 1 tablespoon hot cooking liquid into egg mixture; beat until well combined. Stir egg mixture into remaining cooking liquid. Cook, uncovered, on LOW 20 minutes. Stir in cheese. Divide chicken filling among puff pastry shells. Garnish with chives.

Makes 6 to 8 servings

Pecan and Apple-Stuffed Pork Chops with Apple Brandy

4 **thick-cut, bone-in pork loin chops (about 12 ounces each)**

1 **teaspoon salt, divided**

½ **teaspoon black pepper, divided**

2 **tablespoons vegetable oil**

½ **cup diced green apple**

½ **small onion, minced**

¼ **teaspoon dried thyme**

½ **cup apple brandy or brandy**

⅔ **cup cubed white bread**

2 **tablespoons chopped pecans**

4 **tablespoons frozen butter**

1 **cup unfiltered apple juice**

1. Coat inside of **CROCK-POT®** slow cooker with nonstick cooking spray. Season pork chops with ½ teaspoon salt and ¼ teaspoon pepper. Heat oil in large skillet over medium-high heat. Brown pork chops in batches, if necessary 2 minutes on each side. Remove to plate.

2. Add apple, onion, thyme, remaining ½ teaspoon salt and remaining ¼ teaspoon pepper to skillet and reduce heat to medium. Cook and stir 3 minutes or until onions are translucent. Remove from heat and pour in brandy. Return to medium heat and simmer until most of liquid is absorbed. Stir in bread and pecans; cook 1 minute.

3. Cut each pork chop horizontally to form pocket. Place 1 tablespoon butter into each pocket. Divide stuffing among pork chops. Arrange pork chops in **CROCK-POT®** slow cooker, pocket side up.

4. Pour apple juice around pork chops. Cover; cook on HIGH 1½ to 1¾ hours or until pork reaches an internal temperature of 145°F.

Makes 4 servings

CHOCOLATE HAZELNUT PUDDING CAKE

Chocolate Hazelnut Pudding Cake

1 box (about 18 ounces) golden yellow cake mix
1 cup water
4 eggs
½ cup sour cream
½ cup vegetable oil
1 cup mini semisweet chocolate chips
½ cup chopped hazelnuts
   Whipped cream or ice cream (optional)

1. Coat inside of 6-quart **CROCK-POT®** slow cooker with nonstick cooking spray. Combine cake mix, water, eggs, sour cream and oil; mix smooth. Pour batter into **CROCK-POT®** slow cooker. Cover; cook on HIGH 2 hours or until batter is nearly set.

2. Sprinkle with mini chocolate chips and hazelnuts. Cover; cook on HIGH 30 minutes or until toothpick inserted into center comes out clean or cake begins to pull away from sides of **CROCK-POT®** slow cooker. Turn off heat. Let stand until cooled slightly. Slice or spoon out while warm. Serve with whipped cream, if desired.

Makes 10 servings

Figs Poached in Red Wine

2 cups dry red wine
1 cup packed brown sugar
12 dried Calimyrna or Mediterranean figs (about 6 ounces)
2 (3-inch) cinnamon sticks
1 teaspoon finely grated orange peel
4 tablespoons heavy cream (optional)

1. Combine wine, brown sugar, figs, cinnamon sticks and orange peel in **CROCK-POT®** slow cooker. Cover; cook on LOW 5 to 6 hours or on HIGH 4 to 5 hours.

2. Remove and discard cinnamon sticks. To serve, spoon figs and syrup into serving dish. Top with spoonful of cream, if desired. Serve warm or cold.

Makes 4 servings

Chipotle Cornish Hens

3 small carrots, cut into ½-inch rounds

3 stalks celery, cut into ½-inch pieces

1 onion, chopped

1 can (7 ounces) chipotle peppers in adobo sauce, divided*

2 cups prepared corn bread stuffing

4 Cornish hens (about 1½ pounds each)

Salt and black pepper

Fresh parsley, chopped (optional)

*Jalapeño peppers can sting and irritate the skin, so wear rubber gloves when handling peppers and do not touch your eyes.

1. Coat inside of **CROCK-POT**® slow cooker with nonstick cooking spray. Add carrots, celery and onion.

2. Pour canned chipotles into small bowl. Finely chop 1 chipotle pepper. Remove remaining peppers from adobo sauce and reserve for another use. Mix half of chopped chipotle pepper into prepared stuffing. Add remaining half of chopped chipotle pepper to adobo sauce.**

3. Rinse and dry hens; removing giblets. Season with salt and black pepper inside and out. Fill each hen with about ½ cup stuffing. Rub adobo sauce onto hens. Place in **CROCK-POT**® slow cooker, arranging hens neck down and legs up. Cover; cook on HIGH 3½ to 4½ hours or until hens are cooked through and tender.

4. Transfer hens to serving platter. Remove vegetables with slotted spoon; arrange around hens. Garnish with parsley. Spoon cooking juices over hens and vegetables, if desired.

Makes 4 servings

**For spicier flavor, use 1 chipotle pepper in stuffing and 1 chipotle pepper in sauce.

Tip: Chipotle peppers can be very spicy. Until you know how much spiciness you prefer, use the smaller quantities recommended in recipes. You can always add more the next time you prepare the recipe.

Osso Bucco

1 large onion, cut into thin wedges

2 large carrots, sliced

4 cloves garlic, sliced

4 meaty veal shanks (3 to 4 pounds)

2 teaspoons herbes de Provence*

1 teaspoon salt

½ teaspoon black pepper

½ cup beef broth

¼ cup dry vermouth (optional)

3 tablespoons water

3 tablespoons all-purpose flour

¼ cup minced parsley

1 clove garlic, minced

1 teaspoon grated lemon peel

*Or substitute ½ teaspoon each dried thyme, rosemary, oregano and basil.

1. Coat inside of **CROCK-POT**® slow cooker with nonstick cooking spray. Place onion, carrots and sliced garlic in bottom. Arrange veal shanks over vegetables, overlapping slightly; sprinkle with herbes de Provence, salt and pepper. Add broth and vermouth, if desired. Cover; cook on LOW 8 to 9 hours or on HIGH 5 to 6 hours or until veal and vegetables are tender.

2. Remove veal and vegetables to serving platter; cover with foil to keep warm. Turn **CROCK-POT**® slow cooker to HIGH. Stir water into flour in small bowl until smooth. Whisk into cooking liquid. Cover; cook on HIGH 15 minutes or until sauce thickens. Combine parsley, minced garlic and lemon peel in small bowl.

3. Serve sauce over veal and vegetables; sprinkle with parsley mixture.

Makes 4 servings

CHIPOTLE CORNISH HENS

Chicken Marsala with Fettuccine

4   boneless, skinless chicken breasts
1   tablespoon vegetable oil
1   onion, chopped
½   cup Marsala wine
2   packages (6 ounces each) sliced cremini mushrooms
½   cup chicken broth
2   teaspoons Worcestershire sauce
½   teaspoon salt
½   teaspoon black pepper
½   cup whipping cream
2   tablespoons cornstarch
8   ounces fettuccine, cooked and drained
2   tablespoons chopped fresh parsley (optional)

1. Coat **CROCK-POT**® slow cooker with nonstick cooking spray. Arrange chicken in single layer in **CROCK-POT**® slow cooker.

2. Heat oil in large skillet over medium heat. Add onion; cook and stir until translucent. Add Marsala; cook 2 minutes or until mixture reduces slightly. Stir in mushrooms, broth, Worcestershire sauce, salt and pepper. Pour mixture over chicken. Cover; cook on HIGH 1½ to 1¾ hours or until chicken is cooked through.

3. Remove chicken to cutting board. Cover loosely with foil to keep warm; let stand 10 to 15 minutes. Stir cream into cornstarch in small bowl until smooth. Whisk into cooking liquid. Cover; cook on HIGH 15 minutes or until thickened. Slice chicken. Place fettuccine in large serving bowl. Top with chicken and sauce. Garnish with parsley.

Makes 6 to 8 servings

Tip: Skinless chicken is usually best for recipes using the **CROCK-POT**® slow cooker because the skin can shrivel and curl during cooking.

Jamaica-Me-Crazy Chicken Tropicale

2   sweet potatoes, cut into 2-inch pieces
1   can (20 ounces) pineapple tidbits in pineapple juice, drained and juice reserved
1   can (8 ounces) water chestnuts, drained and sliced
1   cup golden raisins
4   boneless, skinless chicken breasts
4   teaspoons Caribbean jerk seasoning
¼   cup dried onion flakes
3   tablespoons grated fresh ginger
2   tablespoons Worcestershire sauce
1   tablespoon grated lime peel
1   teaspoon whole cumin seeds, slightly crushed
    Hot cooked rice (optional)

1. Place sweet potatoes in **CROCK-POT**® slow cooker. Add pineapple tidbits, water chestnuts and raisins; mix well.

2. Sprinkle chicken with seasoning. Place chicken on top of sweet potato mixture.

3. Combine reserved pineapple juice, onion flakes, ginger, Worcestershire sauce, lime peel and cumin seeds in small bowl; pour over chicken. Cover; cook on LOW 7 to 9 hours or on HIGH 3 to 4 hours or until chicken and sweet potatoes are fork-tender. Serve with rice, if desired.

Makes 4 servings

**CHICKEN MARSALA
WITH FETTUCCINE**

Asian Pork Ribs with Spicy Noodles

1 can (about 14 ounces) beef broth

½ cup water

¼ cup rice wine vinegar

1 ounce (2-inch-piece) fresh ginger, peeled and grated

1 cup (about 1 ounce) dried sliced shiitake mushrooms

¼ teaspoon red pepper flakes

1 tablespoon Chinese five-spice powder*

1 teaspoon ground ginger

1 teaspoon chili powder

1 tablespoon dark sesame oil

2 full racks baby back pork ribs (about 4 pounds total)

½ cup hoisin sauce, divided

1 pound thin spaghetti, cooked and drained

¼ cup thinly sliced green onions

¼ cup chopped fresh cilantro

Chinese five-spice powder is a blend of cinnamon, cloves, fennel seed, anise and Szechuan peppercorns. It is available in most supermarkets and Asian grocery stores.

1. Combine broth, water, vinegar, grated ginger, mushrooms and red pepper flakes into **CROCK-POT®** slow cooker.

2. Stir five-spice powder, ground ginger, chili powder and oil in small bowl to form paste. Pat ribs dry with paper towels. Rub both sides with spice paste and brush with half of hoisin sauce.

3. Place ribs in **CROCK-POT®** slow cooker with prepared cooking liquid (do not stir). Cover; cook on LOW 8 to 10 hours or on HIGH 5 to 6 hours or until tender. Remove ribs to platter and brush lightly with remaining hoisin sauce. Keep warm until serving. Meanwhile, skim off any fat from cooking liquid.

4. Place warm spaghetti in shallow bowl. Ladle small amount of broth over spaghetti; sprinkle with green onions and cilantro. Slice ribs and serve over pasta.

Makes 4 servings

Chicken Tangier

2 tablespoons dried oregano

2 teaspoons seasoning salt

2 teaspoons puréed garlic

¼ teaspoon black pepper

8 skinless chicken thighs (about 3 pounds)

1 lemon, thinly sliced

½ cup dry white wine

2 tablespoons olive oil

1 cup pitted prunes

½ cup pitted green olives

¼ cup currants or raisins

2 tablespoons capers

Hot cooked couscous

Chopped fresh parsley or cilantro (optional)

1. Stir oregano, salt, garlic and pepper in small bowl. Rub onto chicken, coating all sides.

2. Coat inside of **CROCK-POT®** slow cooker with nonstick cooking spray. Arrange chicken in **CROCK-POT®** slow cooker, tucking lemon slices between pieces. Pour wine over chicken; sprinkle with oil. Add prunes, olives, currants and capers. Cover; cook on LOW 7 to 8 hours or on HIGH 4 to 5 hours. Serve over couscous. Garnish with parsley.

Makes 8 servings

Tip: It may seem like a lot, but this recipe really does call for 2 tablespoons dried oregano in order to more accurately represent the powerfully seasoned flavors of Morocco.

ASIAN PORK RIBS
WITH SPICY NOODLES

Indian-Style Apricot Chicken

6 chicken thighs (about 2 pounds)
¼ teaspoon salt, plus additional for seasoning
¼ teaspoon black pepper, plus additional for seasoning
1 tablespoon vegetable oil
1 large onion, chopped
2 cloves garlic, minced
2 tablespoons grated fresh ginger
½ teaspoon ground cinnamon
⅛ teaspoon ground allspice
1 can (about 14 ounces) diced tomatoes
1 cup chicken broth
1 package (8 ounces) dried apricots
1 pinch saffron threads (optional)
  Hot basmati rice
2 tablespoons chopped fresh parsley (optional)

1. Coat **CROCK-POT**® slow cooker with nonstick cooking spray. Season chicken with ¼ teaspoon salt and ¼ teaspoon pepper. Heat oil in large skillet over medium-high heat. Brown chicken on all sides. Transfer to **CROCK-POT**® slow cooker.

2. Add onion to skillet; cook and stir 3 to 5 minutes or until translucent. Stir in garlic, ginger, cinnamon and allspice; cook and stir 15 to 30 seconds or until mixture is fragrant. Add tomatoes and broth; cook 2 to 3 minutes or until mixture is heated through. Pour into **CROCK-POT**® slow cooker.

3. Add apricots and saffron, if desired, to **CROCK-POT**® slow cooker. Cover; cook on LOW 5 to 6 hours or on HIGH 3 to 4 hours or until chicken is tender. Season with salt and pepper, if desired. Serve with basmati rice and garnish with chopped parsley.

Makes 4 to 6 servings

Provençal Lemon and Olive Chicken

2 cups chopped onions
8 chicken thighs (about 2½ pounds)
1 lemon, thinly sliced
1 cup pitted green olives
1 tablespoon olive brine from jar or white vinegar
2 teaspoons herbes de Provence
1 whole bay leaf
½ teaspoon salt
⅛ teaspoon black pepper
1 cup chicken broth
½ cup minced fresh parsley

1. Place onions in **CROCK-POT**® slow cooker. Arrange chicken thighs over onions. Place lemon slice on each thigh. Add olives, brine, herbes de Provence, bay leaf, salt and pepper; slowly pour in broth.

2. Cover; cook on LOW 5 to 6 hours or on HIGH 3 to 3½ hours or until chicken is tender. Remove and discard bay leaf. Stir in parsley before serving.

Makes 8 servings

Tip: If desired, skin chicken easily by grasping the skin with a paper towel and pull away. Repeat with fresh paper towel for each piece of chicken, discarding skins and towels.

**INDIAN-STYLE
APRICOT CHICKEN**

Minestrone alla Milanese

2 cans (about 14 ounces each) reduced-sodium beef broth

1 can (about 14 ounces) diced tomatoes

1 cup diced red potatoes

1 cup coarsely chopped carrots

1 cup coarsely chopped green cabbage

1 cup sliced zucchini

½ cup chopped onion

½ cup sliced fresh green beans

½ cup coarsely chopped celery

½ cup water

2 tablespoons olive oil

1 clove garlic, minced

½ teaspoon dried basil

¼ teaspoon dried rosemary

1 whole bay leaf

1 can (about 15 ounces) cannellini beans, rinsed and drained

Grated Parmesan cheese (optional)

1. Combine all ingredients except cannellini beans and cheese in **CROCK-POT®** slow cooker; mix well. Cover; cook on LOW 5 to 6 hours.

2. Add cannellini beans. Cover; cook on LOW 1 hour or until vegetables are tender.

3. Remove and discard bay leaf. Top with cheese, if desired.

Makes 8 to 10 servings

Chicken Cordon Bleu

¼ cup all-purpose flour

1 teaspoon paprika

½ teaspoon salt

¼ teaspoon black pepper

4 boneless chicken breasts, lightly pounded*

4 slices ham

4 slices Swiss cheese

2 tablespoons olive oil

½ cup dry white wine

½ cup chicken broth

½ cup half-and-half

2 tablespoons cornstarch

Place chicken between two pieces of plastic wrap and flatten with meat mallet or back of skillet.

1. Combine flour, paprika, salt and pepper in large resealable food storage bag.

2. Place flattened chicken on cutting board, skin side down. Place 1 slice ham and 1 slice cheese on each piece. Fold chicken up to enclose filling; secure with toothpick. Place in bag with seasoned flour; shake gently to coat.

3. Heat oil in large skillet over medium-high heat. Brown chicken on all sides. Transfer to **CROCK-POT®** slow cooker.

4. Remove skillet from heat; add wine, stirring to scrape up browned bits. Pour into **CROCK-POT®** slow cooker. Add broth. Cover; cook on LOW 2 hours.

5. Remove chicken with slotted spoon. Cover and keep warm. Stir half-and-half into cornstarch in small bowl until smooth. Stir into cooking liquid. Cover; cook on LOW 15 minutes or until thickened. Remove and discard toothpicks. Serve chicken with cooking liquid.

Makes 4 servings

MINESTRONE ALLA MILANESE

Basque Chicken with Peppers

1 whole chicken (4 pounds), cut into 8 pieces

2 teaspoons salt, divided

1 teaspoon black pepper, divided

1½ tablespoons olive oil

1 onion, chopped

1 medium green bell pepper, cut into strips

1 medium yellow bell pepper, cut into strips

1 medium red bell pepper, cut into strips

8 ounces small brown mushrooms, halved

1 can (about 14 ounces) stewed tomatoes, undrained

½ cup chicken broth

½ cup Rioja wine

3 ounces tomato paste

2 cloves garlic, minced

1 sprig fresh marjoram

1 teaspoon smoked paprika

4 ounces chopped prosciutto

Hot cooked rice pilaf or rice

1. Season chicken with 1 teaspoon salt and ½ teaspoon black pepper. Heat oil in large skillet over medium-high heat. Add chicken in batches; brown well on all sides. Transfer each batch to **CROCK-POT**® slow cooker as it is cooked.

2. Reduce heat to medium-low. Stir in onion; cook and stir 3 minutes or until softened. Add bell peppers and mushrooms; cook 3 minutes. Add tomatoes with juice, broth, wine, tomato paste, garlic, marjoram, remaining 1 teaspoon salt, paprika and remaining ½ teaspoon black pepper to skillet; bring to simmer. Simmer 3 to 4 minutes; pour over chicken. Cover; cook on LOW 5 to 6 hours or on HIGH 4 hours or until chicken is tender.

3. Serve chicken over rice. Ladle vegetables and sauce over chicken. Sprinkle with prosciutto.

Makes 4 to 6 servings

Middle Eastern-Spiced Beef, Tomatoes and Beans

6 teaspoons extra virgin olive oil, divided

1½ pounds boneless beef chuck roast, cut into 1-inch pieces, divided

1 can (about 14 ounces) diced tomatoes with peppers and onions

1 cup chopped onion

6 ounces green beans, trimmed and broken into 1-inch pieces

1½ teaspoons sugar

½ teaspoon ground cinnamon

¼ teaspoon ground allspice

¼ teaspoon garlic powder

½ teaspoon salt

¼ teaspoon black pepper

Hot cooked couscous or rice

1. Heat 2 teaspoons oil in large skillet over medium-high heat. Working in batches, brown beef on all sides. Add additional 2 teaspoons oil as needed. Transfer to **CROCK-POT®** slow cooker.

2. Stir in tomatoes, onion, green beans, sugar, cinnamon, allspice and garlic powder. Cover; cook on LOW 8 hours or on HIGH 4 hours.

3. Turn off heat. Stir salt, pepper and remaining 2 teaspoons oil into **CROCK-POT®** slow cooker. Let stand, uncovered, 15 minutes to allow flavors to absorb and thicken slightly. Serve over couscous.

Makes about 4 servings

Autumn Herbed Chicken with Fennel and Squash

3 to 4 pounds chicken thighs
   Salt and black pepper
   All-purpose flour
2 tablespoons olive oil
1 fennel bulb, thinly sliced
½ butternut squash, cut into ½-inch cubes
1 teaspoon dried thyme
½ cup walnuts (optional)
½ cup chicken broth
½ cup apple cider or juice
   Hot cooked rice
¼ cup fresh basil, sliced
2 teaspoons fresh rosemary, finely minced

1. Season chicken on all sides with salt and pepper; lightly coat chicken with flour. Heat oil in large skillet over medium heat. Working in batches, brown chicken 3 to 5 minutes on each side. Transfer to **CROCK-POT**® slow cooker using slotted spoon.

2. Stir fennel, squash and thyme into **CROCK-POT**® slow cooker. Add walnuts, if desired, broth and cider to **CROCK-POT**® slow cooker. Cover; cook on LOW 5 to 7 hours or on HIGH 2½ to 4½ hours. Serve with rice. Garnish with basil and rosemary.

Makes 6 servings

Beef Roast with Dark Rum Sauce

1 teaspoon ground allspice

½ teaspoon salt

½ teaspoon black pepper

¼ teaspoon ground cloves

2 tablespoons extra virgin olive oil

1 beef rump roast (about 3 pounds)*

1 cup dark rum, divided

½ cup beef broth

2 cloves garlic, minced

2 whole bay leaves, broken in half

½ cup packed dark brown sugar

¼ cup lime juice

*Unless you have a 5-, 6- or 7-quart CROCK-POT®
slow cooker, cut any roast larger than 2½ pounds
in half so it cooks completely.

1. Combine allspice, salt, pepper and cloves in small bowl. Rub spices onto all sides of roast.

2. Heat oil in large skillet over medium heat. Brown beef on all sides, turning as it browns. Transfer to **CROCK-POT**® slow cooker. Add ½ cup rum, broth, garlic and bay leaves. Cover; cook on LOW 1 hour.

3. Combine remaining ½ cup rum, brown sugar and lime juice in small bowl. Pour over roast. Cover; cook on LOW 4 to 6 hours or until beef is fork-tender. Baste beef occasionally with sauce.

4. Remove roast to cutting board. Cover loosely with foil; let stand 10 to 15 minutes before slicing. Remove and discard bay leaves. Serve with sauce.

Makes 6 servings

Greek Chicken and Orzo

2 medium green bell peppers, cut into thin strips

1 cup chopped onion

2 teaspoons extra virgin olive oil

8 chicken thighs, rinsed and patted dry

1 tablespoon dried oregano

½ teaspoon dried rosemary

½ teaspoon garlic powder

½ teaspoon salt, divided

½ teaspoon black pepper, divided

8 ounces uncooked orzo pasta

Juice and grated peel of 1 medium lemon

½ cup water

2 ounces crumbled feta cheese (optional)

Chopped fresh parsley (optional)

1. Coat **CROCK-POT**® slow cooker with nonstick cooking spray. Add bell peppers and onion.

2. Heat oil in large skillet over medium-high heat. Brown chicken on both sides. Transfer to **CROCK-POT**® slow cooker, overlapping slightly if necessary. Sprinkle chicken with oregano, rosemary, garlic powder, ¼ teaspoon salt and ¼ teaspoon black pepper. Cover; cook on LOW 5 to 6 hours or on HIGH 3 to 4 hours or until chicken is tender.

3. Remove chicken to plate. Stir orzo, lemon juice, lemon peel, water, remaining ¼ teaspoon salt and ¼ teaspoon black pepper into **CROCK-POT**® slow cooker. Top with chicken. Cover; cook on HIGH 30 minutes or until pasta is tender. Garnish with cheese and parsley.

Makes 4 servings

Tip: Browning skin-on chicken not only adds flavor and color, but also prevents the skin from shrinking and curling during the long, slow cooking process.

Brioche and Amber Rum Custard

- 2 tablespoons unsalted butter
- 3½ cups heavy cream
- 4 eggs
- ½ cup packed dark brown sugar
- ⅓ cup amber or light rum
- 2 teaspoons vanilla
- 1 loaf (20 to 22 ounces) brioche bread, torn into pieces or 5 large brioche, cut into thirds*
- ½ cup coarsely chopped pecans
  Caramel or butterscotch topping (optional)

If desired, trim and discard heels.

1. Coat inside of **CROCK-POT®** slow cooker with butter. Combine cream, eggs, brown sugar, rum and vanilla in large bowl; stir well.

2. Mound one fourth of brioche pieces in bottom of **CROCK-POT®** slow cooker. Ladle one fourth of cream mixture over brioche. Sprinkle with one third of pecans. Repeat layers with remaining brioche, cream mixture and pecans.

3. Cover; cook on LOW 3 to 3½ hours or on HIGH 1½ to 2 hours until custard is set and toothpick inserted into center comes out clean.

4. Serve warm. Drizzle with caramel or butterscotch topping, if desired. Serve warm.

Makes 4 to 6 servings

MIXED BERRY COBBLER

Sweet Endings

Mixed Berry Cobbler

1 package (16 ounces) frozen mixed berries
½ cup granulated sugar
2 tablespoons quick-cooking tapioca
2 teaspoons grated lemon peel
1½ cups all-purpose flour
½ cup packed light brown sugar
2¼ teaspoons baking powder
¼ teaspoon ground nutmeg
½ cup milk
⅓ cup butter, melted
    Vanilla ice cream or whipped cream

1. Coat **CROCK-POT**® slow cooker with nonstick cooking spray. Stir together berries, granulated sugar, tapioca and lemon peel in medium bowl. Transfer to **CROCK-POT**® slow cooker.

2. For topping, combine flour, brown sugar, baking powder and nutmeg in medium bowl. Add milk and butter; stir just until blended. Drop spoonfuls of dough on top of berry mixture. Cover; cook on LOW 4 hours. Turn off heat. Uncover; let stand about 30 minutes. Serve with ice cream.

Makes 8 servings

Tip: Cobblers are year-round favorites. Experiment with seasonal fresh fruits, such as pears, plums, peaches, rhubarb, blueberries, raspberries, strawberries or gooseberries.

Cran-Apple Orange Conserve

2 medium oranges
5 large tart apples, peeled, cored and chopped
2 cups sugar
1½ cups fresh cranberries
1 tablespoon grated lemon peel

1. Remove thin slice from both ends of both oranges for easier chopping. Finely chop unpeeled oranges (remove any seeds) to yield about 2 cups chopped oranges.

2. Combine chopped oranges, apples, sugar, cranberries and lemon peel in **CROCK-POT**® slow cooker. Cover; cook on LOW 4 hours or on HIGH 2 hours.

3. Slightly crush fruit with potato masher. Cook, uncovered, on LOW 2 hours or on HIGH 1 to 1½ hours or until very thick, stirring occasionally. Turn off heat. Cool at least 2 hours. Serve over pound cake or with waffles or pancakes.

Makes about 5 cups

Tip: Fruit conserve can also be served with roast pork or poultry.

Cran-Cherry Bread Pudding

- 1½ cups light cream
- 3 egg yolks, beaten
- ⅓ cup sugar
- ¼ teaspoon kosher salt
- 1½ teaspoons cherry extract
- ⅔ cup dried sweetened cranberries
- ⅔ cup golden raisins
- ½ cup whole candied red cherries, halved
- ½ cup dry sherry
- 9 cups unseasoned stuffing mix
- 1 cup white chocolate baking chips
  Whipped cream

1. Prepare foil handles by tearing off three 18 × 3-inch strips heavy foil (or use regular foil folded to double thickness). Crisscross foil strips in spoke design; place in **CROCK-POT®** slow cooker. Spray 2-quart baking dish that fits inside **CROCK-POT®** slow cooker with nonstick cooking spray.

2. Cook and stir cream, egg yolks, sugar and salt in medium heavy saucepan over medium heat until mixture coats back of spoon. Remove from heat. Set saucepan in bowl of ice water; stir to cool. Stir in cherry extract. Transfer custard to large bowl; press plastic wrap onto surface of custard; refrigerate.

3. Combine cranberries, raisins and cherries in small bowl. Heat sherry in small saucepan until warm. Pour over fruit; let stand 10 minutes.

4. Fold bread cubes and baking chips into custard. Drain fruit, reserving sherry; stir into custard. Pour into prepared dish. Top with reserved sherry; cover tightly with foil. Place on foil handles in **CROCK-POT®** slow cooker. Add water to come 1 inch up side of dish. Cover; cook on LOW 3½ to 5½ hours or until pudding springs back when touched. Carefully remove dish using foil handles. Turn off heat. Uncover and let stand 10 minutes. Serve warm with whipped cream.

Makes 12 servings

Baked Fudge Pudding Cake

- 6 tablespoons unsweetened cocoa powder
- ¼ cup all-purpose flour
- ⅛ teaspoon salt
- 4 eggs
- 1⅓ cups sugar
- 1 cup (2 sticks) butter, melted
- 1 teaspoon vanilla
  Grated peel of 1 orange
- ½ cup whipping cream
  Chopped toasted pecans*
  Whipped cream or vanilla ice cream

*To toast pecans, spread in single layer in heavy skillet. Cook over medium heat 1 to 2 minutes or until nuts are lightly browned, stirring frequently.

1. Coat inside of 4½-quart **CROCK-POT®** slow cooker with nonstick cooking spray. Preheat **CROCK-POT®** slow cooker on LOW. Combine cocoa, flour and salt in small bowl.

2. Beat eggs in large bowl with electric mixer at medium-high speed until thickened. Gradually add sugar, beating 5 minutes or until very thick and pale yellow. Mix in butter, vanilla and orange peel. Stir cocoa mixture into egg mixture. Add cream; mix until blended. Pour batter into **CROCK-POT®** slow cooker.

3. Line lid with two paper towels. Cover; cook on LOW 3 to 4 hours.

4. Spoon into dishes; sprinkle with pecans and top with whipped cream. Refrigerate leftovers.

Makes 6 to 8 servings

Tip: Refrigerate leftover pudding cake in a covered container. To serve, reheat individual servings in the microwave on HIGH 15 seconds. Or make fudge truffles by rolling leftover cake into small balls and dipping them into melted chocolate. Let stand until chocolate is set.

CRAN-CHERRY BREAD PUDDING

Chocolate Malt Pudding Cake

2 tablespoons unsalted butter

1 cup all-purpose flour

½ cup packed brown sugar

2 tablespoons unsweetened cocoa powder

1½ teaspoons baking powder

½ cup milk

2 tablespoons vegetable oil

½ teaspoon almond extract

½ cup coarsely chopped malted milk balls

½ cup semisweet chocolate chips

½ cup granulated sugar

¼ cup malted milk powder

2 cups boiling water

4 ounces cream cheese, cubed, at room temperature

¼ cup sliced almonds (optional)

Vanilla ice cream (optional)

1. Generously butter 4½-quart **CROCK-POT®** slow cooker. Combine flour, brown sugar, cocoa and baking powder in medium bowl. Add milk, oil and almond extract; stir until smooth.

2. Stir in malted milk balls and chocolate chips. Spread batter in **CROCK-POT®** slow cooker.

3. Combine granulated sugar and malted milk powder in medium bowl. Mix boiling water and cream cheese in separate medium bowl. Stir into malted milk mixture. Pour evenly over batter in **CROCK-POT®** slow cooker. Do not stir. Cover; cook on HIGH 2 to 2½ hours or until toothpick inserted in center comes out clean.

4. Turn off heat. Let stand, uncovered, 30 minutes. Spoon into dessert dishes. Garnish with almonds and serve with ice cream, if desired.

Makes 6 to 8 servings

Chocolate Chip Lemon Loaf

1⅔ cups all-purpose flour

1½ teaspoons baking powder

¼ teaspoon salt

½ cup granulated sugar

½ cup shortening

2 eggs

½ cup milk

½ cup semisweet chocolate chips

Grated peel of 1 lemon

Juice of 1 lemon

¼ to ½ cup powdered sugar

Melted semisweet chocolate (optional)

1. Make foil handles using three 18 × 3-inch strips of heavy-duty foil or use regular foil folded to double thickness. Place in 4½-quart **CROCK-POT®** slow cooker; crisscross foil to form spoke design across bottom and up sides. Preheat **CROCK-POT®** slow cooker on LOW. Prepare 2-quart casserole or soufflé dish that fits inside **CROCK-POT®** slow cooker with nonstick cooking spray. Combine flour, baking powder and salt in medium bowl.

2. Beat granulated sugar and shortening in large bowl with electric mixer at medium-high speed until blended. Add eggs, one at a time, beating well after each addition. Add flour mixture and milk alternately. Stir in chocolate chips and lemon peel.

3. Spoon batter into prepared casserole. Cover with greased foil. Place dish in **CROCK-POT®** slow cooker. Cover; cook on LOW 3 to 4 hours or on HIGH 1½ to 2 hours or until edges are golden and knife inserted into center of loaf comes out clean. Remove dish from **CROCK-POT®** slow cooker; remove foil. Cool completely on wire rack.

4. Combine lemon juice and ¼ cup powdered sugar in small bowl until smooth. Add more sugar as needed to reach desired glaze consistency. Pour glaze over loaf. Drizzle with melted chocolate, if desired.

Makes 8 servings

**CHOCOLATE MALT
PUDDING CAKE**

Rum and Cherry Cola Fudge Spoon Cake

CAKE

- ½ cup cola
- ½ cup dried sour cherries
- 1 cup chocolate milk
- ½ cup (1 stick) unsalted butter, melted
- 2 teaspoons vanilla
- 1½ cups all-purpose flour
- ½ cup ground sweet chocolate
- ½ cup granulated sugar
- 2½ teaspoons baking powder
- ½ teaspoon salt

TOPPING

- 1¼ cups vanilla cola
- ¼ cup dark rum
- ½ cup ground sweet chocolate
- ½ cup granulated sugar
- ½ cup packed brown sugar
  Ice cream

1. Coat inside of **CROCK-POT**® slow cooker with nonstick cooking spray. Bring cola and dried cherries to a boil in small saucepan. Remove from heat; let stand 30 minutes.

2. Combine chocolate milk, melted butter and vanilla in small bowl. Combine flour, ½ cup ground chocolate, ½ cup granulated sugar, baking powder and salt in medium bowl; stir well. Make a well in center of dry ingredients; add milk mixture and stir until smooth. Stir cherry mixture into batter. Pour into **CROCK-POT**® slow cooker.

3. Prepare topping: Bring vanilla cola and rum to a boil in small saucepan. Remove from heat. Add ½ cup ground chocolate and sugars; stir until smooth. Gently pour over batter. Do not stir. Cover; cook on HIGH 2½ hours or until cake is puffed and top layer has set. Turn off heat. Let stand, covered, 30 minutes. Serve with ice cream.

Makes 8 to 10 servings

Apple Crumble Pot

FILLING

- ⅔ cup packed dark brown sugar
- 2 tablespoons biscuit baking mix
- 1½ teaspoons ground cinnamon
- ¼ teaspoon ground allspice
- 4 Granny Smith apples (about 2 pounds), cored and cut into 8 wedges each
- ½ cup dried cranberries
- 2 tablespoons butter, cubed
- 1 teaspoon vanilla

TOPPING

- 1 cup biscuit baking mix
- ½ cup rolled oats
- ⅓ cup packed dark brown sugar
- 3 tablespoons cold butter, cubed
- ½ cup chopped pecans
  Whipped cream or ice cream (optional)

1. Coat inside of **CROCK-POT**® slow cooker with nonstick cooking spray. For filling, combine ⅔ cup brown sugar, 2 tablespoons baking mix, cinnamon and allspice in large bowl. Add apples, cranberries, 2 tablespoons butter and vanilla; toss gently to coat. Transfer to **CROCK-POT**® slow cooker.

2. For topping, combine 1 cup baking mix, oats and ⅓ cup brown sugar in large bowl. Cut in 3 tablespoons butter with pastry blender or two knives until mixture resembles coarse crumbs. Sprinkle evenly over filling in **CROCK-POT**® slow cooker. Top with pecans. Cover; cook on HIGH 2¼ hours or until apples are tender. Do not overcook.

3. Turn off heat. Let stand, uncovered, 15 to 30 minutes before serving. Top with whipped cream, if desired.

Makes 6 to 8 servings

**RUM AND CHERRY COLA
FUDGE SPOON CAKE**

EASY CHOCOLATE PUDDING CAKE

Easy Chocolate Pudding Cake

- 1 package (6-serving size) instant chocolate pudding and pie filling mix
- 3 cups milk
- 1 package (about 18 ounces) chocolate fudge cake mix, plus ingredients to prepare mix

  Crushed peppermint candies (optional)

  Whipped topping or ice cream (optional)

1. Coat inside of 4-quart **CROCK-POT®** slow cooker with nonstick cooking spray. Place pudding mix in **CROCK-POT®** slow cooker. Whisk in milk.

2. Prepare cake mix according to package directions. Carefully pour cake mix into **CROCK-POT®** slow cooker. Do not stir. Cover; cook on HIGH 1½ hours or until toothpick inserted into center comes out clean.

3. Spoon into cups or onto plates; serve warm with crushed peppermint candies and whipped topping, if desired.

Makes 16 servings

Tip: Allow breads, cakes and puddings to cool at least 5 minutes before scooping or removing them from the **CROCK-POT®** slow cooker.

Pineapple Daiquiri Sundae Topping

- 1 pineapple, peeled, cored and cut into ½-inch chunks
- ½ cup sugar
- ½ cup dark rum
- 3 tablespoons lime juice

  Peel of 2 limes, cut into long strips
- 1 tablespoon cornstarch

  Ice cream, pound cake or shortcake

  Fresh raspberries (optional)

1. Place pineapple, sugar, rum, lime juice, lime peel and cornstarch in 1½-quart **CROCK-POT®** slow cooker; mix well. Cover; cook on HIGH 3 to 4 hours.

2. Serve hot over ice cream, pound cake or shortcake. Garnish with raspberries.

Makes 4 to 6 servings

Tip: Substitute 1 can (20 ounces) crushed pineapple, drained, for the fresh pineapple.

CHERRY DELIGHT

Cherry Delight

1 can (21 ounces) cherry pie filling
1 package (about 18 ounces) yellow cake mix
½ cup (1 stick) butter, melted
⅓ cup chopped walnuts
    Whipped topping or vanilla ice cream (optional)

1. Place pie filling in **CROCK-POT®** slow cooker. Mix together cake mix and butter in medium bowl. Spread evenly over pie filling. Sprinkle with walnuts.

2. Cover; cook on LOW 3 to 4 hours or on HIGH 1½ to 2 hours. Spoon into serving dishes. Serve warm with whipped topping or ice cream, if desired.

Makes 8 to 10 servings

Decadent Chocolate Delight

1 package (about 18 ounces) chocolate cake mix
1 container (8 ounces) sour cream
1 cup semisweet chocolate chips
1 cup water
4 eggs
½ cup vegetable oil
1 package (4-serving size) instant chocolate pudding and pie filling mix
    Vanilla ice cream

1. Coat inside of **CROCK-POT®** slow cooker with nonstick cooking spray.

2. Combine all ingredients except ice cream in medium bowl; mix well. Transfer to **CROCK-POT®** slow cooker.

3. Cover; cook on LOW 3 to 4 hours or on HIGH 1½ to 1¾ hours. Serve warm with ice cream.

Makes 12 servings

CARAMEL
AND APPLE
POUND CAKE

Caramel and Apple Pound Cake

 4 medium baking apples, cored, peeled and cut into wedges
 ½ cup apple juice
 ½ pound caramels, unwrapped
 ¼ cup creamy peanut butter
 1½ teaspoons vanilla
 ½ teaspoon ground cinnamon
 ⅛ teaspoon ground cardamom
 1 prepared pound cake, sliced
   Whipped cream (optional)

1. Coat inside of **CROCK-POT®** slow cooker with nonstick cooking spray. Layer apples, apple juice and caramels in **CROCK-POT®** slow cooker.

2. Mix together peanut butter, vanilla, cinnamon and cardamom in small bowl. Drop by teaspoons onto apples. Cover; cook on LOW 6 to 8 hours or on HIGH 3 to 4 hours. Stir. Cover; cook on LOW 1 hour. Spoon apples over cake slices. Top with whipped cream.

Makes 6 to 8 servings

Citrus Chinese Dates with Toasted Hazelnuts

 2 cups pitted dates
 ⅔ cup boiling water
 ½ cup sugar
   Strips of peel from 1 lemon
   Whipped cream (optional)
 ¼ cup hazelnuts, shelled and toasted*

*To toast hazelnuts, spread in single layer in heavy skillet. Cook over medium heat 1 to 2 minutes or until nuts are lightly browned, stirring frequently.

1. Place dates in medium bowl and cover with water. Soak overnight to rehydrate. Drain; place dates in **CROCK-POT®** slow cooker.

2. Add ⅔ cup boiling water, sugar and lemon peel to **CROCK-POT®** slow cooker. Cover; cook on HIGH 3 hours.

3. Remove and discard peel. Place dates in serving dishes. Top with whipped cream, if desired. Sprinkle with hazelnuts.

Makes 4 servings

Hot Fudge Cake

- 2 **cups all-purpose flour**
- 1½ **cups packed light brown sugar, divided**
- ¼ **cup plus 3 tablespoons unsweetened cocoa powder, divided, plus additional for dusting**
- 2 **teaspoons baking powder**
- 1 **teaspoon salt**
- 1 **cup milk**
- ¼ **cup (½ stick) butter, melted**
- 1 **teaspoon vanilla**
- 3½ **cups boiling water**

1. Coat 4½-quart **CROCK-POT®** slow cooker with nonstick cooking spray. Mix flour, 1 cup brown sugar, 3 tablespoons cocoa, baking powder and salt in medium bowl. Stir in milk, butter and vanilla; mix until well blended. Pour into **CROCK-POT®** slow cooker.

2. Blend remaining ½ cup brown sugar and ¼ cup cocoa in small bowl. Sprinkle evenly over mixture in **CROCK-POT®** slow cooker. Pour in boiling water. Do not stir.

3. Cover; cook on HIGH 1¼ to 1½ hours or until toothpick inserted into center comes out clean. Turn off heat. Let stand 10 minutes; invert onto serving platter or scoop into serving dishes. Dust with additional cocoa, if desired.

Makes 6 to 8 servings

"Peachy Keen" Dessert Treat

- 1⅓ **cups old-fashioned oats**
- 1 **cup sugar**
- 1 **cup packed light brown sugar**
- ⅔ **cup buttermilk baking mix**
- 2 **teaspoons ground cinnamon**
- ½ **teaspoon ground nutmeg**
- 2 **pounds fresh peaches (about 8 medium), sliced**

Combine oats, sugars, baking mix, cinnamon and nutmeg in large bowl. Stir in peaches until well blended. Pour mixture into **CROCK-POT®** slow cooker. Cover; cook on LOW 4 to 6 hours.

Makes 8 to 12 servings

Triple Chocolate Fantasy

2 pounds white almond bark, broken into pieces

1 bar (4 ounces) sweetened chocolate, broken into pieces*

1 package (12 ounces) semisweet chocolate chips

3 cups lightly toasted, coarsely chopped pecans**

Use your favorite high-quality chocolate candy bar.

**To toast pecans, spread in single layer in heavy skillet. Cook over medium heat 1 to 2 minutes or until nuts are lightly browned, stirring frequently.*

1. Place bark, sweetened chocolate and chocolate chips in **CROCK-POT®** slow cooker. Cover; cook on HIGH 1 hour. Do not stir.

2. Turn **CROCK-POT®** slow cooker to LOW. Cover; cook on LOW 1 hour, stirring every 15 minutes. Stir in nuts.

3. Drop mixture by tablespoonfuls onto baking sheet covered with waxed paper; cool. Store in tightly covered container.

Makes 36 pieces

Tip: Here are a few ideas for other imaginative items to add in along with or instead of pecans: raisins, crushed peppermint candy, candy-coated baking bits, crushed toffee, peanuts or pistachio nuts, chopped gum drops, chopped dried fruit, candied cherries, chopped marshmallows or sweetened coconut.

Steamed Southern Sweet Potato Custard

1 can (16 ounces) cut sweet potatoes, drained

1 can (12 ounces) evaporated milk, divided

½ cup packed brown sugar

2 eggs, lightly beaten

1 teaspoon ground cinnamon

½ teaspoon ground ginger

¼ teaspoon salt

Whipped cream (optional)

Ground nutmeg (optional)

1. Place sweet potatoes and ¼ cup evaporated milk in food processor or blender; process until smooth. Add remaining evaporated milk, brown sugar, eggs, cinnamon, ginger and salt; process until well blended. Pour into ungreased 1-quart soufflé dish. Cover tightly with foil. Crumple large sheet (15 × 12 inches) of foil; place in bottom of **CROCK-POT®** slow cooker. Pour 2 cups water over foil. Make foil handles. (See Note.)

2. Transfer dish to **CROCK-POT®** slow cooker using foil handles. Cover; cook on HIGH 2½ to 3 hours or until knife inserted into center comes out clean.

3. Use foil strips to transfer dish to wire rack. Uncover; let stand 30 minutes. Garnish with whipped cream and nutmeg.

Makes 4 servings

Note: To make foil handles, tear off three 18 × 3-inch strips of heavy-duty foil or use regular foil folded to double thickness. Crisscross strips in spoke design and place in **CROCK-POT®** slow cooker to make lifting dish easier.

TRIPLE CHOCOLATE FANTASY

Fruit Ambrosia with Dumplings

4 cups fresh or frozen fruit, prepared for use and cut into bite-size pieces*

½ cup plus 2 tablespoons granulated sugar, divided

½ cup warm apple or cran-apple juice

2 tablespoons quick-cooking tapioca

1 cup all-purpose flour

1¼ teaspoons baking powder

¼ teaspoon salt

3 tablespoons butter or margarine, cubed

½ cup milk

1 egg

2 tablespoons packed light brown sugar, plus additional for garnish

Vanilla ice cream, whipped cream or fruity yogurt (optional)

1. Combine fruit, ½ cup granulated sugar, juice and tapioca in **CROCK-POT**® slow cooker. Cover; cook on LOW 5 to 6 hours or on HIGH 2½ to 3 hours or until thick sauce forms.

2. Combine flour, remaining 2 tablespoons granulated sugar, baking powder and salt in medium bowl. Cut in butter using pastry blender or two knives until mixture resembles coarse crumbs. Whisk milk and egg in small bowl. Pour milk mixture into flour mixture. Stir until soft dough forms.

3. Drop dough by teaspoonfuls on top of fruit. Sprinkle with 2 tablespoons brown sugar. Cover; cook on HIGH 30 minutes to 1 hour or until toothpick inserted into centers of dumplings comes out clean.

4. Serve warm. Sprinkle dumplings with additional brown sugar, if desired. Top with ice cream, if desired.

Makes 4 to 6 servings

Peanut Fudge Pudding Cake

1 cup all-purpose flour

1 cup sugar, divided

1½ teaspoons baking powder

⅔ cup milk

½ cup peanut butter

2 tablespoons vegetable oil

1 teaspoon vanilla

¼ cup unsweetened cocoa powder

1 cup boiling water

Chopped peanuts

Vanilla ice cream (optional)

1. Coat 4½-quart **CROCK-POT**® slow cooker with nonstick cooking spray. Combine flour, ½ cup sugar and baking powder in medium bowl. Stir in milk, peanut butter, oil and vanilla until well blended. Pour batter into **CROCK-POT**® slow cooker.

2. Combine remaining ½ cup sugar and cocoa in small bowl. Stir in boiling water. Pour into **CROCK-POT**® slow cooker. Do not stir.

3. Cover; cook on HIGH 1¼ to 1½ hours or until toothpick inserted into center comes out clean. Turn off heat. Let stand 10 minutes; scoop into serving dishes or invert onto serving platter. Serve warm with peanuts and ice cream, if desired.

Makes 4 servings

Tip: Because this recipe makes its own fudge topping, be sure to spoon some of it from the bottom of the **CROCK-POT**® slow cooker when serving or invert the cake for a luscious chocolatey finish.

**FRUIT AMBROSIA
WITH DUMPLINGS**

BANANAS FOSTER

Bananas Foster

12 bananas, cut into quarters
1 cup flaked coconut
1 cup dark corn syrup
⅔ cup butter, melted
¼ cup lemon juice
2 teaspoons grated lemon peel
2 teaspoons rum
1 teaspoon ground cinnamon
½ teaspoon salt
12 slices pound cake
1 quart vanilla ice cream

Combine bananas and coconut in **CROCK-POT®** slow cooker. Stir together corn syrup, butter, lemon juice, lemon peel, rum, cinnamon and salt in medium bowl; pour over bananas. Cover; cook on LOW 1 to 2 hours. To serve, arrange bananas on pound cake slices. Top with ice cream and warm sauce.

Makes 12 servings

Cinnamon-Ginger Poached Pears

3 cups water
1 cup sugar
10 slices fresh ginger
2 whole cinnamon sticks
1 tablespoon chopped candied ginger (optional)
6 Bosc or Anjou pears, peeled and cored

1. Combine water, sugar, ginger, cinnamon sticks and candied ginger, if desired, in **CROCK-POT®** slow cooker. Add pears. Cover; cook on LOW 4 to 6 hours or on HIGH 1½ to 2 hours.

2. Remove pears with slotted spoon. Cook syrup, uncovered, on LOW 30 minutes or until thickened. Remove and discard cinnamon sticks.

Makes 6 servings

FRESH BOSC
PEAR GRANITA

Fresh Bosc Pear Granita

1 pound fresh Bosc pears, peeled, cored and cubed

1¼ cups water

¼ cup sugar

½ teaspoon ground cinnamon

1 tablespoon lemon juice

1. Place pears, water, sugar and cinnamon in **CROCK-POT®** slow cooker. Cover; cook on HIGH 2½ to 3½ hours or until pears are very soft and tender. Stir in lemon juice.

2. Transfer pears and syrup to blender or food processor; blend until smooth. Strain mixture, discarding any pulp. Pour liquid into 11 × 9-inch baking pan. Cover tightly with plastic wrap. Place pan in freezer.

3. Stir every hour, tossing granita with fork. Crush any lumps in mixture as it freezes. Freeze 3 to 4 hours or until firm. You may keep granita in freezer up to 2 days before serving; toss granita every 6 to 12 hours.

Makes 6 servings

Hot Tropics Sipper

4 cups pineapple juice

2 cups apple juice

1 container (about 11 ounces) apricot nectar

½ cup packed dark brown sugar

1 medium orange, thinly sliced

1 medium lemon, thinly sliced

3 whole cinnamon sticks

6 whole cloves

Additional lemon or orange slices (optional)

1. Combine pineapple juice, apple juice, nectar, brown sugar, orange slices, lemon slices, cinnamon sticks and cloves in **CROCK-POT®** slow cooker. Cover; cook on HIGH 3½ to 4 hours or until very fragrant.

2. Strain immediately (beverage will turn bitter if fruit and spices remain after cooking is complete). Remove and discard cinnamon sticks. Serve with additional fresh lemon slices, if desired.

Makes 8 servings

PUMPKIN-CRANBERRY CUSTARD

Pumpkin-Cranberry Custard

- **1 can (30 ounces) pumpkin pie filling**
- **1 can (12 ounces) evaporated milk**
- **1 cup dried cranberries**
- **4 eggs, beaten**
- **1 cup crushed or whole gingersnap cookies (optional)**
- **Whipped cream (optional)**

Combine pumpkin, evaporated milk, cranberries and eggs in **CROCK-POT®** slow cooker; mix thoroughly. Cover; cook on HIGH 4 to 4½ hours. Serve with crushed or whole gingersnaps and whipped cream, if desired.

Makes 4 to 6 servings

Streusel Pound Cake

- **1 package (16 ounces) pound cake mix, plus ingredients to prepare mix**
- **¼ cup packed light brown sugar**
- **1 tablespoon all-purpose flour**
- **¼ cup chopped nuts**
- **1 teaspoon ground cinnamon**
- **Strawberries, blueberries and raspberries (optional)**

Coat 4½-quart **CROCK-POT®** slow cooker with nonstick cooking spray. Prepare cake mix according to package directions; stir in brown sugar, flour, nuts and cinnamon. Pour batter into **CROCK-POT®** slow cooker. Cover; cook on HIGH 1½ to 1¾ hours or until toothpick inserted into center comes out clean. Serve with berries, if desired.

Makes 6 to 8 servings

Glazed Orange Poppy Seed Cake

CAKE

- 1½ cups biscuit baking mix
- ½ cup granulated sugar
- 2 tablespoons poppy seeds
- ½ cup sour cream
- 1 egg
- 2 tablespoons milk
- 2 teaspoons orange peel
- 1 teaspoon vanilla

GLAZE

- ¼ cup orange juice
- 2 cups powdered sugar, sifted
- 2 teaspoons poppy seeds

1. Coat inside of 4-quart **CROCK-POT®** slow cooker with nonstick cooking spray. Cut waxed paper circle to fit bottom of **CROCK-POT®** slow cooker (trace insert bottom and cut slightly smaller to fit). Spray lightly with nonstick cooking spray.

2. To prepare batter, whisk baking mix, granulated sugar and 2 tablespoons poppy seeds in medium bowl; set aside. Blend sour cream, egg, milk, orange peel and vanilla in separate medium bowl. Whisk dry ingredients into sour cream mixture until thoroughly blended.

3. Spoon batter into **CROCK-POT®** slow cooker; smooth top. Line lid with paper towels. Cover; cook on HIGH 1½ hours or until cake is no longer shiny and toothpick inserted into center comes out clean.

4. Invert cake onto wire rack; peel off waxed paper. Cool completely.

5. To prepare glaze, whisk orange juice into powdered sugar in small bowl. Cut cake into wedges; place on wire rack with tray underneath to catch drips. Spread glaze over top and sides of each wedge. Sprinkle 2 teaspoons poppy seeds over wedges; let stand until glaze is set.

Makes 8 servings

Brownie Bottoms

½ cup packed brown sugar

½ cup water

2 tablespoons unsweetened cocoa powder

2½ cups packaged brownie mix

1 package (2½ ounces) instant chocolate pudding mix

½ cup milk chocolate chips

2 eggs, beaten

3 tablespoons butter or margarine, melted

1. Coat inside of **CROCK-POT**® slow cooker with nonstick cooking spray. Combine brown sugar, water and cocoa in small saucepan over medium heat; bring to a boil over medium-high heat.

2. Meanwhile, combine brownie mix, pudding mix, chocolate chips, eggs and butter in medium bowl; stir until well blended. Spread batter in **CROCK-POT**® slow cooker; pour boiling sugar mixture over batter. Cover; cook on HIGH 1½ hours.

3. Turn off heat. Let stand 30 minutes. Serve warm.

Makes 6 servings

Tip: Serve this warm chocolate dessert with whipped cream or ice cream.

Tip: Recipe can be doubled for a 5-, 6- or 7-quart **CROCK-POT**® slow cooker.

Spiked Sponge Cake

CAKE

1 package (about 18 ounces) yellow cake mix

1 cup water

4 eggs

½ cup vegetable oil

1 tablespoon grated orange peel

1 package (6 ounces) golden raisins and cherries or other chopped dried fruit (about 1 cup)

SAUCE

1 cup chopped pecans

½ cup sugar

½ cup (1 stick) butter

¼ cup bourbon or apple juice

1. Coat inside of 5-quart **CROCK-POT**® slow cooker with nonstick cooking spray.

2. Combine cake mix, water, eggs and oil in large bowl; stir well. (Batter will be lumpy). Stir in orange peel. Pour two thirds of batter into **CROCK-POT**® slow cooker. Sprinkle raisins and cherries evenly over batter. Top evenly with remaining batter. Cover; cook on HIGH 1½ to 1¾ hours or until toothpick inserted into center of cake comes out clean.

3. Immediately remove stoneware and cool 10 minutes on wire rack. Run flat rubber spatula around edge of cake, lifting bottom slightly. Invert onto serving plate.

4. For sauce, heat large skillet over medium-high heat. Add pecans; cook and stir 2 to 3 minutes or until pecans are golden brown. Add sugar, butter and bourbon; bring to a boil, stirring constantly. Cook 1 to 2 minutes or until sugar dissolves. Pour over cake.

Makes 8 to 10 servings

Tip: Allow breads, cakes and puddings to cool at least 5 minutes before scooping or removing them from the **CROCK-POT**® slow cooker.

BROWNIE BOTTOMS

Chai Tea Cherries 'n' Cream

2 cans (15½ ounces each) pitted cherries in pear juice

2 cups water

½ cup orange juice

1 cup sugar

4 cardamom pods

2 cinnamon sticks (broken in half)

1 teaspoon grated orange peel

¼ ounce coarsely chopped candied ginger

4 whole cloves

2 black peppercorns

4 green tea bags

1 container (6 ounces) fat-free black cherry yogurt

1 quart vanilla ice cream

Sprigs fresh mint (optional)

1. Drain cherries, reserving juice. Combine reserved juice, water and orange juice in **CROCK-POT®** slow cooker. Mix in sugar, cardamom pods, cinnamon sticks, orange peel, ginger, cloves and peppercorns. Cover; cook on HIGH 1½ hours.

2. Remove spices with slotted spoon and discard. Stir in tea bags and reserved cherries. Cover; cook on HIGH 30 minutes.

3. Turn off heat. Remove and discard tea bags. Remove cherries from liquid; set aside. Let liquid cool until just warm. Whisk in yogurt until smooth.

4. To serve, divide warm cherries and yogurt sauce among wine or cocktail glasses. Top each serving with small scoop of ice cream; swirl lightly. Garnish with mint.

Makes 8 servings

Warm and Spicy Fruit Punch

4 cinnamon sticks

1 orange

1 square (8 inches) double-thickness cheesecloth

1 teaspoon whole allspice

½ teaspoon whole cloves

7 cups water

1 can (12 ounces) frozen cran-raspberry juice concentrate, thawed

1 can (6 ounces) frozen lemonade concentrate, thawed

2 cans (5½ ounces each) apricot nectar

1. Break cinnamon sticks into pieces. Remove strips of orange peel with vegetable peeler or paring knife. Squeeze juice from orange; set juice aside.

2. Rinse cheesecloth; squeeze out water. Wrap cinnamon sticks, orange peel, allspice and cloves in cheesecloth. Tie bag securely with cotton string or strip of cheesecloth.

3. Combine reserved orange juice, water, juice concentrates and apricot nectar in **CROCK-POT®** slow cooker; add spice bag. Cover; cook on LOW 5 to 6 hours. Remove and discard spice bag before serving.

Makes about 14 servings

Tip: To keep punch warm during a party, place your **CROCK-POT®** slow cooker on the buffet table and turn the setting to LOW or WARM.

CHAI TEA CHERRIES 'N' CREAM

Fudge and Cream Pudding Cake

2 tablespoons unsalted butter

1 cup all-purpose flour

½ cup packed light brown sugar

5 tablespoons unsweetened cocoa powder, divided

2 teaspoons baking powder

½ teaspoon ground cinnamon

⅛ teaspoon salt

1 cup light cream

1 tablespoon vegetable oil

1 teaspoon vanilla

1½ cups hot water

½ cup packed dark brown sugar

Whipped cream or ice cream (optional)

1. Coat inside of 4½-quart **CROCK-POT**® slow cooker with butter. Combine flour, light brown sugar, 3 tablespoons cocoa, baking powder, cinnamon and salt in medium bowl. Add cream, oil and vanilla; stir well to combine. Pour batter into **CROCK-POT**® slow cooker.

2. Combine hot water, dark brown sugar and remaining 2 tablespoons cocoa in medium; stir well. Pour sauce over cake batter. Do not stir. Cover; cook on HIGH 2 hours.

3. Spoon pudding cake onto plates. Serve with whipped cream, if desired.

Makes 8 to 10 servings

Coconut Rice Pudding

2 cups water

1 cup uncooked converted long grain rice

1 tablespoon unsalted butter

Pinch salt

2¼ cups evaporated milk

1 can (14 ounces) cream of coconut

½ cup golden raisins

3 egg yolks, beaten

Grated peel of 2 limes

1 teaspoon vanilla

Toasted shredded coconut (optional)*

*To toast coconut, spread evenly on ungreased baking sheet. Toast in preheated 350°F oven 5 to 7 minutes or until light golden brown, stirring occasionally.

1. Place water, rice, butter and salt in medium saucepan. Bring to a boil over high heat, stirring frequently. Reduce heat to low. Cover; cook 10 to 12 minutes. Remove from heat. Let stand, covered, 5 minutes.

2. Meanwhile, coat inside of **CROCK-POT®** slow cooker with nonstick cooking spray. Add evaporated milk, cream of coconut, raisins, egg yolks, lime peel and vanilla; mix well. Add rice; stir until blended.

3. Cover; cook on LOW 4 hours or on HIGH 2 hours. Stir every 30 minutes, if possible. Pudding will thicken as it cools. Garnish with shredded coconut. Sprinkle with coconut.

Makes 6 servings

Recipe Index

Metric Chart

VOLUME MEASUREMENTS (dry)

$\frac{1}{8}$ teaspoon = 0.5 mL
$\frac{1}{4}$ teaspoon = 1 mL
$\frac{1}{2}$ teaspoon = 2 mL
$\frac{3}{4}$ teaspoon = 4 mL
1 teaspoon = 5 mL
1 tablespoon = 15 mL
2 tablespoons = 30 mL
$\frac{1}{4}$ cup = 60 mL
$\frac{1}{3}$ cup = 75 mL
$\frac{1}{2}$ cup = 125 mL
$\frac{2}{3}$ cup = 150 mL
$\frac{3}{4}$ cup = 175 mL
1 cup = 250 mL
2 cups = 1 pint = 500 mL
3 cups = 750 mL
4 cups = 1 quart = 1 L

VOLUME MEASUREMENTS (fluid)

1 fluid ounce (2 tablespoons) = 30 mL
4 fluid ounces ($\frac{1}{2}$ cup) = 125 mL
8 fluid ounces (1 cup) = 250 mL
12 fluid ounces ($1\frac{1}{2}$ cups) = 375 mL
16 fluid ounces (2 cups) = 500 mL

WEIGHTS (mass)

$\frac{1}{2}$ ounce = 15 g
1 ounce = 30 g
3 ounces = 90 g
4 ounces = 120 g
8 ounces = 225 g
10 ounces = 285 g
12 ounces = 360 g
16 ounces = 1 pound = 450 g

DIMENSIONS

$\frac{1}{16}$ inch = 2 mm
$\frac{1}{8}$ inch = 3 mm
$\frac{1}{4}$ inch = 6 mm
$\frac{1}{2}$ inch = 1.5 cm
$\frac{3}{4}$ inch = 2 cm
1 inch = 2.5 cm

OVEN TEMPERATURES

250°F = 120°C
275°F = 140°C
300°F = 150°C
325°F = 160°C
350°F = 180°C
375°F = 190°C
400°F = 200°C
425°F = 220°C
450°F = 230°C

BAKING PAN AND DISH EQUIVALENTS

Utensil	Size in Inches	Size in Centimeters	Volume	Metric Volume
Baking or Cake Pan (square or rectangular)	8×8×2	20×20×5	8 cups	2 L
	9×9×2	23×23×5	10 cups	2.5 L
	13×9×2	33×23×5	12 cups	3 L
Loaf Pan	$8\frac{1}{2}\times4\frac{1}{2}\times2\frac{1}{2}$	21×11×6	6 cups	1.5 L
	9×9×3	23×13×7	8 cups	2 L
Round Layer Cake Pan	$8\times1\frac{1}{2}$	20×4	4 cups	1 L
	$9\times1\frac{1}{2}$	23×4	5 cups	1.25 L
Pie Plate	$8\times1\frac{1}{2}$	20×4	4 cups	1 L
	$9\times1\frac{1}{2}$	23×4	5 cups	1.25 L
Baking Dish or Casserole			1 quart/4 cups	1 L
			$1\frac{1}{2}$ quart/6 cups	1.5 L
			2 quart/8 cups	2 L
			3 quart/12 cups	3 L